Winning With Leasing!

by Sudhir P. Amembal

AMEMBAL & ASSOCIATES
The World's Foremost Authority in Lease Education and Consulting

Publisher:	Amembal & Associates
Production Manager:	Cesar Rios
Layout and Design:	Contact Business Communications
Printing:	Jostens

ISBN: 0-9776654-1-0

Printed in the United States of America

Copyright © 2006 Amembal & Associates

All rights reserved. No part of this publication may be reproduced, stored in a retrieval system or transmitted, in any form or by any means, electronic, mechanical, photocopying, recording or otherwise, without prior written permission of the copyright owner.

*Dedicated to the three girls in my life –
Kiran, my wife; Tofa and Amy, my four-footed children.*

ACKNOWLEDGEMENTS

Winning with Leasing! has been a collective effort. It could not have been published without the tremendous assistance I have received from three individuals here in beautiful San Miguel de Allende, Mexico.

My assistant, Cesar Rios, spent countless hours over a 12-month period through five drafts, often working late evenings and weekends. He suffered through my terrible handwriting and scribbles. To him I owe the most for his incredible patience, a continuous positive attitude and, of course, his skills. Without Cesar, I would have continued to teach *Winning with Leasing!*, not publish it.

My administrative assistant, Laura Hernandez, helped in the editing as well as in guiding and managing the publication in many different ways.

As always, my wife Kiran was a pillar of strength, support and encouragement. Late dinners were the norm not the exception; weekends were consumed more with writing and rewriting than with family and social activities. Her tolerance and patience were priceless.

Beyond those who assisted, as noted above, my deepest gratitude is extended to the global equipment leasing industry that has expressed its trust and confidence in me over the past three decades.

Sudhir Amembal
San Miguel de Allende, Mexico
January 1, 2006

ABOUT AMEMBAL & ASSOCIATES

Sudhir P. Amembal is Chairman and CEO of Amembal & Associates. He began his professional career in lease education, consulting and publications by cofounding Amembal & Isom in 1978, the first entity in the world to serve the global leasing industry.

Entities under his stewardship became the world's most highly respected training and consulting firms in the field of equipment leasing. These entities have trained over 60,000 leasing professionals throughout the world. Mr. Amembal has conducted technical presentations on leasing in over 60 countries. He currently focuses on emerging lease economies.

As a government advisor, Mr. Amembal has spearheaded lease consultancy engagements, conducted on behalf of the governments of Albania, Bosnia and Herzegovina, China, Croatia, Estonia, Indonesia, Korea, Kyrgyz Republic, Latvia, Lithuania, Macedonia, Mongolia, Nicaragua, Nigeria, Poland, Romania, Russia, Sri Lanka, Tajikistan, Turkmenistan, Uzbekistan, and Yugoslavia. These engagements required him to review the overall leasing industry in each country and devise strategic recommendations to facilitate the growth of the industry.

He has coauthored 15 books on leasing: 2006 *Asian Leasing Yearbook* (published by Amembal & Associates, 2005), *Operating Leases: The Complete Guide* (published by Amembal & Associates, 2000), *International Leasing: The Complete Guide* (published by Amembal & Associates, 2000), *The Handbook of Equipment Leasing* (published by A&H, 1995), *Lease Securitization* (published by A&H, 1994), *A Guide to Accounting for Leases* (published by A&H, 1992), *Equipment Leasing: A Complete Handbook* (published by McGraw Hill, 1992), *Leasing Applications for the HP-12C* (published by A&H, 1991), *Leasing Applications for the HP-17B* (published by A&H, 1991), *The Handbook of Equipment Leasing* (published by A&H, 1988), *Guide to Captive Finance Company Equipment Leasing* (published jointly by A&H and the AAEL, 1984), *Handbook of Leasing: Techniques and Analysis* (published by Petrocelli Books, Inc., 1982), *Leasing Series*

Applications for the HP-12C Calculator (published by Hewlett Packard Inc., 1982), *Lease Payment Tables* (published by Vestigrowth 2000, 1982), and *Leasing For Profit* (published by American Management Association's Extension Institute, 1980).

He has appeared as a keynote speaker at numerous domestic and international conferences. He has addressed conventions held by all four of the global regional associations—African Leasing Association, AsiaLease, Leaseurope, and the Latin American Leasing Association. He serves as the Patron as well as a member of the Governing Council of the African Leasing Association. He has chaired each of the annual World Leasing Conventions from 1993 to date.

He is chairman of the recently formed Asian Centre for Lease Education (ACLE). ACLE offers a Certified Professional in Leasing (CPL) programme in the Asian region. He serves as a technical advisor to Odessa Technologies, developers of the lease management software, Leasewave; as well as to LeaseInspection.com, a U.S. entity specializing in the arena of lease inspections.

For a period of five years from 1997 to 2002, Mr. Amembal was Chairman of Amembal Capital Corporation, a middle-market leasing company. Prior to 1978, he was a member of the faculty at the College of Business, University of Utah prior to which he worked with Ernst & Young in New York City.

Born in Bangalore, India, he now lives with his wife, Kiran, in San Miguel de Allende, Mexico.

He can be reached at Sudhir@amembalandassociates.com

www.amembalandassociates.com

A PERSONAL NOTE

I have had the privilege of serving the global equipment leasing industry since 1978. What started as a career became an adventure; and soon a passion. Through almost three decades of traveling and teaching in over 60 countries, my life has been vastly enhanced by the thousands of leasing professionals I have encountered in my seminars. I taught them leasing as well as I could; they challenged me continually with their questions and thoughts and humbled me with their presence.

I have continued to witness leasing's growth in developing markets and participated in its birth in nascent ones. It has indeed been a joy to witness and take part in the growth of an extremely dynamic, vibrant and resilient industry that has grown from approximately $40 billion in volume when I first served it to over $570 billion today.

Winning with Leasing! is dear to my heart. Under a different title, this was the first commercially developed leasing seminar in the world, co-created by me in 1978. Twenty-eight years later, I saw the need to convert its most updated version into this publication so that it would continue to help guide the industry that I have had the privilege and honour to serve.

I would be delighted to hear from you; particularly after you have read this publication.

You may contact me at Sudhir@amembalandassociates.com.

SUDHIR AMEMBAL
SAN MIGUEL DE ALLENDE, MEXICO
JANUARY 1, 2006

INTRODUCTION

WINNING WITH LEASING! has been written in the same informal style that I chose to adopt in teaching this seminar over the past 28 years. I felt that a Q & A approach would be simple, clear and hopefully interesting!

In choosing its content, I had many objectives in mind:

- to help acquaint the novice
- to fine-tune the experienced
- to assist the service provider
- to guide the customer

but, the single most important objective is to provide simple yet powerful tools to lessors to increase their sales and/or profits. In this context, the publication is replete with ideas that can be instantly implemented to win additional deals.

The publication is intended for lessors, lessees, service providers and the professionals who serve the leasing industry. It has been written in a manner that its style and jargon as well as its illustrations are conducive to international readership. Yet, given the significance of the U.S. leasing industry, adequate effort has been taken to specifically incorporate U.S. tax and accounting nuances.

The illustrations use $ signs for no particular reason. The HP12C and the HP17BII+ were chosen as the calculators for the quantitative parts as these calculators are universally used. While no effort has been made to instruct the reader in using the calculators, the keystrokes in the Lease Finance Section include all set-up keystrokes as well as detailed explanations.

If the reader wishes to receive material for either of the two calculators, an e-mail should be sent to Cesar@amembalandassociates.com.

The material can only be sent for either of the two specified calculators and it can only be sent via e-mail. Readers wishing to receiving periodic electronic newsletters from Amembal & Associates should also write to the same e-mail address. The newsletters will provide the reader with major technical developments as well as our training schedule.

Each section contains a summary and a glossary. Also, homework has been provided at the end of each section with homework answers following.

Thank you for having purchased the publication. I hope you enjoy reading it as much as I enjoyed writing it!

TABLE OF CONTENTS

Section One
OVERVIEW
    Significance and Evolution of Leasing   18
    Definition of a Lease   23
    The Types of Leases   24
    The Types of Lessors   34
    Summary   37
    Glossary   39
    Homework!   42
    Homework Answers   46

Section Two
LEASE FINANCE
    Preface   52
    Overview   53
    Present Value   55
    Internal Rate of Return   75
    Varied Applications   87
    Summary   88
    Glossary   89
    Homework!   91
    Homework Answers   94

Section Three
LEASE MARKETING
    The Types of Lessees   110
    The Benefits of Leasing   112
    The Equipment Acquisition Process   130
    Lease Versus Purchase Analysis   134
    Lease Versus Lease Analysis   172
    Countering Common Objections   185
    Summary   192
    Glossary   198
    Homework!   202
    Homework Answers   208

Section Four
LEASE ACCOUNTING
    The Two Types of Leases   218
    The Accounting Impact on Lessees   220
    The Accounting Impact on Lessors   224
    Criteria Distinguishing Finance and
        Operating Leases   228
    Techniques to Structure
        Off Balance Sheet Financing   246
    The Future of Lease Accounting   266
    Summary   269
    Glossary   273
    Homework!   276
    Homework Answers   283

Section Five
LEASE TAXATION
    Defining a Lease   294
    Depreciation and its Value   302
    U.S. Tax Nuances   316
    Summary   334
    Glossary   337
    Homework!   339
    Homework Answers   344

Section Six:
PRICING AND STRUCTURING
    Difference Between
        Pricing and Structuring   350
    Arriving at Lessor IRR   355
    Lease Pricing   362
    Lease Structuring   377
    Summary   393
    Glossary   395
    Homework!   397
    Homework Answers   401

Section Seven
OPERATING LEASES
   Defining the Product   416
   Unique Advantages to Lessees   427
   Unique Advantages to Lessors   443
   Managing Varied Risks   448
   Residual Risk   470
   Techniques to Mitigate Residual Risk   476
   Operating Leases Without Asset Risk   479
   Summary   481
   Glossary   484
   Homework!   487
   Homework Answers   492

Advertisements   495
ACC Capital Corporation
Amembal/Odessa Software
Asian Leasing School
Asian Leasing Yearbook 2006
Contact Business Communications
Kropschot Financial Services
LeaseInspection.com
Lease Publications
Lease Training
Monitor
Odessa Technologies
Odessa Technologies
Vision Commerce
Winning With Leasing Seminars

Overview

Overview

Significance and Evolution of Leasing

Definition of a Lease

The Types of Leases

The Types of Lessors

Summary

Glossary

Homework!

Homework Answers

SIGNIFICANCE AND EVOLUTION OF LEASING

1. What makes leasing significant?
Varied statistics strongly suggest that leasing is extremely significant. In the year 2004, the latest year for which global statistics exist, leasing accounted for over US $570 billion in volume as measured by equipment cost. Twenty-six years ago in 1978, the volume was only US $40 billion. The compound annual growth rate between 1978 and 2004 has been approximately 11%.

Equipment leasing contributes significantly to economic growth

2. What percentage of total equipment acquisition is attributed to leasing?
On a global basis, leasing accounts for approximately 20% of the total investment in equipment. Generally, "equipment" means personal property (movables) and therefore excludes real property—land and buildings.

3. What exactly is meant by the expression "penetration percentage"?
The penetration percentage is the volume of leasing expressed as a percentage of total investment in equipment.

Whereas the global average for leasing penetration is 20%, the percentage is almost invariably higher in mature markets such as the U.S. and Australia. The U.S. has the highest penetration percentage; approximately 30%. In the U.S., leasing is the single largest source of external financing. On the other hand, emerging lease markets, particularly in Asia and Latin America, have a single-digit penetration percentage as leasing is typically newer and/or the psychology of ownership is still a barrier to its development.

4. What is leasing's contribution to GDP?

On a global basis leasing's contribution to gross domestic product is approximately 1.5%.

5. How does leasing evolve in any one country?

The following diagram illustrates this:

STAGES IN THE EVOLUTION OF LEASING MARKETS

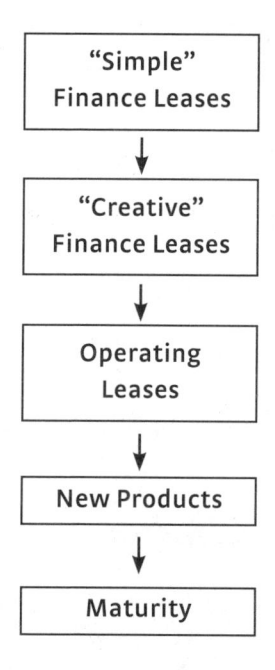

"Simple" Finance Leases
↓
"Creative" Finance Leases
↓
Operating Leases
↓
New Products
↓
Maturity

The evolution of leasing is the same regardless of which country one looks at. When leasing is first introduced, the product is invariably the "simple" full payout finance lease. During this stage, leases are noncancellable and net (where the onus of maintaining, insuring, repairing and performing other responsibilities of ownership falls on the lessee).

Net means the lessor is only providing one thing—the financing, which is why the lease is referred to as a finance lease. Lessee intent is to eventually buy the asset, typically for a nominal amount of consideration, at the end of the lease.

Leases during this stage are typically linear where one rental equals another.

6. What comes after the "simple" finance lease?

To begin with, there is no such thing in the real world as a "simple" finance lease. The expression is being used here to explain the evolution from this stage to the next stage where the finance lease is offered with themes and variations; a stage referred to as the "creative" finance lease stage. As leasing becomes competitive, lessors become creative. During this stage, some finance leases begin to be structured (as versus being linear in the previous stage) and some others have varied end of term variations (such as a balloon or bullet payment that can either be paid at the end of the lease or the bullet amount can be refinanced, say over 12 months).

Some finance leases are also offered on a full-service basis where the lessor bundles items such as maintenance and insurance into the lease. The largest amount of growth in leasing volume takes place during this stage.

7. What is the next stage?

The next stage (stage three) is the introduction of operating leases. Operating leases come about for a variety of reasons:

- Increased competition causing some lessors to offer a new product
- Lessee demand particularly from large listed companies as well as from multinationals
- Developing or developed secondary markets which are essential for the success of operating leases
- Denial of tax benefits on finance leases

- Introduction of international accounting standards requiring finance leases to be capitalized by the lessee; thus, operating leases become the only product offering off balance sheet financing

8. What are the characteristics of the operating lease?

The product is invariably nonfull payout given the lessor's reliance on residual; the asset is often returned at the end of the lease term (unlike in the finance lease, where it is almost invariably purchased); and the lease is often a full-service lease (unlike the finance lease which is almost always net).

9. What is the next stage in the evolution of leasing after operating leases?

As leasing develops, some lessors enter stage four—the new products stage. During this stage, products such as synthetic leases, leveraged leases, cross-border leases, venture leases as well as securitization are introduced.

New products are introduced owing to continued lessor creativity.

10. Then what?

Stage five—maturity—is experienced by well-developed leasing markets such as the U.S. and Australia.

11. What are the characteristics of this stage?

In maturity, the big become bigger (through mergers and acquisitions); margins are thinner (due to extreme competition); there is flatness in leasing's penetration percentage (the U.S. is a perfect example, where penetration of approximately 30% has remained constant for the past decade or so); there is a focus on alliances and joint ventures (for synergy); and lastly, lessors concentrate on becoming value added.

In maturity the big become bigger and there is flatness in penetration.

12. Do the five stages apply to all lessors?
Not at all. They apply to the industry as a whole on a country by country basis. Whereas the industry enters successive phases with the passage of time, many lessors by choice opt not to evolve with the industry. As an example, many do not strategically wish to go beyond finance leases. They are content, and rightfully so, to remain as finance lease lessors. Also, the five stages are not mutually exclusive. A lessor who decides to enter the operating lease stage does not necessarily stop offering finance leases. What is important to note is that the leasing industry as a whole in each country evolves sequentially.

DEFINITION OF A LEASE

13. What is the simplest definition of a lease?
A one word answer would be "rental" or "hire." However, as seen later, there is a clear distinction between a lease and a rental or a hire.

14. How does leasing work?
A lease typically involves four parties as best seen in the diagram below:

THE FOUR PARTIES TO A LEASE

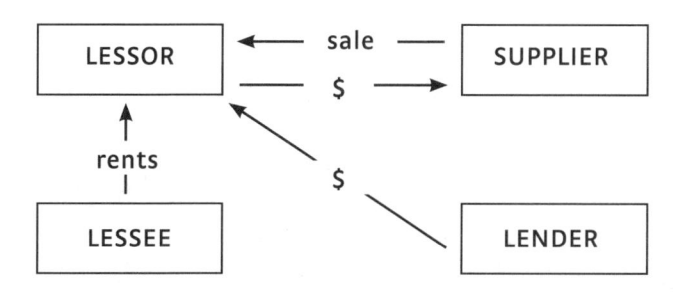

```
  ┌─────────┐  ←── sale ──  ┌──────────┐
  │ LESSOR  │               │ SUPPLIER │
  └─────────┘  ─── $ ──→    └──────────┘
       ↑  ↖
     rents  ↖  $
       │      ↖
  ┌─────────┐     ┌──────────┐
  │ LESSEE  │     │  LENDER  │
  └─────────┘     └──────────┘
```

The lessor, who is the legal owner of the equipment, purchases the equipment (generally selected by the lessee) from the supplier (also generally selected by the lessee) and pays for the equipment. The lessee, via a lease agreement, leases the equipment from the lessor and pays periodic rents to the lessor.

Leasing relies on leverage (also known as gearing). Leverage/gearing entails the insertion of debt. The average debt to equity ratio in the world is about 6:1; in emerging lease economies, it is typically lower as capital markets are not fully developed. In such markets, the average debt to equity ratio is approximately 4:1. This means for every $5 of equipment cost, $4 comes from debt, $1 comes from equity.

THE TYPES OF LEASES

15. How many types of leases are there?
There really are only two types of leases—finance leases and operating leases.

There really are only two types of leases—finance and operating. Other than where a brief reference is made to accounting in QUESTIONS 16 & 17 below, the entire discussion in this subsection is from a marketplace point of view and not from an accounting point of view. At the onset, it is important to note that marketplace means the world of leasing in the commercial arena without any regard to the accounting, tax or legal arenas.

16. What is the distinction between the two types of leases?
A finance lease has three characteristics: to begin with, it has a term equal to or greater than 12 months. This characteristic is important in distinguishing a lease from a rental. A rental is generally considered to be an instrument with a term less than 12 months. This distinction is from an accounting point of view and in some countries from a legal point of view as well.

17. What is the accounting distinction between a lease and a rental?
Rentals (less than 12 months) are neither shown on the balance sheet of the one renting the equipment for usage nor do they appear as a footnote to financial statements. On the other hand, finance leases (capital leases, as they are referred to in the U.S.) do appear on the balance sheet of the lessee and additional detailed disclosure is contained in the footnotes to the financial statements. Operating leases, though some of these do not appear on the balance sheet of the lessee, are disclosed in the footnotes to financial statements. It will be explained later in the

Accounting Section that some marketplace operating leases are actually finance leases from an accounting point of view.

Thus, the key difference from an accounting point of view is that rentals do not appear anywhere; operating leases are footnoted; finance leases are capitalized (and footnoted).

18. What are the other two characteristics of finance leases?

Finance leases are almost invariably "net." Net means that the lessee is responsible for the incidence of ownership; items such as maintenance and repairs. In fact net leases typically contain a "hell or high water" clause which states that even if the equipment fails to function, the lessee is still responsible to make the rental payments. Net means the lessor is providing only one thing—the money or the financing. This is why these leases are called finance leases.

19. And the last characteristic?

Finance leases are full payout. This is a critical characteristic as will be illustrated later. Full payout means that the sum of the rentals will always be equal to the equipment cost plus the lessor's targeted profit (or interest) in the transaction.

20. What happens after all the rentals are paid?

At the end of the lease the lessee will almost invariably purchase the equipment from the lessor for a nominal sum, say $1. This is typically done through a $1 purchase option. The reason for the nominal consideration is obvious—there needs to be consideration paid for legal transfer of title and it is nominal in amount as the lessee has fully paid the lessor through the rentals. Almost always, the nominal purchase option will be exercised; the reason is obvious, the lessee would be a fool not to! After all, the lessee has fully paid the principal and the interest. $1 purchase option leases are referred to as dollar out leases in the U.S.

End of term practices vary throughout the world. In many countries title is transferred upon the payment of a nominal percentage of equipment cost, say one percent; in some others, title is transferred upon the payment of the last rental. Australia has a nuance where, for tax purposes, lessors are required to have a minimum residual value on leases and it is upon payment of this amount that the title is transferred.

21. An illustration of a finance lease?
A simple one will do. Let's assume:

Equipment cost	$100.00
Term in months	48
Monthly rental in advance	$2.52
Lessor interest rate	10%
Transfer price at end	$1.00

The $2.52 was arrived at using an interest rate of 10%. Once all 48 rentals have been paid the lessor has received a total of $120.96 which is comprised of $100 of equipment cost (or principal) and $20.96 of interest. The lessor is fully paid out; it has recovered the entire principal and earned the 10% desired interest on the transaction.

22. Can a finance lease have a purchase option greater than 1% of equipment cost?
This type of lease is not uncommon in the U.S. Lessors do these types of transactions with lessees who are not too sophisticated or who are not creditworthy enough to qualify for a bank loan. A 10% purchase option on a full payout finance lease is not uncommon.

23. Perhaps an illustration would help?
Let's take the earlier illustration from QUESTION 21 forward as follows:

Equipment cost	$100.00
Term in months	48
Monthly rental in advance	$2.52
Lessor interest rate	10%
Purchase option	$10.00

Note that the rental is still the same as in the earlier illustration. What has changed is the end of term amount. In the earlier illustration, the lessee paid $1 for the transfer of ownership. In the above illustration, a different lessee is presented with a 10% purchase option. If the option is not exercised and the equipment is returned, the lessor has been fully paid out through the 48 rentals and is now receiving an asset which has value causing the lease to be better than a full payout lease.

24. What if the purchase option is exercised?

If the lessee pays $10, the lessor will have received 48 rentals plus $10. The 48 rentals alone gave the lessor its desired 10% yield (or rate); the extra $10 enhances the yield—the lessor's interest rate is 13.48%. In essence, the lessee is paying 13.48% for financing.

25. What is meant by a PUT?

Some leases, particularly in the U.S., have a PUT at the end of the lease. Let's use a 10% PUT. PUT stands for Purchase Upon Termination. Such a clause in the lease agreement requires the lessee to pay 10% at the end of lease term; it is not an option. From a yield (or rate) point of view, the lessor achieves the same 13.48% as seen above.

26. What is the difference, again, between a purchase option and a PUT?

A purchase option is an example of a call option. A call option is one where it is left to the lessee to determine whether to exercise the option or not. PUT is a "put" (it is a coincidence that the two words are the same); in a put the lessee has no choice, it must pay the stated amount.

27. What type of risk does the lessor have in a finance lease?

Full payout leases entail only one type of risk—credit risk or the risk of default.

Full payout leases entail only one type of risk— the risk of default.

28. Moving on to operating leases, what are the characteristics of this type of a lease?

Operating leases, as contrasted with rentals, have a tenor or term equal to or greater than 12 months. As noted earlier, this is true with finance leases as well. It could therefore be said that rentals are short-term leases and leases are long-term rentals!

29. What are the other characteristics of operating leases?

Operating leases can either be net or "full-service." Full-service is the opposite of net. In full-service leases the lessor is responsible for items such as maintenance, repairs, insurance and the like.

30. But are not operating leases always full-service?

This is not true. Some, in fact many, operating leases are net. A good example is an operating lease of aircraft. Almost invariably the lessee (the airline) is responsible for maintenance, repairs and the like. On the other hand, a lease involving a fleet of vehicles will be full-service if the lessee desires outsourcing—where they merely want to use the vehicles. The lessor then takes responsibility for maintenance, repairs, insurance, etc.

Thus, whether an operating lease is net or full-service depends on what the lessee desires.

31. Any other characteristics?

The third and last characteristic of operating leases is the one that distinguishes a finance lease from an operating lease and this has to do with the nonfull payout nature of operating leases. In fact, this is the sole difference between the two types of leases. The nonfull payout characteristic occurs as a result of the lessor taking a residual position in the lease.

The sole difference between a finance and an operating lease is residual.

32. What is meant by residual?

Residual, in an operating lease, means the estimated fair market value (FMV) of the asset at the end of the lease. This estimate is arrived at by the lessor when pricing the lease.

33. Can this be illustrated?

Let's use the earlier example of the finance lease from QUESTION 21 with one change: the lessor assumes that the estimated FMV of the equipment at the end of the lease term is $30. Given that residual conceptually is the same as a balloon or bullet payment, it will cause the rentals to be lower than $2.52. The new rental is $2.01.

Equipment cost	$100.00
Term in months	48
Monthly rental in advance	$2.01
Lessor interest rate	10%
Residual	$30.00

34. What is the impact of residual on the lessor?

The 48 rentals in the above example do not even recover equipment cost; they aggregate to $96.48. Thus the existence of residual causes the lease to be nonfull payout in nature. A lower than $30 residual will cause the rental to be greater than $2.01 conceivably allowing the lessor to recover equipment cost; but, the lease will still be a nonfull payout lease as there is reliance on residual for the lessor to fully recover equipment cost and earn a 10% interest rate.

35. What type of risk does the lessor have?

Over and above the credit risk in a finance lease the operating lease imposes an asset risk. When (or if) the asset is returned, it may not be worth $30; it could be worth say $27. The lessor will lose $3 on residual thus impairing the final rate of return to the lessor. Of course, there is residual upside as well.

To summarize, the sole difference between a finance lease and an operating lease is the full payout versus nonfull payout nature or to put it differently, finance leases have credit risk; operating leases have both credit and asset risk.

36. It was stated earlier that in operating leases, lessees often do not return the equipment?

Yes, the lessee may purchase the equipment or renew the lease.

37. At what amount does the lessee purchase the equipment?
Using the earlier illustration, and depending on how the lease is structured, the lessee can purchase it at the end of term either for a fixed $30 (if contractually stated) or at the then FMV, which could be equal to $30, less than $30, or more than $30.

38. How about renewals?
Let's assume the actual value of the asset at the end of the lease term is indeed $30. Further let's assume it is a two year renewal with the expected FMV being zero at the end of two years. With an interest rate of 10%, the monthly renewal rental would be $1.37.

39. Other than finance and operating leases are there any other types of leases?
Yes and no. There are themes and variations; but, at the end of the day all leases are either finance or operating.

40. What would be a few examples of "themes and variations"?
One example would be a sale leaseback. In a sale leaseback an equipment user who purchased equipment some time ago now sells the equipment to a lessor and leases it back as diagramed below:

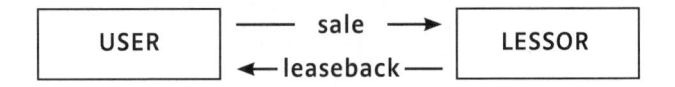

```
┌────────┐   ─── sale ──▶   ┌────────┐
│  USER  │                  │ LESSOR │
└────────┘   ◀─ leaseback ─ └────────┘
```

41. Why would someone want to do this?
There are many reasons, for example: liquidity, where the entity is seeking to use leasing to refinance equipment that has no debt against it; or, it could be for financial reporting purposes where the entity is seeking to sell an asset (that has debt associated with it) to a lessor and lease it back through a lease that would qualify as off balance sheet financing (discussed further in the Accounting Section); or it could be for tax reasons where the entity is desirous of a tax gain on a fully (or partially) depreciated asset.

Tongue in cheek, a sale leaseback is defined as "I wish I had leased to begin with"!

42. So is the leaseback a finance or an operating lease?

The lease can be either; it depends on full payout or nonfull payout status.

43. Any other "themes and variations"?

Another example would be a leveraged lease where the lessor borrows on a nonrecourse basis. Nonrecourse means the lessor borrows funds from a lender but is not obliged to pay it back!

44. That sounds too good—can this be embellished?

This is best done through an example diagramed below:

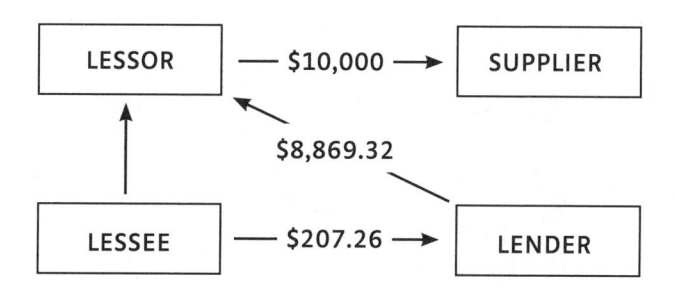

```
    LESSOR  ── $10,000 ──▶  SUPPLIER
       ▲  ◀── $8,869.32
       │
    LESSEE  ── $207.26 ──▶  LENDER
```

Equipment cost	$10,000.00
Term in months	48
Lessor interest rate	8%
Residual	$2,000.00
Rental in advance	$207.26
Loan proceeds at 6%	$8,869.32

45. It looks too complicated. Can it be explained?

The lessee is an entity that wants to lease (to seek certain unique benefits of leasing; for example off balance sheet financing). The lessee's lender (say, a bank) is not in the leasing business. Thus, the need for a lessor. Enter a lessor who is willing to lease to the lessee. However, the lessee has an excellent relationship with its lender who would otherwise have loaned monies to the lessee. The lender, therefore on the basis of the lessee's creditworthiness, loans monies to the lessor. The loan is generally the present value of the rentals discounted at the lender's interest rate.

In this example, the present value of the 48 rents discounted at 6% is $8,869.32.

46. But if the lessor receives $8,869.32, how does it come up with the difference to pay the supplier $10,000?
The difference, $1,130.68, comes from the lessor's equity.

47. Why would a lender lend on a nonrecourse basis? How is the lender protected?
The lender in essence is loaning against the creditworthiness of the lessee. The protection comes from the fact that the monthly lease rentals are assigned to it; in other words, the lessee makes the monthly rental payment directly to the lender. Upon payment of the last rental, the loan is paid off.

A leveraged lease, by definition, has nonrecourse debt.

48. What if the lessee defaults?
If this happens the lessor is not obliged to pay the balance to the lender. The lender, who has a lien or mortgage on the equipment, would foreclose and sell the equipment, proceeds from which would pay off the remaining loan principal. If there is a deficit this is borne by the lender.

49. Why would the lessor make an equity investment of $1,130.68 without having any benefit of cash for 48 months?
Two reasons: in this example the lease is an operating lease and the lessor has invested $1,130.68 to eventually realize an expected residual of $2,000 (keep in mind that the lessor as the legal owner "owns" the

residual); the second reason is that leveraged leases are a tax play. For a small investment, the lessor gains 100% of the tax benefits.

50. Are leveraged leases done by lessors only when the lessee's lender is not in the leasing business?

No. The example given was to facilitate understanding of one way that a leveraged lease arises. Such leases can be initiated by a lessor who borrows from its own lender on a nonrecourse basis. The concepts would remain the same as explained above.

51. What is a TRAC lease?

TRAC stands for Terminal Rental Adjustment Clause. The expression is uniquely used in the U.S. Essentially it means a lease where the residual is partially or fully guaranteed by the lessee.

52. Why would a lessee guarantee a lessor's residual?

On large transactions, particularly those involving fleets (cars, trucks, delivery vans and the like), lessees understand assets as well as lessors do—often even better. As an example, an electric utility company, that has been using trucks say for 100 years, will have a good understanding on expected fair market values of used trucks at the end of a lease. Given this, such lessees are often willing to guarantee the residual and in return negotiate for a lower rental.

53. Are TRAC leases common outside of the U.S.?

Yes they are, except they are not called TRAC leases.

54. Any more "themes and variations"?

One last one: a synthetic lease. This is a "hybrid" lease; an operating lease for accounting purposes and a loan for tax purposes.

55. A further explanation?

Too complex for this publication!

THE TYPES OF LESSORS

56. Are there different types of lessors?
Yes, there are basically two types of lessors—independents and captives.

57. What is the difference?
The independent is so labeled because this type of lessor works with a variety of suppliers, vendors, dealers, distributors and manufacturers. The independent lessor is not beholden to any one party.

The diagram embellishes:

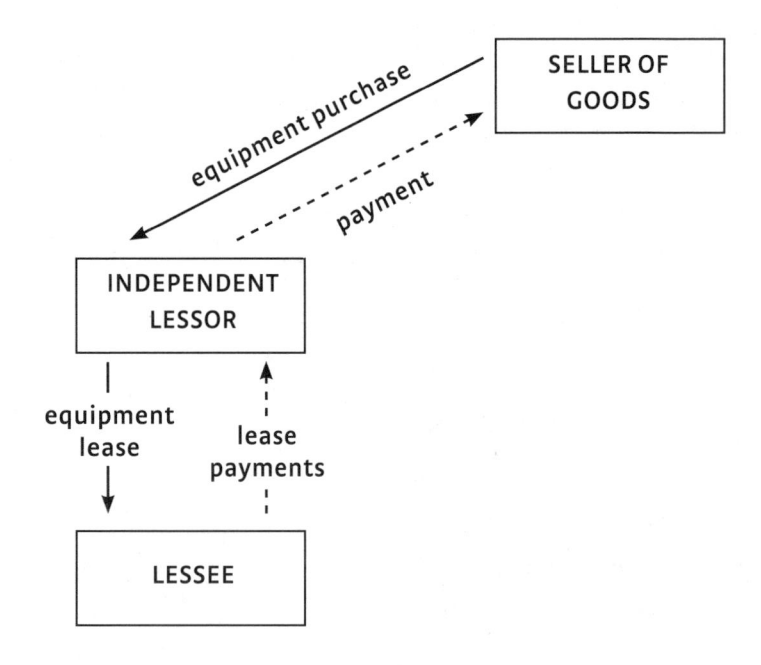

```
                    equipment purchase      ┌──────────────┐
                    ─────────────────────→  │  SELLER OF   │
                 ←                           │    GOODS     │
                    ←─ ─ ─ ─ ─ ─ ─ ─ ─ ─    └──────────────┘
                         payment
        ┌──────────────┐
        │ INDEPENDENT  │
        │    LESSOR    │
        └──────────────┘
            │      ▲
  equipment │      │  lease
    lease   │      │  payments
            ▼      │
        ┌──────────────┐
        │    LESSEE    │
        └──────────────┘
```

34 Winning With Leasing!

58. Are there various types of independents?

Yes, basically there are two types of independents—banks and nonbanks. Nonbanks are often broken out into the following categories: finance companies and specialized leasing companies.

59. What is different between the independents and the captives?

Captives are typically wholly owned finance subsidiaries of a dealer, distributor or manufacturer—entities such as Hewlett Packard Finance, Caterpillar Finance, etc.

The diagram embellishes:

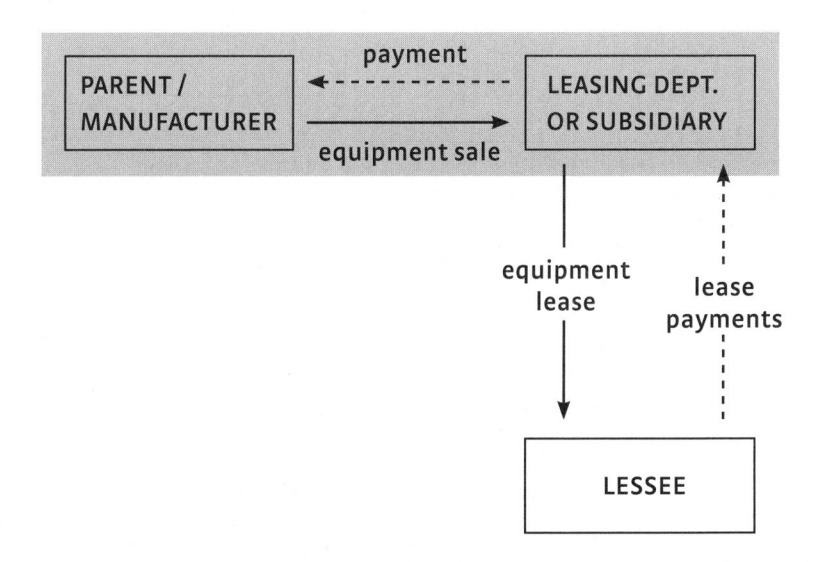

```
                    payment
  PARENT /      ←----------      LEASING DEPT.
  MANUFACTURER   ---------→      OR SUBSIDIARY
                 equipment sale
                         |              ↑
                         |              |
                   equipment          lease
                     lease          payments
                         |              |
                         ↓              |
                            LESSEE
```

The finance subsidiary purchases equipment from its manufacturing parent and leases it to the lessee.

60. Do captives only lease or finance their parents' products?

The principal objective of forming a captive is to facilitate sales for the parent; in fact, this is referred to as sales-aid leasing. Generally, at least

Overview **35**

to begin with, captives lease or finance their parents' products. After a few years, some captives (wanting to avail of economies of scale or for other strategic reasons) diversify into other products.

61. Are captives always a subsidiary?
If a separate company is formed it is almost invariably a wholly-owned subsidiary; yet, once in a while a parent may not form another entity in which case leasing will be done through a department or division of the parent itself.

62. What is meant by the expression vendor leasing?
Vendor leasing could have two meanings—first, it is another expression for captive leasing; yet, the more common meaning is when an independent leasing company enters into an agreement with a vendor (generally on an exclusive basis) to finance the vendor's equipment. The lessor generally receives a right of first refusal to finance any transaction that needs financing.

63. What about lease brokers?
Lease brokers do exist in many countries and do serve an extremely useful purpose. A broker typically helps lessors to originate transactions. The broker finds the interested lessee, does the initial credit due diligence, helps the lessee fill out the credit application and then submits the lessee's financial package to a lessor.

64. How are they paid?
Generally, after the transaction is funded, they are paid an upfront fee – x% of equipment cost. Also, it is not uncommon for brokers to participate in residual profit.

SUMMARY

1. Leasing is a significant industry. In the year 2004, it accounted for over $570 billion in new originations as measured by equipment cost. This represented approximately 20% of the total investment in equipment.

2. The U.S. is the most mature leasing market in the world; it has a penetration rate exceeding 30%. Leasing in the U.S. is the single largest source of external financing. Emerging lease markets generally have a single digit penetration percentage.

3. There are five stages to the evolution of leasing. These are:

   - "Simple" finance lease
   - "Creative" finance lease
   - Operating lease
   - New products
   - Maturity

4. There are only two basic types of leases in the marketplace—the finance and the operating lease. Finance leases are generally net. At the end of the lease term, the lessee generally purchases the equipment for a nominal amount.

5. Operating leases can either be net or full service; it depends on what the lessee desires. At the end of an operating lease the lessee either returns the equipment, purchases it or renews the lease.

6. The sole difference between a marketplace finance lease and an operating lease has to do with full payout/nonfull payout. Finance leases are full payout where the sum of the rentals will equal equipment cost plus the lessor's desired return. Operating leases are nonfull payout owing to the existence of residual.

7. Residual is the estimated value of the equipment at the end of the lease term on an operating lease. It causes the lessor to have an asset risk in the lease. Thus, operating leases have both credit and asset risk while finance leases only have credit risk.

8. A sale leaseback can either be a finance lease or an operating lease.

9. A leveraged lease is one with nonrecourse debt.

10. A synthetic lease has not been defined in this publication!

11. There are two types of lessors: independent (as they purchase goods from a variety of suppliers) and captives. Independents can either be banks or bank affiliates or they can be nonbank lessors.

GLOSSARY

call option
An option exercisable at the discretion of the lessee.

capitalize
To record an asset (and in the case of a finance or capital lease, the corresponding liability) on the balance sheet.

captive lessor
A lessor which is a department, division or subsidiary of a seller of goods.

cross-border lease
A transaction where the lessor and lessee are domiciled in different countries.

dollar out lease
A full payout lease with a $1 purchase option.

finance lease
A transaction that is typically net but invariably full payout.

full payout
Where the sum of the rentals, without any reliance on residual, fully pays the lessor the equipment cost (principal) plus the desired interest in the transaction.

full-service
A finance or operating lease where the lessor bundles other services (besides financing) such as insurance and maintenance into the lease. Also known, at times, as a wet lease.

independent lessor
A lessor who purchases equipment, on behalf of its lessees, from a variety of dealers, distributors and manufacturers.

leverage
The benefit (or detriment) that stems from procuring debt. Also known as gearing.

leveraged lease
A transaction where the lessor's debt is nonrecourse.

net
A finance or operating lease where the responsibilities of ownership, such as insurance, maintenance and repairs, are the lessee's burden. Also known, at times, as a dry lease.

nonfull payout
Where the sum of the rentals does not fully pay the lessor the equipment cost (principal) plus the desired interest in the transaction; thus, a lease where the lessor is residual reliant to be fully paid out.

nonrecourse
Without recourse or without being obligated as in a nonrecourse loan.

off balance sheet
Where certain operating leases are not recorded on the balance sheet of the lessee.

operating lease
A transaction that is either net or full-service but invariably nonfull payout.

purchase option
An option given to the lessee whereby the lessee, at the end of lease term, can either purchase the leased asset or return it.

put
An end of term event which the lessee is required to perform.

residual
The estimated market value of the leased asset at the end of the lease term; an amount the lessor has to estimate at the inception of the lease agreement.

sale leaseback
A transaction where an entity sells used equipment to a lessor and simultaneously enters into a lease for the same equipment.

securitization
A process whereby the lessor sells a part of its lease receivables generally through a special purpose vehicle.

synthetic lease
A lease which is an operating lease for accounting purposes and a loan for tax purposes.

TRAC lease
A lease where the lessee guarantees the lessor's residual. TRAC stands for Terminal Rental Adjustment Clause.

vendor leasing
An arrangement between a seller of goods and a lessor whereby the lessor typically obtains an exclusive agreement to finance the vendor's sales.

venture lease
A hybrid transaction that encompasses the characteristics of venture capital and equipment leasing.

HOMEWORK!

1. What is the accounting difference between a rental and a lease?

2. What is the accounting treatment of a rental?

3. What are the three characteristics of a finance lease?

4. What is meant by full payout?

5. Why does the lessee almost invariably purchase the asset at a nominal amount at the end of term on a finance lease?

6. What type of risk does a lessor have in a finance lease?

7. What are the three characteristics of an operating lease?

8. What is meant by the word "residual"?

9. What type of risk(s) does the lessor have on operating leases?

10. What are the motivations for a sale leaseback transaction?

11. What exactly is a leveraged lease?

12. What is a TRAC lease?

13. What are the two types of lessors?

HOMEWORK ANSWERS

Answer 1
Rentals are generally considered to be a product with a term less than 12 months; leases, on the other hand, have a term of 12 months or more. Rentals are short-term leases; leases are long-term rentals.

Answer 2
Rentals neither appear on the balance sheet nor are footnoted.

Answer 3
Finance leases have the following three characteristics:

- Equal to or longer than 12 months in tenor
- Net
- The lessee buys the asset at the end of the lease term

Answer 4
Full payout is where the sum of the rentals is equal to equipment cost plus the lessor's targeted profit (interest) in the lease.

Answer 5
Merely because the lessee has already fully paid the lessor the equipment cost plus interest through all the lease rentals!

Answer 6
As the lessor assumes residual to be zero, the only risk it has is the risk of default or credit risk.

Answer 7
Operating leases have the following three characteristics:

- Equal to or longer than 12 months in tenor
- Net or full-service
- Asset is either purchased or returned at the end of term or lease is renewed

Answer 8
Residual, on an operating lease, is the expected fair market value of the asset at the end of lease term.

Answer 9
Credit risk and asset risk.

Answer 10
Generally cash flow (liquidity); tax (need to show a gain for tax purposes to offset existing losses); or financial reporting (to get rid of any existing debt pertaining to the asset).

Answer 11
A leveraged lease is one which has nonrecourse debt—where the lessor borrows based on the creditworthiness of the lessee and is not obliged to pay the loan back if the lessee defaults.

Answer 12
A TRAC lease is one where the lessee guarantees the lessor's residual. TRAC stands for Terminal Rental Adjustment Clause.

Answer 13
Independents and captives.

Lease Finance

Lease Finance

Preface

Overview

Present Value

Internal Rate of Return

Varied Applications

Summary

Glossary

Homework!

Homework Answers

PREFACE

The author has chosen to use the HP12C and the HP17BII+ calculators throughout this publication. The choice is based on the fact that these two calculators are universally used; moreover, they are inexpensive to purchase and simple to use.

Though it is beyond the scope of this publication to provide detailed instruction on how to use the calculators, this section on Lease Finance provides the reader with needed set-up entries as well as detailed explanations for each keystroke.

For those using the HP17BII+, the calculator should first be turned on, after which the first keystroke may need to be ☐ (the yellow shift key above the ON keystroke) MAIN. This brings the calculator to the main menu showing:

       FIN   BUS   SUM   TIME   SOLVE   CURR

After this ☐ CLR DATA will help clear any previous clutter.

Those readers who wish for Amembal & Associates to e-mail them material for either the HP12C or the HP17BII+ should e-mail cesar@amembalandassociates.com clearly specifying which of the two calculators is being chosen. The material can only be sent via e-mail. The material provides insight into the mechanics of the calculators.

OVERVIEW

65. What exactly is meant by the expression "lease finance"?
Leasing is a quantitative subject and a lease invariably involves future cash flows. Two financial concepts, present value and internal rate of return (IRR), come in to play.

66. The cash flow in a lease can either be in arrears or in advance. Can this be explained?
A lease is best looked upon as a time line. Assume a 36-month lease where the monthly rentals are in arrears. The time line would be as follows:

```
▼                                                    ▼
─────────────────────────────────────────────────────────
0   1                                              35  36
```

The triangle shows when the rentals are received. Note that the first rental is being received at the end of the first period after the lessee has used the equipment for a month. Similarly, the last rental is being received at the end of the 36th month. The rentals are in arrears as they are received after each period of usage.

67. How about rentals in advance?
Let's take the same timeline as seen above and change the rentals from arrears to advance. The time line is shown below:

```
▼ ▼                                                  ▼   0
─────────────────────────────────────────────────────────
0   1                                              35  36
```

Lease Finance   53

Rentals in a lease can either be in advance or in arrears; advance is more common.

In the time line above, the first rental is being received in advance for the first month's usage and the last is being received in advance of the 36th month's usage; in total there are still 36 rentals with no rental being received at the end of the 36th month. The basic difference between arrears and advance is that the very last rental in the arrears mode is received up front in advance for the first month's usage.

68. Are there any variations to advance or arrears?
Occasionally a lessor may take multiple rentals in advance. This is how it would look, using the same time line used above:

```
   ▼
 ▼ ▼                              ▼   0   0
───────────────────────────────────────────
 0  1                             34  35  36
```

At time zero the lessor receives the equivalent of two rentals (if each rental is $100, the amount received at time zero is $200); thereafter, there are 34 additional rentals (each being $100). Note the total number of rentals is still 36 with no rentals being received at point 35 and point 36.

69. Are rentals always monthly?
Not at all. Monthly rentals are the most common; however, rentals can be received quarterly, semiannually or even annually.

PRESENT VALUE

70. What exactly is meant by the expression present value?
Present value is a concept that is commonly used in the analysis of many financial transactions including leasing. Examples of present value applications include capital budgeting, lease versus purchase analysis and alternative investment analysis.

If one were evaluating two alternative investments, present value would be the process used to bring all future cash flows to today's dollar value. If this were not done one would have to compare one set of future cash flows to another set of future cash flows perhaps occurring over different terms (where one investment say had future cash flows over 36 months and the other say over 48 months). Given the expression that a dollar received today is not equal to a dollar received in the future, present value would bring all future cash flows to a common denominator—today, or time zero.

The above process facilitates the proper analysis of the two alternative investments as one is looking at the answers at the same common point—today.

71. How does one arrive at present value?
Future cash flows are discounted to time zero.

72. What exactly is meant by discounting?
There are many ways to explain this term. One way is to simply state that discounting is the process used to bring all future cash flows to a common denominator—today. Another way is to state that discounting is the process used to arrive at present value.

The best way to really explain this term is to state that discounting is the opposite of compounding!

73. Can this be embellished?

It's best done through a simple example. Let's assume one puts $100 into a bank account on January 1. If this sum of money were to earn interest at say 10% compounded annually, at the end of the year on December 31 the $100 would have grown to be $110. The example is so simple that a calculator is not necessary. The time line is shown below:

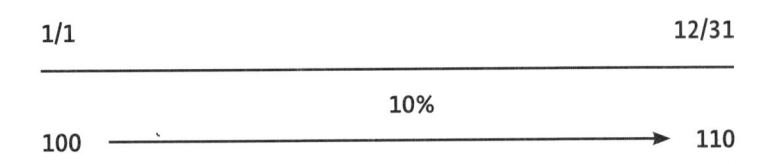

```
    1/1                                              12/31
    ─────────────────────────────────────────────────────
                          10%
    100  ──────────────────────────────────────▶  110
```

When money compounds, the original amount grows to become a larger amount.

With discounting, one starts with future dollars. Let's go through the example as follows:

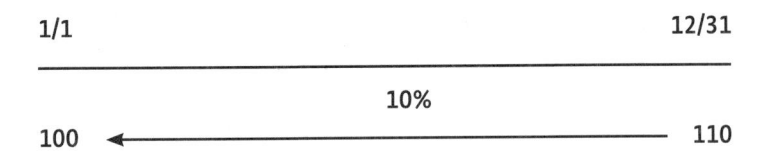

```
    1/1                                              12/31
    ─────────────────────────────────────────────────────
                          10%
    100  ◀──────────────────────────────────────  110
```

The $110 of future value is being brought back to 1/1 (time zero) at 10%. Common sense would suggest that if $100 grows to become $110 at 10%; $110 shrinks to become $100 at 10%. Discounting is indeed the opposite of compounding.

It is through this simple example that one arrives at the golden rule of finance: when the discount rate in a transaction is equal to the interest rate in the transaction, present value equals principal!

74. Again?

In the above example $100 is the principal; through compounding at 10% it grew to $110. When $110 was discounted at 10%, the present value shrunk to $100. Present value equals principal when the discount rate is equal to the interest rate.

> *Discounting is the opposite of compounding; when the discount rate is equal to the interest rate, present value equals principal.*

This golden rule will help in understanding many practical applications in the world of leasing including lease versus purchase analysis as well as pricing and structuring.

75. How about some present value examples?

Present value has two applications: present value of a single sum and present value of a series of cash flows. Let's begin with present value of a single sum.

Through all of the following examples the objective is not to understand present value necessarily as it applies to leasing; the objective is simply to understand present value.

What is the present value of $100,000 received at the end of a 48-month lease discounted at 10% per annum?

Time line:

```
0                                            48
|_____|
                                        100,000
```

Explanation:

The transaction has been subtly stated as a 48-month transaction implying that there are 48 monthly rentals (which remain unseen for purpos-

Lease Finance   57

es of this illustration). Given that the transaction is a 48-month transaction the annual discount rate needs to be converted into its monthly equivalent. Thus, the discount rate is not 10% but (10÷12) %.

Keystrokes:

> HP12-C

	f	REG	To clear all registers
100,000	CHS	FV	To enter future value
48		n	To enter term
10	g	12÷	To enter discount rate
PV		<u>67,143.20</u>	The answer is 67,143.20

> HP17BII+

	☐	CLEAR DATA	To clear old data
		FIN	To enter FIN menu
		TVM	To enter TVM menu
		OTHER	To enter OTHER menu
12		P/YR	To enter number of payments per year
		EXIT	To exit OTHER menu
48		N	To enter term
10		I%YR	To enter discount rate
100,000	+/-	FV	To enter future value
PV		<u>67,143.20</u>	The answer is 67,143.20

58 Winning With Leasing!

Analysis:

$67,143.20 is the present value of $100,000 discounted at .8333% per month over 48 months. In other words, under the concept that discounting is the opposite of compounding, $67,143.20 of principal compounded at .8333% per month will grow to be $100,000 at the end of the 48 months.

In the above illustration, whether the calculator is at the begin mode or end mode is irrelevant; the answer will be the same. The reason for this is that when a single sum is being discounted, such single sum is at a specific point in time and it is being brought back to time zero from that specific point in time.

76. How about one more example for present value of a single sum?

What is the present value of $100,000 received at the end of a four-year lease discounted at 10% per annum?

Time line:

```
0                                                    4
                                                100,000
```

Explanation:

In this transaction where the period is stated as four years it is implied that there are four annual rentals (which again remain unseen for purposes of this illustration). Given that the transaction is a four-year transaction, the discount rate remains at 10% and does not have to be divided by 12.

Lease Finance

Keystrokes:

> HP12-C

	f	REG	To clear all registers
100,000	CHS	FV	To enter future value
	4	n	To enter term
	10	i	To enter discount rate
	PV	68,301.35	The answers is 68,301.35

> HP17BII+

		CLEAR DATA	To clear old data
		FIN	To enter FIN menu
		TVM	To enter TVM menu
		OTHER	To enter OTHER menu
	1	P/YR	To enter number of payments per year
		EXIT	To exit OTHER menu
	4	N	To enter term
	10	I%YR	To enter discount rate
100,000	+/-	FV	To enter future value
	PV	68,301.35	The answer is 68,301.35

60 Winning With Leasing!

Analysis:

$68,301.35 is the present value of $100,000 discounted at 10% per year over four years. It should be obvious that this answer is greater than the answer in the earlier illustration ($67,143.20). The reason why this is so is because of the golden rule of finance (remember?): discounting is the opposite of compounding. In the earlier illustration one needs $67,143.20 to put into a hypothetical bank account which then at .8333% per month will grow to become $100,000; in the latter transaction, one needs to put a larger amount in the bank account, $68,301.35, to have it become $100,000 as the interest rate at which this principal compounds is 10% per year and not .8333% per month. In the first example the frequency of compounding being monthly means more interest on interest.

77. Does all of the above have to do with the difference between nominal interest rates and effective interest rates?

Yes it does! .8333% per month is effectively greater than the annual nominal 10%. Once again, as mentioned above, this is because when the frequency of compounding is monthly (as versus say annual), the effective (or true) interest earned is not .8333 x 12 = 10 but a larger number. One way to convert a monthly nominal rate of .8333% to its annual effective rate is to assume one is putting $100 into a bank account and that the banker is giving .8333% interest per month over a 12 month period. One can see below that the accumulation at the end of 12 months is $110.47.

Effective rates are always greater than nominal rates as they take into account frequent periodic compounding.

Lease Finance

> HP12-C

	f	REG	To clear all registers
	g	END	To set the calculator in arrears mode
100	CHS	PV	To enter principal
.8333		i	To enter monthly interest rate
12		n	To enter number of months in a year
		FV	110.47 — The answer is 110.47

> HP17BII+

		☐ CLEAR DATA	To clear old data
		FIN	To enter FIN menu
		TVM	To enter TVM menu
		OTHER	To enter OTHER menu
12		P/YR	To enter number of payments per year
		END	To set the calculator in arrears mode
		EXIT	To exit OTHER menu
100	+/-	PV	To enter principal
10		I%YR	To enter interest rate
12		N	To enter number of months in a year
		FV	110.47 — The answer is 110.47

62 Winning With Leasing!

Subtracting the principal of $100 from the total gives the amount of interest earned as $10.47. The effective or true return is not 10% but 10.47% as $100 of principal has earned $10.47. This means that a nominal rate of 10% compounded monthly is the same as an effective rate of 10.47% annually.

Thus, going back to QUESTION 76, if the discount rate were to be set at 10.47%, setting aside any rounding, the answer would be exactly equal to $67,143.20. Try it!

78. Another example of nominal and effective rates would be helpful?

Assume that a bank will give 12% per year compounded monthly. The monthly nominal rate is 1% (12÷12); however, as the customer earns interest on interest each month the annual effective rate is greater than 12%. Here is how it is calculated:

> HP12-C

	f	REG	
	g	END	To set the calculator in arrears mode
100	CHS	PV	To enter principal
1		i	To enter monthly interest rate
12		n	To enter number of months in a year
FV		112.68	The answer is 112.68

(first row description: To clear all registers)

> HP17BII+

		CLEAR DATA	To clear old data
		FIN	To enter FIN menu
		TVM	To enter TVM menu
		OTHER	To enter OTHER menu
12		P/YR	To enter number of payments per year
		END	To set the calculator in arrears mode
		EXIT	To exit OTHER menu
100	+/-	PV	To enter principal
12		I%YR	To enter interest rate
12		N	To enter number of months in a year
		FV	112.68	The answer is 112.68

Thus, with a monthly rate of 1% (or an annual nominal of 12%), the annual effective rate is 12.68%.

79. Time to move on to understand the present value of a series of cash flows?

A series of cash flows that takes place over regular intervals is called an annuity. Let's start with an annuity in arrears.

What is the present value of 48 rents each amounting to $5,000 to be received in arrears discounted at 17% per annum?

64 Winning With Leasing!

Time line:

```
0   1                                                48
─────────────────────────────────────────────────────
0   5,000  - - - - - - - - - - - - - - - - - - -    5,000
```

Explanation:

The rents are in arrears, thus there is no cash flow at time zero.

Keystrokes:

> HP12-C

		f	REG	To clear all registers
		g	END	To set calculator in arrears mode
48			n	To enter # of rentals
5,000			PMT	To enter rental amount
17		g	12÷	To enter discount rate
PV			-173,279.94	The answer is 173,279.94

Lease Finance **65**

> HP17BII+

		CLEAR DATA	To clear old data
		FIN	To enter FIN menu
		TVM	To enter TVM menu
		OTHER	To enter OTHER menu
12		P/YR	To enter number of payments per year
		END	To set the calculator in arrears mode
		EXIT	To exit OTHER menu
48		N	To enter number of months
5,000		PMT	To enter rental amount
17		I%YR	To enter discount rate
		PV	-173,279.94 The answer is 173,279.94

Analysis:

$173,279.94 is the present value of 48 rents in arrears discounted at the monthly equivalent of a 17% annual rate.

In other words, under the concept that discounting is the opposite of compounding, $173,279.94 of principal today in a hypothetical bank account would allow for the withdrawal of 48 payments in advance each amounting to $5,000 with the money earning 17% per annum compounded monthly. At the end of 48 months the principal would have been totally used up.

66 Winning With Leasing!

80. Perhaps the next illustration is a series of cash flows in advance?

What is the present value of 48 rents, each amounting to $5,000, in advance, discounted at 17% per annum. This obviously is the same illustration as in QUESTION 79; the only difference is that rents are in advance, not in arrears.

Time line:

```
0                                              47   48
────────────────────────────────────────────────────
5,000    ----------------------------    5,000   0
```

Explanation:

The rents are in advance; thus, there is no rental at point 48.

Keystrokes:

> HP12-C

	f	REG	To clear all registers
	g	BEGIN	To set the calculator in advance mode
5,000	CHS	PMT	To enter rental amount
17	g	12÷	To enter discount rate
48		n	To enter # of rentals
PV		175,734.74	The answer is 175,734.74

Lease Finance 67

> HP17BII+

		CLEAR DATA	To clear old data
		FIN	To enter FIN menu
		TVM	To enter TVM menu
		OTHER	To enter OTHER menu
12		P/YR	To enter number of payments per year
		BEG	To set the calculator in advance mode
		EXIT	To exit OTHER menu
48		N	To enter number of months
17		I%YR	To enter discount rate
5,000	+/-	PMT	To enter rental amount
	PV	**175,734.74**	The answer is 175,734.74

Analysis:

$175,734.74 is the present value of 48 rents in advance discounted at the monthly equivalent of a 17% annual rate.

This answer, $175,734.74, is greater than $173,279.94 in the earlier illustration where rentals were in arrears. This is logical, as when rentals are received sooner (in advance), the present value will be greater, all other variables being equal.

81. Both of the illustrations (in arrears and in advance) had even cash flows. Perhaps the next several illustrations will have uneven cash flows?

What is the present value of 36 rents with the rents in advance, where the first 12 rents are $1,000 and the remaining 24 rents are $1,500? The discount rate is 14% per annum.

Time line:

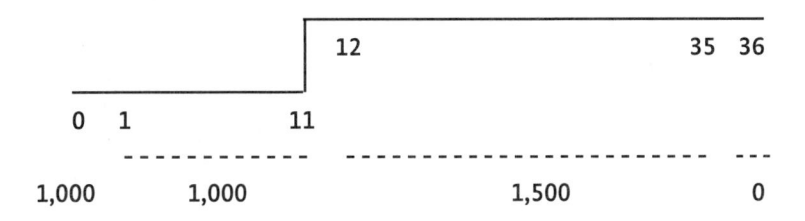

```
                        12                          35  36
   _____|
   0    1             11
                 ------------   -------------------------  ---
  1,000      1,000                      1,500               0
```

Explanation:

Given that the rents are in advance the first rent takes place at time zero. Thereafter there are 11 additional $1,000 rentals. After this there are 24 remaining rentals at $1,500 each. As the lease rentals are in advance, there is no cash flow at month 36.

Keystrokes:

> HP12-C

	f	REG	To clear all registers
14	g	12÷	To enter discount rate
1,000	g	CFo	To enter first cash flow at time zero
1,000	g	CFj	To enter next cash flow
11	g	Nj	To enter number of such flows
1,500	g	CFj	To enter next cash flow
24	g	Nj	To enter number of such flows
	f	NPV	<u>38,766.69</u> The answer is 38,766.69

The process cannot be done with the white keyboard. The blue keyboard must be used when one has uneven cash flows. Also the cash flows must be entered sequentially. Lastly, when using the blue keyboard for input the answer is always found on the gold keyboard. Whether the calculator is at the begin or end mode the answer will be the same. The blue keyboard designates cash flows and thus the mode is irrelevant.

70 Winning With Leasing!

> HP17BII+

		CLEAR DATA	To clear old data
		FIN	To enter FIN menu
		CFLO	To enter CFLO menu
		CLEAR DATA	To clear CFLO data
		YES	To affirm
1,000		INPUT	Inputs 1,000 for initial cash flow
1,000		INPUT	Inputs 1,000 for flow 1
11		INPUT	Indicates that flow 1 occurs 11 times
1,500		INPUT	Inputs 1,500 for flow 2
24		INPUT	Indicates that flow 2 occurs 24 times
		EXIT	To go to CALC
		CALC	To enter CALC menu
14 ÷ 12 = 1.1667		I%	To enter discount rate
NPV		38,766.69	The answer is 38,766.69

The process cannot be done with the TVM menu. The CFLO menu must be used when one has uneven cash flows. Also the cash flows must be entered sequentially. Lastly, the interest rate must be entered on a consistent basis with the cash flows. A monthly equivalent rate must be entered for monthly cash flows. Whether the calculator is at the begin or end mode, the answer will be the same. The CFLO menu designates cash flow and thus the mode is irrelevant.

It should be noted in both of the above calculations the answer was arrived at by pressing NPV. This is a mechanical quirk with both calculators. In reality, one is solving for present value and not net present value. Net present value (NPV), as will be seen later, is the difference between the present value of cash outflow and cash inflow.

82. Another illustration? Perhaps one with residual?

What is the present value of the cash flows in the following lease: in arrears, 60 months, first 24 rents at $1,000 per month, next 36 at $1,500 per month and residual of $10,000 at the end of the lease. The discount rate is 10% per annum.

Time line:

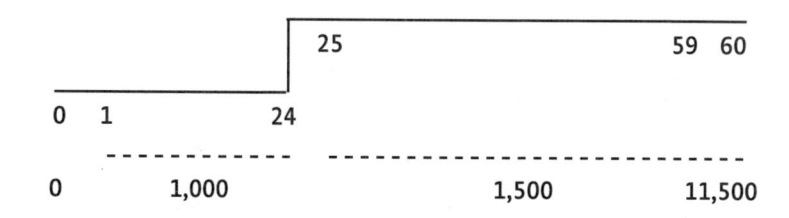

```
                        25                      59  60
    _____|                              
    0   1           24
    - - - - - - - - -    - - - - - - - - - - - - - - -
    0       1,000              1,500           11,500
```

Explanation:

Given that the rents are in arrears there is no cash flow at time zero. Thereafter one has 24 rents of $1,000 each. Though after this there are 36 rents of $1,500 each, the first 35 are shown separately; the last rent plus residual are shown together.

Keystrokes:

> HP12-C

	f	REG	To clear all registers
10	g	12÷	To enter discount rate
0	g	CFo	To enter zero as rentals are in arrears
1,000	g	CFj	To enter first cash flow
24	g	Nj	To enter number of such flows
1,500	g	CFj	To enter next cash flow
35	g	Nj	To enter number of such flows
11,500	g	CFj	To enter last rental plus residual
	f	NPV	65,840.51 — The answer is 65,840.51

Lease Finance 73

> HP17BII+

		CLEAR DATA	To clear old data
		FIN	To enter FIN menu
		CFLO	To enter CFLO menu
	☐	CLEAR DATA	To clear CFLO data
		YES	To affirm
0		INPUT	Inputs initial cash flow
1,000		INPUT	Inputs 1,000 for next cash flow
24		INPUT	Indicates that flow 1 occurs 24 times
1,500		INPUT	Inputs 1,500 for flow 2
35		INPUT	Indicates that flow 2 occurs 35 times
11,500		INPUT	Inputs last cash flow plus residual
1		INPUT	Indicates that flow 3 occurs once
		EXIT	To go to CALC
		CALC	To enter CALC menu
10 ÷ 12 = .8333		I%	To enter discount rate
NPV		<u>65,840.51</u>	The answer is 65,840.51

Analysis:

$65,840.51 is the present value of the 60 rents and the residual.

74 Winning With Leasing!

INTERNAL RATE OF RETURN

83. What is meant by the expression "internal rate of return"?
In its simplest form, setting aside the word "internal," the expression "rate of return" is synonymous to the interest rate in the lease.

84. What then is meant by the word "internal" as it pertains to the expression "internal rate of return"?
The word "internal" as it pertains to the expression "internal rate of return" has to do with a critical assumption that is an integral part of the expression "internal rate of return."

85. What is the assumption?
In a lease or for that matter in any financial transaction the lessor or investor receives cash flow back over a period of time. As this cash flow is received on an ongoing basis, each cash flow is reinvested by the lessor in other lease transactions.

The rate at which this external investment takes place (external to the transaction in question) is not known at the inception of the transaction in question. In fact, say over a 36-month lease as cash flow is being received each month, each cash flow is invested in varied lease transactions at rates unknown at the time the transaction in question is incepted.

Therefore to compute the rate of return of the transaction in question an assumption is made that all successive cash flows received are reinvested at the rate that the transaction itself has. This is what is meant by the word internal; the reinvestment is assumed to take place internally.

86. Is this a realistic assumption?
No it is not. In reality, as stated above, all cash flows are indeed reinvested externally in other leases; however, since it is truly impossible to

Lease Finance   75

know what these various reinvestment rates will be, the best assumption one can make is that the cash flows are reinvested internally. This assumption is universal to the world of IRR.

87. An example might help?
Let's use a simple one. Assume a lease has the following variables:

Equipment cost	$1,000.00
Annual rentals in arrears	$402.11
Term in years	3
Interest rate or IRR	10%

The time line would look as follows:

0	1	2	3
(1,000)	402.11	402.11	402.11

Let's proceed with the assumption that all cash flows generated are reinvested internally at 10%. The first cash flow is received at the end of the first year and therefore needs to be reinvested for a period of two years as follows:

> HP12-C

	f	REG	To clear all registers
402.11	CHS	PV	To enter cash flow received
2		n	To enter # of periods
10		i	To enter interest rate
FV		486.55	402.11 grows to become 486.55

76   Winning With Leasing!

> HP17BII+

		CLEAR DATA	To clear old data
		FIN	To clear all registers
		TVM	To enter TVM menu
		OTHER	To enter OTHER menu
	1	P/YR	To enter number of payments per year
		EXIT	To exit OTHER menu
402.11	+/-	PV	To enter cash flow received
	2	N	To enter # of periods
	10	I%YR	To enter interest rate
	FV	**486.55**	402.11 grows to become 486.55

Thus the first cash flow of $402.11 reinvested at 10% over two years has compounded to $486.55 at the end of the lease term.

88. The second cash flow needs to be reinvested for how long?

The second cash flow is received at the end of the second year—only one year remains in the lease. Thus it needs to be reinvested for one year at 10% which means it will compound to $442.32 ($402.11 x 1.10).

89. What about the last cash flow?

The third and last cash flow of $402.11 is received at the end of the lease term and therefore it does not need to be reinvested—the lease has expired.

Lease Finance   77

The above computations where two of three cash flows were reinvested at the internal rate of 10% can be summarized through the following time line:

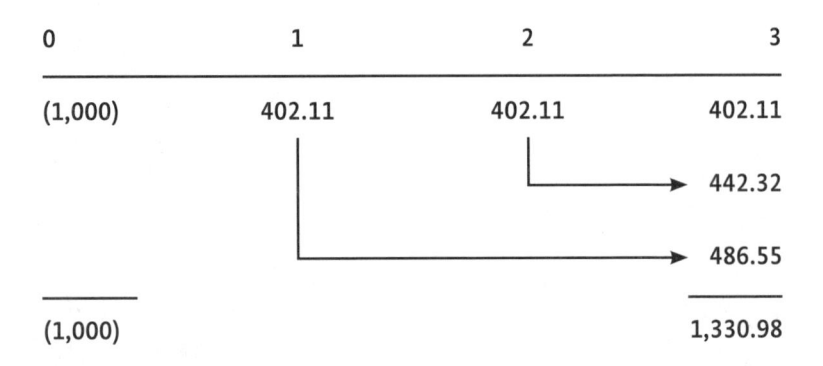

```
0                1              2                3

(1,000)         402.11         402.11           402.11
                  │              │
                  │              └──────────▶   442.32
                  │
                  └─────────────────────────▶   486.55
                                               ───────
(1,000)                                         1,330.98
```

90. So what is the conclusion to the above?
One should conclude that a $1,000 investment (in equipment cost) realized a total amount at the end of the lease equal to $1,330.98 under the premise that cash flows in the lease were reinvested at 10%.
Let's compute the IRR of the above cash flows as follows:

> **HP12-C**

	f	REG	To clear all registers
1,000	CHS	PV	To enter equipment cost
3		n	To enter # of periods
1,330.98		FV	To enter future value
	i	<u>10%</u>	10% is the IRR

78 Winning With Leasing!

> HP17BII+

		CLEAR DATA	To clear old data
		FIN	To enter FIN menu
		TVM	To enter TVM menu
		OTHER	To enter OTHER menu
1		P/YR	To enter number of payments per year
		EXIT	To exit OTHER menu
1,000	+/-	PV	To enter equipment cost
3		N	To enter # of periods
1,330.98		FV	To enter future value
I%YR		<u>10%</u>	10% is the IRR

91. The same rate as the IRR in the lease?

Yes! What the above computations prove is that when cash flows in a lease (or any other investment) are assumed to be reinvested at the same rate as in the lease, the eventual IRR of the cash flows is indeed the same as that which the lease was written for—in this case, 10%. Any other reinvestment rate would give a different IRR.

The word "internal" in the context of the expression "internal rate of return" assumes that all successive cash flows are reinvested at the IRR.

92. What is the technical definition of IRR?

IRR is that unique rate in a transaction which gives a net present value (NPV) of zero.

93. Wow! Can this be explained?
This is really best explained through a simple example. Assume the following: a banker writes a loan for $10,000 at 10% with three annual payments in arrears of $4,021.15 each.

The present value of the cash outflow to the banker is obviously $10,000; to be precise, it is a negative $10,000.

Let's compute the present value of the cash inflows to the banker.

94. At what discount rate?
Let's discount the cash inflows at 10% (which is the IRR in the transaction) as follows:

> HP12-C

	f	REG	To clear all registers
	g	END	To set the calculator in arrears mode
4,021.15	CHS	PMT	To enter payment
3		n	To enter # of payments
10		i	To enter discount rate
PV		10,000	The present value is 10,000

> HP17BII+

			CLEAR DATA	To clear old data
			FIN	To enter FIN menu
			TVM	To enter TVM menu
			OTHER	To enter OTHER menu
	1		P/YR	To enter number of payments per year
			END	To set the calculator to arrears mode
			EXIT	To exit OTHER menu
4,021.15		+/-	PMT	To enter payment
	3		N	To enter # of payments
	10		I%YR	To enter discount rate
	PV		<u>10,000</u>	The present value is 10,000

$10,000 is the present value of the three cash flows discounted at 10%, the IRR in the lease.

95. But that number is the same as the amount of the loan?
Remember the golden rule of finance?

96. Vaguely! It has been too long since that was mentioned. What is the golden rule of finance?
The golden rule of finance is as follows: discounting is the opposite of compounding; or in other words, when the discount rate in a transaction is the same as the interest rate in a transaction, present value equals principal!

Lease Finance   81

This is why when the cash flows were discounted at the interest rate (IRR) in the transaction, the present value equaled principal.

97. What about NPV?

The NPV in the transaction is shown below:

Present value of cash outflow	- 10,000
Present value of cash inflow	+ 10,000
NPV	0

NPV is the difference between the present value of cash outflow and cash inflow.

Thus NPV, as can be seen above, is simply the difference between the present value of cash outflow and cash inflow.

98. What explains the zero?

Given that the discount rate for the inflows is the same as the IRR, the present value will always be equal to principal; thus the zero. To embellish: if the discount rate for the cash inflows is a number different than 10%, the present value will no longer be $10,000; it will be a different number and zero will not be zero! Again, this proves that IRR is that unique rate in a transaction which gives a NPV of zero.

99. A few illustrations of IRR would now be helpful?

Let's start with a simple one: A 36-month lease has 36 rents of $1,800 each in arrears. The equipment cost is $50,000. What is the IRR?

Time line:

```
   0          1                                           36
  ─────────────────────────────────────────────────────────
(50,000)   1,800   - - - - - - - - - - - - - - - - -   1,800
```

Explanation:

Equipment cost, $50,000, is the outflow for the lessor; thus, logically shown as a negative cash flow. This takes place at time zero. Thereafter, there are 36 rents of $1,800 each in arrears from month 1-36.

Keystrokes:

> HP12-C

	f	REG	To clear all registers
	g	END	To set the calculator in arrears mode
50,000	CHS	PV	To enter equipment cost
36		n	To enter # of payments
1,800		PMT	To enter rental amount
	i	1.47	The monthly IRR is 1.47
12	x	17.70	The annual IRR is 17.70

Lease Finance 83

> HP17BII+

		CLEAR DATA	To clear old data
		FIN	To enter FIN menu
		TVM	To enter TVM menu
		OTHER	To enter OTHER menu
		END	To set calculator to arrears mode
12		P/YR	To enter number of payments per year
		EXIT	To exit OTHER menu
36		N	To enter # of months
1,800		PMT	To enter rental
50,000	+/-	PV	To enter equipment cost
I%YR		<u>17.70</u>	The annual IRR is 17.70

Analysis:

The IRR in the lease is 17.70%. When working with the white keyboard (HP12-C) for even cash flows, one solves for [i] keeping in mind that i and IRR mean the same thing.

100. Another illustration?

A lease has equipment cost of $90,000 with 48 payments in advance where the first 12 payments are $2,000 and the remaining 36 payments are $2,500. What is the IRR?

84 Winning With Leasing!

Time line:

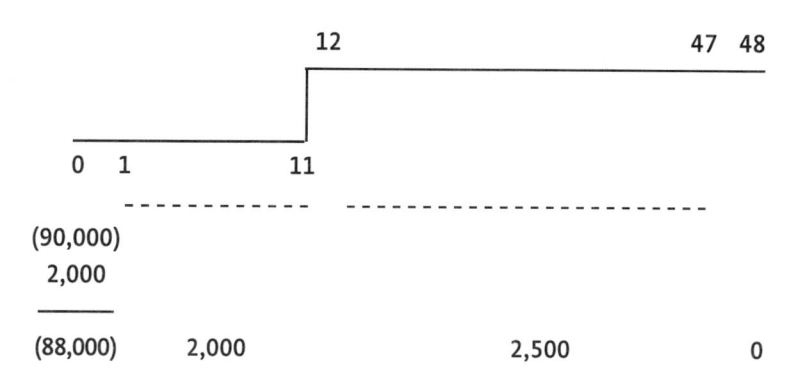

```
                    12                    47  48
                     ┌─────────────────────┐
                     │                     │
 0    1             11
 ──────────────     ──────────────────────────
(90,000)
 2,000
 ───────
(88,000)    2,000                  2,500        0
```

Explanation:

Two things occur at time zero: the lessor pays the supplier $90,000 and receives the first rental of $2,000. Thus the outflow at time zero is $88,000. After this there are 11 remaining cash flows of $2,000 (not 12 as the first was collected at time zero) followed by 36 cash flows of $2,500. There is no cash flow at point 48 as the rentals are in advance.

Key strokes:

> HP 12-C

	f	REG	To clear all registers
88,000	CHS g	CFo	To enter first cash flow at time zero
2,000	g	CFj	To enter next cash flow
11	g	Nj	To enter # of such flows
2,500	g	CFj	To enter next cash flow
36	g	Nj	To enter # of such flows
	f	IRR	1.01 The monthly IRR is 1.01
12	x	12.12	The annual IRR is 12.12

Lease Finance

› HP17BII+

	☐	CLEAR DATA	To clear old data
		FIN	To enter FIN menu
		CFLO	To enter CFLO menu
	☐	CLEAR DATA	To clear CFLO data
		YES	To affirm
88,000	+/-	INPUT	Inputs initial cash flow
2,000		INPUT	Inputs 2,000 for flow 1
11		INPUT	Indicates that flow 1 occurs 11 times
2,500		INPUT	Inputs 2,500 for flow 2
36		INPUT	Indicates that flow 2 occurs 36 times
		EXIT	To go to CALC
		CALC	To enter CALC menu
IRR%		1.01	The monthly IRR is 1.01
x12	=	12.12	The annual IRR is 12.12

Analysis:

12.12% is the IRR in the lease.

VARIED APPLICATIONS

101. In the real world of leasing when is present value used?
Present value, at least as it applies to this publication, is used in the following applications:

- Lease versus purchase analysis
- Lease pricing and structuring
- Lease accounting (the 90% present value test)
- Lease taxation (the value of depreciation)

102. What about IRR?
IRR is extensively used in portfolio analysis. In this publication it is used in the following applications:

- Lease versus purchase analysis (breakeven IRR)
- Lease accounting (lessor implicit rate)

SUMMARY

1. Rentals in a lease can either be in advance or arrears. Also they can either be monthly, quarterly, semiannually or annually.

2. Present value is the process of discounting future cash flows to today—time zero.

3. Discounting is the opposite of compounding; when the discount rate in a transaction equals the interest rate in the transaction, present value equals principal.

4. Annual effective rates are greater than annual nominal rates as the effective rates take into account the frequent periodic compounding.

5. Discount rates must be in sync with the periods over which cash flows are discounted; if cash flows are monthly, the discount rate is the monthly equivalent of the annual rate.

6. IRR in its simplest form is the interest rate in the lease.

7. The word "internal" within the expression "internal rate of return" means that all successive cash flows in a lease are assumed to be reinvested internally within the transaction.

8. IRR is that unique rate in a transaction that results in NPV equal to zero.

GLOSSARY

advance
Where rentals are received in advance of the period of usage.

annuity
A series of cash flows received/paid over regular intervals.

arrears
Where rentals are received at the end of the period of usage.

discounting
The process used to obtain present value. Also, discounting is the opposite of compounding; when the discount rate in a transaction equals the interest rate in the same transaction, present value equals principal.

effective rate
A rate which takes into account frequent periodic compounding. Example: if the monthly interest rate is 1% and money is to be compounded monthly, the annual effective rate will be 12.68%. Effective rates are always greater than nominal rates.

internal rate of return
Also IRR. In its simplest form, it is the interest rate in the lease. Technically, it is that unique discount rate in a transaction which gives a net present value (NPV) of zero.

net present value
The difference between the present value of cash outflow and cash inflow.

nominal rate
A rate which does not take into account the frequency of compounding. Example: if the monthly interest rate is 1% and money is to be compounded monthly, the annual nominal rate will be 1x12 = 12%.

present value
The value today of future cash flows.

HOMEWORK!

1. What is the present value of $200,000 at the end of 36 months discounted at 15% per annum?

2. What is the present value of $200,000 at the end of three years discounted at 15% per annum?

3. What is the present value of 48 rents of $1,500 in advance discounted at 14% per annum?

4. What is the present value of 48 rents of $1,500 in advance; two up-front, 46 remaining discounted at 14% per annum?

5. What is the present value of 48 rents of $1,500 in advance; two up-front, 46 remaining with residual of $10,000 discounted at 14% per annum?

6. What is the present value of 48 rents in advance, where the first 18 rents are $2,000 and the remaining 30 rents are $2,500 each? The discount rate is 16% per annum.

7. What is the present value of 60 rents in arrears, with the first 24 at $1,000 each and the remaining at $750 each along with a residual of $5,000? The discount rate is 13.5% per annum.

8. A 48-month lease has rents in advance of $1,000 each. Equipment cost is $36,000. What is the IRR?

9. A lease has equipment cost of $100,000 with 48 payments in arrears. The first 12 payments are $2,000 each, the remaining 36 months are $2,500 each. The residual is $10,000. What is the IRR?

HOMEWORK ANSWERS

Answer 1
Time line:

```
0                                    36
─────────────────────────────────────
                                200,000
```

> **HP 12-C**

	f	REG
200,000	CHS	FV
36		n
15	g	12 ÷
PV		**127,881.83**

> **HP17BII+**

	☐	CLEAR DATA
		FIN
		TVM
200,000	+/-	FV
36		N
15		I%YR
PV		**127,881.83**

Winning With Leasing!

Answer 2
Time line:

```
0                                           3
─────────────────────────────────────────────
                                      200,000
```

> HP 12-C

	f	REG
200,000	CHS	FV
3		n
15		i
PV		131,503.25

> HP17BII+

		CLEAR DATA
		FIN
		TVM
		OTHER
1		P/YR
		EXIT
200,000	+/-	FV
3		N
15		I%YR
PV		131,503.25

Lease Finance 95

Answer 3
Time line:

```
0                                              47  48
─────────────────────────────────────────────────────
1,500  - - - - - - - - - - - - - - - - - - -  1,500  0
```

› HP 12-C

	f	REG
	g	BEGIN
48		n
14	g	12 ÷
1,500	CHS	PMT
	PV	<u>55,532.22</u>

› HP17BII+

		CLEAR DATA
		FIN
		TVM
		OTHER
12		P/YR
		BEG
		EXIT
48		N
14		I%YR
1,500	+/-	PMT
	PV	<u>55,532.22</u>

96 Winning With Leasing!

Answer 4
Time line:

```
 0    1                           46  47  48
-----------------------------------------------
                -----------------------
3,000         1,500                  0   0
```

> HP 12-C

	f	REG
3,000	g	CFo
1,500	g	CFj
46	g	Nj
14	g	12÷
	f	NPV 56,162.60

> HP17BII+

		CLEAR DATA
		FIN
		CFLO
	☐	CLEAR DATA
		YES
3,000		INPUT
1,500		INPUT
46		INPUT
		EXIT
		CALC
14 ÷ 12	=	I%
NPV		56,162.60

Answer 5
Time line:

```
0    1                                    46  47  48
----------------------------------------- --- ---
3,000     1,500                            0  10,000
```

> HP 12-C

	f	REG
3,000	g	CFo
1,500	g	CFj
46	g	Nj
0	g	CFj
10,000	g	CFj
14	g	12÷
	f	NPV	**61,893.24**

> HP17BII+

	☐	CLEAR DATA
		FIN
		CFLO
	☐	CLEAR DATA
		YES
3,000		INPUT
1,500		INPUT
46		INPUT
0		INPUT
1		INPUT
10,000		INPUT
1		INPUT
		EXIT
		CALC
14 ÷ 12	=	I%
NPV		61,893.24

Lease Finance

Answer 6
Time line:

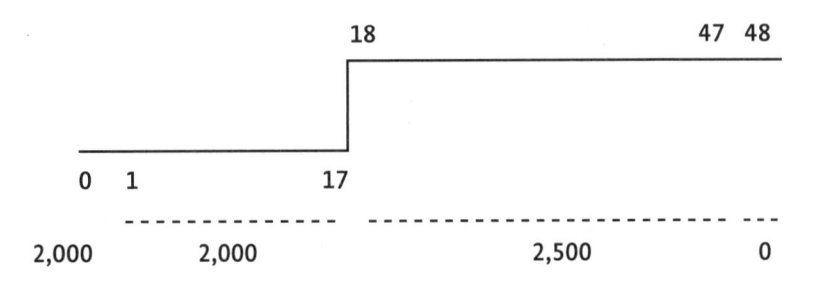

```
                    18                  47  48
                    ┌─────────────────────┐
                    │
     0   1          17
   ─ ─ ─ ─ ─ ─ ─ ─ ─    ─ ─ ─ ─ ─ ─ ─ ─ ─ ─ ─ ─ ─ ─ ─
  2,000    2,000                  2,500            0
```

> **HP 12-C**

	f	REG
16	g	12÷
2,000	g	CFo
2,000	g	CFj
17	g	Nj
2,500	g	CFj
30	g	Nj
	f	NPV **81,329.15**

100 Winning With Leasing!

> HP17BII+

		CLEAR DATA
		FIN
		CFLO
		CLEAR DATA
		YES
2,000		INPUT
2,000		INPUT
17		INPUT
2,500		INPUT
30		INPUT
		EXIT
		CALC
16 ÷ 12		I%
NPV		<u>81,329.15</u>

Lease Finance

Answer 7
Time line:

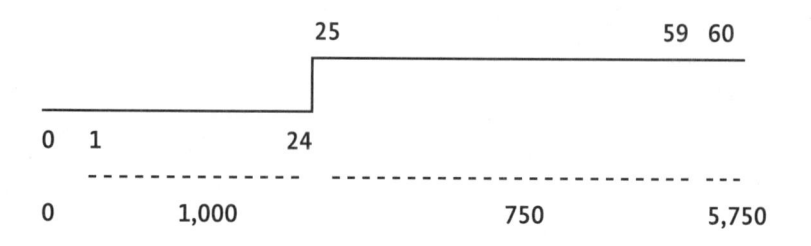

```
                25                    59  60
    ────────────┘                         
    0   1       24
    ─ ─ ─ ─ ─ ─ ─    ─ ─ ─ ─ ─ ─ ─ ─ ─ ─ ─  ─ ─ ─
    0       1,000              750           5,750
```

> **HP 12-C**

	f	REG
1,000	g	CFj
24	g	Nj
750	g	CFj
35	g	Nj
5,750	g	CFj
13.5	g	12÷
	f	NPV 40,382.78

> HP17BII+

	☐	CLEAR DATA
		FIN
		CFLO
	☐	CLEAR DATA
		YES
0		INPUT
1,000		INPUT
24		INPUT
750		INPUT
35		INPUT
5,750		INPUT
1		INPUT
		EXIT
		CALC
13.5 ÷ 12	=	I%
NPV		<u>40,382.78</u>

Lease Finance

Answer 8

> HP 12-C

	f	REG
	g	BEG
48		n
1,000		PMT
36,000	CHS	PV
	i	1.30
	12x	__15.61__

> HP17BII+

	☐	CLEAR DATA
		FIN
		TVM
		OTHER
12		P/YR
		BEG
		EXIT
48		N
1,000		PMT
36,000	+/-	PV
	I%YR	__15.61__

104 Winning With Leasing!

Answer 9
Time line:

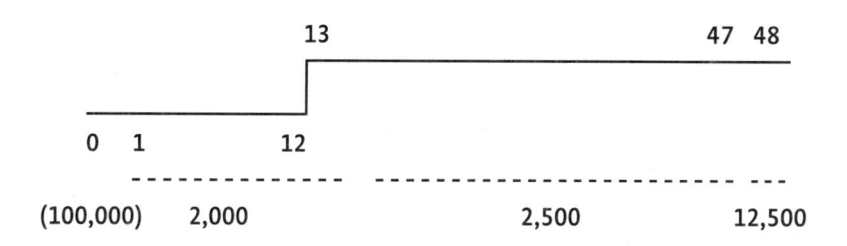

```
                    13                      47  48
                    ┌──────────────────────────
                    │
 0    1             12
 ┼────┼─────────────┼────────────────────────┼───┼
(100,000)  2,000                     2,500      12,500
```

> HP 12-C

	f	REG
100,000	CHS g	CFo
2,000	g	CFj
12	g	Nj
2,500	g	CFj
35	g	Nj
12,500	g	CFj
f IRR		.82
12x		<u>9.81</u>

> HP17BII+

	☐	CLEAR DATA
		FIN
		CFLO
	☐	CLEAR DATA
		YES
100,000	+/-	INPUT
2,000		INPUT
12		INPUT
2,500		INPUT
35		INPUT
12,500		INPUT
1		INPUT
		EXIT
		CALC
IRR%		0.82
x12	=	<u>9.81</u>

Lease Marketing

Lease Marketing

The Types of Lessees

The Benefits of Leasing

The Equipment Acquisition Process

Lease Versus Purchase Analysis

Lease Versus Lease Analysis

Countering Common Objections

Summary

Glossary

Homework!

Homework Answers

THE TYPES OF LESSEES

103. Are there different types of lessees?
There are two types of lessees – those who want to lease and those who need to lease.

104. What is the difference between these two types?
The first type, the ones who want to lease, are the types who realize that leasing offers certain benefits and though they have the ability to acquire equipment through other means, such as cash or a bank loan, they lease because they want to.

Those who need to lease do so because they have no other options; those who want to lease do so as they recognize the benefits that leasing provides.

105. What about the other type?
The second type, the ones who need to lease, are typically the types who have difficulty in obtaining other means of financing such as a bank loan and thus they lease because they need to.

106. Why would a leasing company lease to an entity that has difficulty in obtaining other means of financing?
Typically independent nonbank lessors, who are often not regulated (or in some countries less regulated than banks), are willing to take on higher risk clients for two reasons.

107. What are the two reasons?
First of all, many lessors position themselves in below investment grade quality credits or SME (small and medium-sized enterprise) markets. This is because these lessors generally cannot compete in the

"blue chip" lessee market as these types of lessees are able to get lower cost loans or leases from banks or large lessors who have access to low cost funding.

Secondly, as independent nonbank lessors are either not regulated or are lightly regulated, they are in a better position to take on poorer quality credits by taking the risk-reward approach where the IRRs are quite high and the spreads are quite generous. Banks generally are unwilling to take on such credits as they have to monitor their delinquencies for doubtful accounts as required by the regulators.

THE BENEFITS OF LEASING

108. What are the main reasons why lessees do lease?
There are six major reasons for leasing—they follow:

- Cash flow
- Financial reporting
- Financial
- Technology
- Tax
- Convenience

The above six reasons are universal.

109. Which is the single most important reason for leasing?
This is difficult to conclude as different lessees lease for different reasons. Only one country, the U.S., has conducted formal surveys to gauge why lessees do lease. The Equipment Leasing Association of the U.S. in two surveys done over the years concluded that cash flow is the number one reason for leasing. Based on the author's experience and exposure, it is believed this is generally true with most, if not all, other countries.

Of the six reasons to lease, cash flow or cash management is the number one reason throughout the world.

110. Can each of the above six categories be explained in greater detail?
It is important to do so as it is only through such detail that one fully understands the popularity of leasing.

111. Why not start sequentially?

From a cash flow or cash management point of view there are many benefits that leasing offers. To begin with, leasing often finances 100% of equipment cost. Other financing alternatives generally require the borrower to make a down payment.

100% financing facilitates affordability whereby lessees are able to acquire equipment they could otherwise not afford.

112. What is meant by the expression "more than 100% financing"?

Often when it comes to IT systems, a large part of the total cost has to do with software, installation and training – these items constitute soft collateral. Soft collateral at times can exceed 50% of the total cost; yet, lessors will typically finance 100% of the total cost. Comparing the amount financed to the total of hard collateral this amounts to "more than 100% financing."

113. Any other benefits of cash flow?

Leasing conserves working capital. Working capital is current assets minus current liabilities. Cash is a major component of current assets and as leasing preserves cash, it preserves working capital. Prudent financial practice would suggest that working capital should not be used for medium-term financing needs.

114. Is that it?

One additional benefit from a cash flow point of view is that leases can be structured to meet the cash flow needs of lessees.

115. What exactly is meant by structuring a lease?

As an example, if the lessee is in a seasonal business the lease can be structured on a skip payment basis. During low cash generation periods, certain rentals are skipped. In essence structuring means giving the lease the pattern most suited to meet the lessee's cash flow needs.

116. What other examples can be provided of structuring a lease?

Leases can be step-up (also referred to as low- high) or step-down (also referred to as high-low). A step-up lease would look as follows:

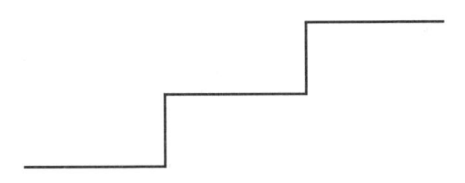

A step-down lease, on the other hand, would look as follows:

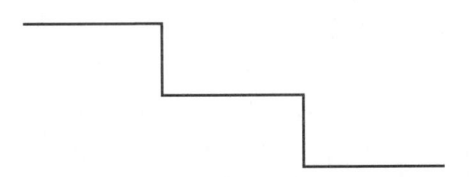

The step-up structure would be of benefit, as an example, to a construction company that has received a government contract to construct a new building. The construction company is likely to be receiving cash from the project on a percentage completion basis; often under such a scenario, the cash flow is deferred and the step-up structure accommodates the pattern of the cash flow.

On the other hand, a step-down structure would be of benefit to an entity which has excess cash on hand and would like the comfort of lower rentals in the future. This is referred to as "buying down the rate."

Structuring leases is substantially embellished in the Pricing and Structuring Section.

117. Are rentals paid to lessors higher than what loan payments would be on a loan?

Assuming one is comparing "apples to apples" (where the lease term is equal to what otherwise would be the loan term), rentals can actually be lower. This is caused because of the existence of residual on operating leases. Higher the residual, lower will be the rental. Also, when lessors pass on the value of tax benefits to the lessee they do so by reducing the rentals. Thus, from a cash flow point of view, the periodic repayment amount on an operating lease can very often be lower than on a loan.

118. A summary of cash flow benefits would be helpful?

The summary follows:

- 100% financing
- 100% plus financing
- Conservation of working capital
- Structured leases tailored to meet cash flow needs
- Lower rentals due to residual and transfer of tax benefits

119. What benefits does the lessee obtain from the financial reporting category?

To begin with, one must understand that the benefit from financial reporting has to do with off balance sheet financing.

This is fully explained in the Accounting Section.

120. Why do lessees prefer off balance sheet financing?

Off balance sheet financing is used by lessees to window dress their financial statements. Window dressing means that the financial statements appear to be stronger than they really are.

121. How is this done?

Let's first summarize that which is detailed later in the Accounting Section. When a lessee has an operating lease which qualifies for off balance sheet financing, the impact of this on the balance sheet is that neither the asset nor the corresponding debt is shown; the income statement shows rent expense. In other words, the lease is treated as though it is a rental.

122. What is the benefit of this treatment?

It leads to ratio enhancement. Let's use three examples: the current ratio, return on assets (ROA) and the debt to equity ratio.

Let's start with the current ratio, the formula for which is:

CURRENT ASSETS
───────────────
CURRENT LIABILITIES

Off balance sheet financing causes the debt to escape the balance sheet; thus, current liabilities (that portion of the debt deemed to be current) are lower than otherwise. This reduces the denominator in the current ratio causing the ratio to be higher than otherwise. Entities almost invariably prefer higher current ratios.

123. What is the impact on ROA?

The formula for ROA is:

NET INCOME
───────────
TOTAL ASSETS

Off balance sheet financing causes the leased asset not to be booked; thus, total assets, the denominator in the ratio, are lower than otherwise which causes ROA to be higher. Entities universally prefer higher ROAs.

124. How does off balance sheet financing help the debt to equity ratio?

The debt to equity ratio, also known as leverage or gearing, is the ratio of an entity's total debt to shareholder's equity. Off balance sheet financing causes the debt component to be lower than otherwise thereby causing the debt to equity ratio to be lower. Entities typically prefer this ratio to be lower than otherwise as it strengthens their capital structure.

Thus, three key ratios, the current ratio (a measure of liquidity); ROA (a measure of profitability); and the debt to equity ratio (a measure of capital structure), are enhanced through operating leases which qualify for off balance sheet financing.

125. Though ratios are enhanced, operating leases are disclosed in the footnotes to the financial statements. Based on this can an astute reader/analyst not reincorporate the assets and liabilities back into the balance sheet and recalculate the ratios?
Not all readers are astute!

Going beyond external financial reporting, off balance sheet financing can increase the quantum of top management's bonuses. As explained earlier, ROA can be enhanced through operating leases. Many entities award performance bonuses based on ROA; therefore, many divisional managers avail of off balance sheet financing from operating leases to improve ROA!

126. What are some other benefits from financial reporting?
Off balance sheet financing can possibly improve the earnings of an entity. Let's compare the impact on the income statement of a lessee from both an off balance sheet operating lease and a finance lease (or for that matter a loan – as finance leases are treated as though they are loans).

When a lessee has an operating lease, rent expense is shown on the income statement typically on a linear basis as follows:

Off balance sheet financing not only strengthens the balance sheet; it improves earnings as well.

RENT EXPENSE
_____

Lease Marketing 117

However when a lessee has a finance lease (or a loan), the income statement shows depreciation plus interest expense. Depreciation, for accounting purposes (as versus tax), is generally linear; interest, however is always a downward sloping line as there is more interest in the earlier periods than in the latter periods.

The impact is shown below:

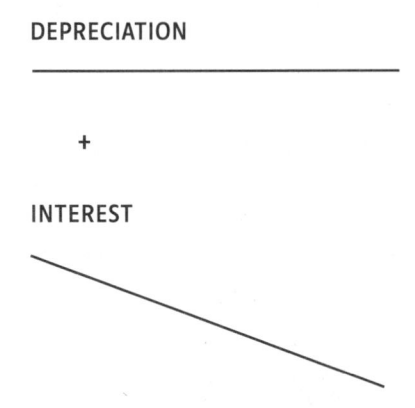

DEPRECIATION
_____

+

INTEREST
‾‾‾‾‾‾‾‾‾‾‾‾‾‾‾‾‾‾‾‾‾‾

Thus, when one compares a straight line (rent expense) to the sum of a straight line plus a downward sloping line (depreciation plus interest expense), more often than not rent expense in the early periods of the lease is likely to be less than depreciation plus interest expense. This causes earnings (and correspondingly, earnings per share) to be higher.

127. But is there not a reversal later as interest expense is lower in latter periods?

Even if such reversal were to take place, lessees typically are earnings conscious in the short term—often from one quarter to another. This is true for most, if not for all, listed companies who are glaringly aware of the correlation between earnings and share price!

128. What type of lessee will generally use off balance sheet financing for ratio enhancement and improvement in earnings?

Any entity that wishes to show stronger financial statements to its lenders and/or shareholders will avail of such benefit.

129. Any other benefits from financial reporting?
Off balance sheet financing can often help avoid trigger restrictive financial covenants imposed by lenders. As explained earlier, operating leases can cause the leverage or gearing to be lower. Thus, if a lender has imposed a debt to equity ceiling, operating leases can come to the rescue.

130. Would not lenders include operating leases as debt?
Some do, some don't!

131. Do operating leases, via off balance sheet financing, have any other benefits?
Operating leases can preclude potential book losses. This is best illustrated. Assume an entity had purchased (not leased) an asset a few years ago (say a computer) for $100. Assume the asset has accumulated depreciation of $60 or a book value of $40. Now further assume that due to technology the asset is worth zero and is useless to the entity. If this is a material transaction, the auditors would require that the asset be written off. Such an unexpected write-off causes a loss which can often be a big hit to earnings.

132. How do operating leases help?
Given that operating leases can be off balance sheet, the asset to begin with is not booked. One cannot write an asset down if there is no asset in the balance sheet to begin with!

133. A summary of the financial reporting benefits would be helpful?
The summary follows:

- Ratio enhancement
- Possible improvement in earnings
- Increased performance bonuses to management
- Avoidance of restrictive financial covenants
- Avoidance of potential book losses

134. The third major reason for leasing was stated as financial. What are the benefits to a lessee from this category?
There are many benefits in this category. To begin with, from a financial point of view, leasing makes financing available to entities who often are not bankable. Banks typically are more conservative in their lending practices primarily because they are strictly regulated via stringent prudential norms. Leasing companies, particularly independent non-bank types, are able to "play" with the risk/reward aspect of lending to a much greater degree than banks. Thus medium-term asset financing is often made available to those who otherwise would not qualify for bank credit. This, indeed, is a benefit.

135. If leasing often caters to the riskier credits, do lessors seek additional collateral beyond the fact that they are the legal owners of the leased asset?
Yes and no. Given the fact that they are indeed the legal owners of assets leased, and if the repossession and recovery process is expedient, lessors often do not seek additional collateral. This is of substantial benefit to many lessees who either do not have additional collateral or do not wish to be burdened with liens and such. Of course, as it would seem obvious, whether or not additional collateral is sought is a case-by-case credit decision.

136. Can leasing be a hedge against inflation?
Leasing can indeed offer such a hedge if the lessor extends a fixed-rate lease to the lessee. This is actually quite common as lessors often are able to hedge such risk (say through match funding) or are willing to bear such risk if they perceive interest rates not to be too volatile over the lease term. In any event a hedge against inflation, or not being subject to the vagaries of fluctuating interest rates, is indeed a financial benefit to the lessee.

137. What are some of the other financial benefits?
There are many others. Leasing offers financial diversification. It is not financially prudent to have an entity, say at one extreme, borrow from just one bank. This is because banks can, and often do, change lending practices either owing to any merger and acquisition that may have

taken place or due to any other internal strategic reasons. A prudent borrower should diversify its borrowing base; ideally, one should have a financial relationship with say two or three banks and two or three lessors. This also enhances the borrower's negotiating abilities.

138. From a financial point of view is leasing always more expensive?

Not at all! It is an unfortunate myth that leasing is always more expensive. Not only does leasing offer many benefits as are being discussed in this subsection; often, it can even be cheaper!

Leasing has many benefits; often, it can be the lowest cost mode of acquisition as well!

139. Cheaper than what?

More often than not leasing is cheaper than cash as cash has an opportunity cost associated with it. Also, depending on other factors such as the tax rate, the tax depreciation life of the asset, the method of depreciation to be used if the asset were to be purchased, the amount of down payment on a loan and finally the choice of a discount rate – leasing is often cheaper on a present value basis than loan financing.

140. Are there any other financial benefits?

Yes. Often captives (whose major focus is to avail of additional gross profit on incremental sales) will lease to entities who are not sufficiently creditworthy to get a bank loan. Or, captives may subsidize a lease rate to manage (which means unload!) the inventory of the parent company. Lessees benefit from a financial point of view in either of the two scenarios presented.

141. A summary of the financial benefits would be helpful?

The summary follows:

- Availability of medium-term financing
- Often no additional collateral
- Hedge against inflation on fixed-rate leases
- Financial diversification
- Often less expensive
- Availability of financing for marginally creditworthy lessees

142. The next major reason for leasing was listed as technology. What are some of the benefits in this category?

Leasing is a hedge against technology. This is true on operating leases where the lessor takes a residual position. This type of a lease makes the leasing arrangement one of usage with the burden of technological risk being borne by the lessor. At the end of the lease term, the lessee has the right to return the asset. If the then fair market value of the asset is less than the residual that the lessor assumed, the lessor bears this loss. Of course lessors are as careful as possible in assuming residual risk and are also able to benefit from many leases where the fair market value of the asset at the end of the lease term is greater than the assumed residual position. Nonetheless, the mere existence of residual causes the lessee to have a hedge against technology.

The former is true even on equipment that is not high technology; for when a lessor assumes a residual position, the lessee is protected from any impairment in the market value of the equipment at the end of the lease term.

143. Can a lessee return the leased asset to the lessor prior to the expiration of the lease term?

This can indeed happen under two different scenarios. The first is known as "technology refresh." This is a benefit typically offered by captives and applies generally to high tech equipment such as computers.

144. What exactly is meant by "technology refresh?"

This is best illustrated. Assume a lessee has leased 100 personal computers on a 36-month lease. Further assume that halfway through the lease the computers, based on new technology that has come about, are not acceptable to the lessee. The lessee desires to shift to newer technology. The lessee approaches the lessor and requests that the 100 personal computers be "taken out" and replaced with newer technology computers.

145. Why would a lessor be willing to do this?

It really is a win-win situation for both parties. The lessor is willing to take out the older computers only after having been assured by its remarketing group that they have located another lessee who would be willing to lease the older computers. That which is obsolete to one is not obsolete to another! Also the lessor will, of course, charge the first lessee a penalty for an early take out. On top of this the lessor can benefit from having placed the first lessee into a new lease!

146. How does the first lessee benefit?

The first lessee avails of the benefit of "technology refresh" and has, of course, ascertained that they are better off paying the penalty than staying with the older computers for the remaining life of the lease.

147. Why is "technology refresh" typically offered only by captive lessors?

Captive lessors are generally willing to take inventory risks (in cases where the returned assets have not yet been remarketed) the type of which other lessors are generally not, as captives are in the business of selling inventory for their parent. This is not to say that certain specialized independents do not offer "technology refresh."

148. What is the other scenario where leased assets can be returned?

Leased assets can be returned simply through the early termination of a lease. In this case, whether it be for technological reasons or otherwise, a lessee may desire to return leased assets prior to the expiration of the lease term. Lessors, again generally captives, would be willing to do this based on some of the same concepts under "technology refresh" other than the fact that the lessee is not replacing older assets with newer assets.

149. A summary of the technology benefits would be helpful?
The summary follows:

- Hedge against technology
- Technology refresh during the term of the lease
- Early termination options

150. The fifth major reason for leasing is Taxation. What are the benefits under this category?
An important benefit under taxation has to do with the fact that, more often than not, lessees can claim rent expense on a lease over a period shorter than the tax depreciation life (had the asset been purchased).

151. Can this be illustrated?
Assume a three-year finance lease in a country where rent expense is fully deductible on such a lease (This is further explained in the Taxation Section). Further assume that if the asset had been purchased it could have been depreciated on a straight line basis over its fiscal life of five years. Other assumptions follow:

Equipment cost	$100.00
Monthly rental	$3.20
Residual	$.00

Leasing can provide substantial tax benefits to tax motivated lessees.

Over each of the three years, assuming the lease was incepted the first day of the fiscal year, the lessee will claim $38.40 ($3.20 x 12) as the rental or lease expense in its tax return. Had the asset been purchased, the depreciation expense for each of the same three years would have been $20. Clearly the lease facilitates a faster write-off and enables lessees to have lower taxable income in the early years.

152. Will the above always be true?
It will, as long as the lease term is shorter than the otherwise deprecia-

ble life, when depreciation is straight line and when there are no special first year investment allowances or bonus depreciation.

153. Any other benefits from taxation?
In those countries where lessors are allowed to claim tax depreciation on leases (this, too, is further explained in the Taxation Section) they often pass on either a part or all of such tax benefits to the lessee. This is done in competitive markets and is accomplished through a reduction in the rentals.

154. Are there not some unique tax benefits from leasing in the United States?
In the U.S., operating leases can prevent a lessee from triggering the alternative minimum tax (AMT) and the midquarter convention under MACRS. The underlying premise here is that operating leases are generally considered to be true (tax) leases from a tax point of view thereby allowing the lessee to claim rent expense in its tax return. In the context of the AMT, depreciation is a preference item; rent expense is not. Large amounts of preferences will tip an entity into AMT which, in essence, is a penalty tax.

In the context of the midquarter convention, it is purchased property (more than 40% in the fourth fiscal quarter) which triggers this convention which then reduces the total amount of MACRS that can be claimed. True leases (operating leases) help an entity not to tip the 40% threshold, thereby avoiding the midquarter convention.

Substantial detail on AMT and midquarter can be found in the Taxation Section; suffice it to note that operating leases mitigate tax damage.

155. A summary of the taxation benefits would be helpful?
The summary follows:

- Faster tax write-off
- Lower rentals due to tax benefit transfer
- Mitigation of AMT and midquarter (in the U.S.)

156. We are down to the last major reason for leasing, "convenience." What various benefits does the lessee derive from this category?
There are numerous benefits under this category. The most important is that more often than not leasing has a faster response time than other alternative means of financing such as loans.

157. Why is this so?
As mentioned earlier, banks are regulated; generally, independent non-bank leasing companies are either not regulated or are lightly regulated. Regulation causes banks to be more cautious. This is not to say that nonbank lessors are frivolous; however, as they compete against banks, who have access to lower cost of funds, they try their best to be more value added. One form of value add is faster response time which is critical to many an entity that desires less red tape and faster processing of credit applications.

Many lease merely because leasing has a faster response time than other financing options.

158. Can leases be approved faster and/or easier at the lessee end as well?
This is true with both large entities as well as governmental organizations. Both typically have two types of budgets – capital and operating. When an asset is to be purchased it is appropriated from the capital budget. This appropriation/approval can be, and often is, time consuming as paperwork has to be shuffled to committees, sign-off is required by many and seeking justification causes untold delays.

On the other hand when an asset is to be leased, it is appropriated from pre-approved operating budgets which have carefully been put together with adequate due diligence. Thus assets can be procured faster when they are leased, not only because of faster response time at the lessor end but faster appropriation at the lessee end!

159. Any other benefits from convenience?

Master lease agreements make it both convenient and expedient for subsequent assets that will be leased. Once a master lease agreement has been negotiated and signed by both the lessor and the lessee, subsequent "draw downs" (additional leased assets) are done on simple addendums, or appendices, without having to go through the whole process of signing another major contract.

160. What is meant by the expression "one stop shopping"?

Full-service leases include services such as maintenance, insurance and the like. In fact some leases can be so full-service that it tantamounts to total outsourcing. Motor car or truck fleet leases are examples where the lessor purchases the vehicles, registers them, obtains special licenses where applicable, provides trained drivers, maintains and repairs the fleet, provides varied types of needed insurance, provides substitute vehicles when one in the fleet is being repaired, provides management reports such as monthly expenses ... the list of services can be endless. Though this may be an extreme example of "one stop shopping," any lease with additional services bundled into it makes it convenient for the lessee to procure all services, including financing, under one roof.

161. Does leasing offer more flexibility than other modes of financing?

Yes it does. Flexibility comes from end of term options inherent in operating leases. Whereas in a full payout finance lease, the lessee almost invariably intends to, and does, purchase the asset at the end of the lease term either after paying the last rental or a nominal amount; on an operating lease, whether it is contractually stated or not, the lessee typically has three options. The lessee can either purchase the leased asset, return it or renew the lease.

This type of flexibility is a tremendous benefit as the entity is not "locked in" forever at the inception of the lease financing arrangement. This is discussed in detail in the Operating Lease Section.

162. A summary of the convenience benefits would be helpful?

The summary follows:

- Faster response time than loans
- Faster appropriation from operating budgets
- Master lease agreements
- One stop shopping
- Flexibility from end of term options

163. There are so many benefits listed, a final summary would be helpful?

CASH FLOW
- 100% financing
- 100% plus financing
- Conservation of working capital
- Structured leases tailored to meet cash flow needs
- Lower rentals due to residual and transfer of tax benefits

FINANCIAL REPORTING
- Ratio enhancement
- Possible improvement in earnings
- Increased performance bonuses to management
- Avoidance of restrictive financial covenants
- Avoidance of potential book losses

FINANCIAL
- Availability of medium-term financing
- Often no additional collateral
- Hedge against inflation on fixed-rate leases
- Financial diversification
- Often less expensive
- Availability of financing for marginally creditworthy lessees

TECHNOLOGY
- Hedge against technology
- Technology refresh during the term of the lease
- Early termination options

TAX
- Faster tax write-off
- Lower rentals due to tax benefit transfer
- Mitigation of AMT and midquarter (in the U.S.)

CONVENIENCE
- Faster response time than loans
- Faster appropriation from operating budgets
- Master lease agreements
- One stop shopping
- Flexibility from end of term options

164. It is easy to see why leasing is popular, is it not?
Yes, leasing indeed offers many significant benefits to lessees. No wonder that it is the single largest source of external financing in the U.S. and captures approximately 20% of all equipment acquisition in the world!

165. Do all of the above benefits appeal to all lessees?
Not at all. It is important to conclude this subsection by noting that different entities lease for different reasons.

THE EQUIPMENT ACQUISITION PROCESS

166. Why is the equipment acquisition process something that a lessor's sales/marketing personnel should be informed about?
Entities who acquire equipment invariably go through their own internal acquisition process. Equipment financing is an integral part of this process and therefore it is important for lessors to not just be informed about the process but to be involved in it.

167. What exactly is the equipment acquisition process?
Let's diagram it first and then explain each phase of the process.

The diagram follows:

CAPITAL EXPENDITURE DECISION	FINANCING DECISION	LESSOR SELECTION PROCESS	LEASE VS LEASE ANALYSIS
Go / No Go	Lease / Purchase	LESSOR ATTRIBUTES	QUANTITATIVE

Phase I is the Capital Expenditure Decision also referred to as the Investment Decision. In this phase the entity decides whether to acquire a particular asset or not. This decision is based on a simple concept that most, if not all, entities have "too few dollars chasing too many projects."

The sooner a lessor gets involved in the equipment acquisition process, the better the chance of winning the deal.

168. How does an entity make the capital expenditure decision?
How exactly the decision is made depends on how sophisticated the entity is. This will be best understood if one takes two extremes. At one extreme let's assume a large and extremely sophisticated entity.

169. What would be a good example of such in the real world?
A large listed entity that has a CFO, a Treasurer and employs many financial analysts who work on projects such as cost/benefit analyses.

170. How exactly would such an entity make this decision?
To begin with, such an analysis would be conducted on "material" transactions. The word material is a relative word for that which is material (large enough to warrant the effort of such an analysis) to one entity is not necessarily material to another. On material transactions a sophisticated entity would do a cost/benefit analysis on a net present value basis. Costs are easier to determine; research is needed to quantify the benefits.

171. What discount rate would be used in the net present value analysis?
Generally the entity would use an internal "hurdle" or "obstacle" rate, typically the firm's cost of capital or cost of capital plus a certain percentage. If the net present value of the costs and benefits is equal to or greater than zero, the entity will proceed with the acquisition.

172. Why is this so?
If the net present value is equal to zero, the hurdle or obstacle rate has been achieved!

173. At the other extreme, how would this decision be made?
First one needs to understand what is meant by the other extreme. These are entities typically very small that are not financially sophisticated. No one in the entity understands what is meant by net present value.

174. So what process do they use?
They "scribble numbers on the back of a napkin" which could also mean that they work it out in their head and decide whether to acquire or not.

Thus regardless of how sophisticated or unsophisticated an entity is, the first step is to decide whether to proceed with acquiring the equipment or not.

175. What is the next step?
Phase II is the Financing Decision. In this stage the entity, having already concluded that the equipment will indeed be acquired, will decide whether to purchase or lease the equipment.

176. How is this decision made?
The next subsection details exactly how this decision is made on a quantitative basis. For purposes of this subsection let's assume that the entity has decided to lease.

177. Then what?
Phase III is the Lessor Selection Process. Once an entity has decided to lease the next step is obvious. It has to decide which lessor to lease from. If the entity has leased before, they are likely to already have a short list of lessors from whom it has leased or at least from whom it has received quotes. At this stage, the entity will ask each of these lessors to submit a lease quote.

178. What if this is a first time lessee?

In fact, for purposes of this subsection, it helps to assume it is a first time lessee in which case the next step is to arrive at a short list of lessors.

179. Why and how is this done?

In most countries there are a large number of lessors. Lessees will not obviously want lease quotations from all the lessors but from a short list of say three or four. The lessee will consider varied lessor attributes or characteristics and based on these decide which lessors to place on the short list.

180. Then what?

The short listed lessors will each give a lease quote to the lessee. This is Phase IV, Lease versus Lease Analysis, where the lessee will quantitatively evaluate the competing bids.

Phase III and Phase IV are the subject matter of another subsection entitled Lease versus Lease Analysis.

LEASE VERSUS PURCHASE ANALYSIS

181. Is leasing more expensive than purchase?
Not at all! Unfortunately this is a myth. The reality is that often leasing is less expensive than purchase; particularly when it is compared to an outright cash purchase.

When it comes to the alternative mode of acquisition, one has to decide whether one is comparing a lease to an outright cash purchase or a loan (or in some countries to a hire-purchase transaction).

182. How does one conclude whether leasing is more expensive or the other way around?
Unfortunately most lessees, and for that matter many lessors, only look at the interest rate in the transaction when they compare a lease to a loan. Given that, more often than not, lease rates are higher than loan rates they erroneously conclude that leasing is more expensive.

183. Why is this conclusion an erroneous one?
Because it is only half the story!

184. What is the other half?
When one compares a lease to a loan the conclusion as to which is cheaper must be made on a present value after-tax basis.

185. Why present value after-tax?
Present value because a lease and a loan both involve cash flows over time. Such flows must be analyzed on a present value basis to address the time value of money issue.

186. Why after-tax?
Taxes are a critical part of the equipment financing decision process in particular when the tax impact of leasing and purchasing is different.

187. What are the differences?
When an entity purchases via a loan, the tax consequence is that depreciation (known as capital allowances in some countries) and interest are tax deductible; while if an entity leases the equipment, generally the lease expense or rent

No leasing company should do without spreadsheets or software that can do lease versus purchase analyses.

expense is deductible. (In some countries as noted in the Tax Section, finance leases are treated as loans for tax purposes, in which case depreciation and interest expense are deductible on such a lease. However on operating leases, the tax treatment throughout the world is for the lessee to claim rent expense as a deduction on the tax return).

188. What about the comparison between a lease and an outright cash purchase?
Here, too many lessees erroneously believe that cash is cheaper as they ignore the opportunity cost of tying up cash.

189. Would a lease versus cash analysis also be done on a present value after-tax basis?
Absolutely yes! A lease is always a time line as the rentals are paid over time; however, a cash purchase is also a time line as the tax savings of depreciation come over time. Thus, one is indeed analyzing two time lines and once again the time value of money needs to be filtered out, present value being the only correct approach.

190. What information does one need to perform the lease versus purchase analysis on a present value after-tax basis?
One needs some simple information which is not difficult to obtain. Most of the information must be procured from the lessee.

191. But would the lessee be willing to give such information to the lessor?
Yes, as the lessee benefits from the process. Many lessees are, of course, capable of conducting a lease versus purchase analysis themselves, yet the majority of lessees are either not sophisticated to perform such

Lease Marketing 135

analysis, or do not have the time to do so or do not take the time to do so.

192. Some lessees do not even understand present value. How does one deal with such as a customer?

In such cases, one has to use discretion. Is the lessee teachable? If not, present value will do nothing but confuse. Present value analysis should be used with quasi-sophisticated and sophisticated lessees.

193. Would sophisticated lessees not always do their own analysis?

Perhaps. But even in this situation many such "sophisticated" lessees often do the analysis erroneously, as will be explained later, by using an incorrect discount rate to present value the cash flows. An incorrect discount rate will give an incorrect answer!

194. Can we proceed to list the data that needs to be gathered for the analysis?

The list is presented below:

- Equipment cost
- Lease quote
- Alternative mode of acquisition – cash or loan
- If loan, a loan quote
- Tax rate
- Depreciation details
- Useful life of asset
- End of term assumption (EOT)
- Salvage value
- Differential costs
- Discount rate

195. Perhaps it is best to go over each item?

Yes, and in sequence. Equipment cost is, of course, needed as this forms the basis of the lease and the loan quotes and in the case of an outright cash purchase, this is the amount to be paid to the supplier. Next, one must have a real world lease quote that has all the quantitative information such as the term, the periodic rental, closing fee (if any), etc.

196. With regard to the alternative mode of acquisition, does one compare leasing to a loan or to cash?

It obviously depends on what the entity is considering. If the entity is considering cash as the alternative, then one compares leasing to cash; if the entity is considering a loan, then one compares leasing to a loan. Sometimes an entity may desire to compare leasing to both a loan and cash simply to better understand the dynamics of varied modes of acquisition.

197. What information should the loan quote contain?

Any and all quantitative information such as the down payment (if any), interest rate, the periodic loan payments, closing fees (if any), etc.

198. With regards to the tax rate, how does one come up with such a rate particularly given that the analysis is over a period of time?

In the year in which the analysis is being done, it is not difficult for an entity to know its tax rate; thereafter, an assumption has to be made. One generally assumes that the tax rate remains constant unless one has information to the contrary.

199. What about depreciation details?

If the entity purchases either via a loan or outright cash, depreciation is deductible for tax purposes. Thus one needs to know the depreciation life and method for the asset in question. The method varies from country to country; sometimes straight line, sometimes accelerated.

200. Is the useful life of the asset the same as the economic life?

No. Whereas economic life is the life in the hands of multiple users, useful life is the assumed life over which the entity doing the analysis is likely to use the asset. At the end of such period the entity will sell the asset for an assumed salvage value.

201. What exactly is meant by the expression "end of term assumption"?

This is an important assumption made in the lease versus purchase analysis and it needs to be illustrated with both a finance lease as well as an operating lease. On a finance lease given the full payout nature it is assumed, and logically so, that the lessee at the end of the lease term will buy the asset for a nominal amount. Once the asset is purchased is when the useful life assumption really needs to be made. Let's assume a 48-month finance lease. In the context of useful life it is fair to assume that the useful life of the asset to the lessee is at least 48 months, otherwise the lessee would not ask for a 48-month lease. At the end of the 48-month term, given the earlier comment, the lessee is assumed to be purchasing the asset, at which stage the remaining useful life is assumed to be say 12 months. The lease line can be diagramed as follows:

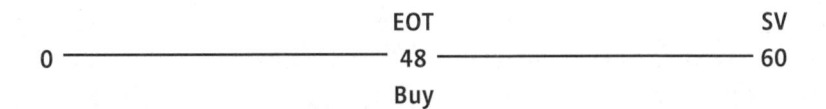

```
                        EOT                        SV
0 ————————————————— 48 ————————————————— 60
                        Buy
```

At the end of the 60 months the asset will be sold for an assumed salvage value.

202. A number of assumptions have been made. Is there not a likelihood that some or all of these are incorrect?

Of course there is such a likelihood. With assumptions what matters is not whether they are entirely correct but that they are consistent. Using the same example as above on the purchase side, say an outright cash purchase, the purchase line would look as follows:

The assumptions in the analysis may not always be correct; they need to be consistent.

```
                                                        SV
0 ─────────────────────────────── 60
```

Note under both time lines the useful life is assumed to be 60 months after which the asset is sold for the same assumed salvage value. The assumptions are consistent.

203. What about an operating lease?

With operating leases the useful life can logically be assumed to be at least the lease term (even though with high tech equipment this may not necessarily be true). At the end of such term one needs to make an end of term assumption. Generally the most common assumption is that the asset will be returned to the lessor. The lease line would look as follows:

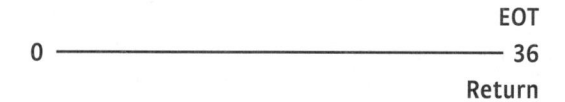

```
                                        EOT
0 ─────────────────────────────── 36
                                      Return
```

204. What about consistency on the purchase side?

On the purchase side the useful life is also assumed to be 36 months and at the end of such useful life the asset will be sold for the assumed salvage value:

```
                                         SV
0 ─────────────────────────────── 36
```

Note that in either case the useful life is 36 months at the end of which period the entity does not have the asset; on the lease side, it has been returned while on the purchase side, it has been sold. This is consistency.

205. Can it be assumed at the end of an operating lease that the lessee will purchase the asset?

If this is the most likely EOT event, then such assumption can certainly be made. However, this creates the need to assume an extended useful life beyond the lease term as follows:

	EOT	SV
0	36	48
	Buy	

In the illustration above where it is assumed that the lessee will purchase the asset at the end of a 36-month operating lease, it is further assumed that the total useful life is 48 months at the end of which period the asset will be sold for its assumed salvage value.

In the above case an assumption may also have to be made with regard to the purchase price at the end of the 36 months unless the lessee has a fixed purchase option.

206. What about consistency on the purchase side?

This is simple:

	SV
0	48

Note that in both time lines the useful life is 48 months at the end of which the entity sells the asset for the same assumed salvage value.

Often a lease versus purchase analysis on an operating lease may be done twice: once where it is assumed the asset is returned; once where it is assumed it is purchased at the end of the lease term. The dual analyses provide the lessee with answers that might lead to conclusions as to whether they should return or purchase the asset!

207. What are differential costs?

These are costs that are different in quantum or timing based on whether the entity leases or purchases.

208. What are some examples of differential costs?

One common example would be VAT. This tax is paid up-front say on an outright cash purchase; yet in most countries, it is paid over time on a lease similar to sales tax in many states as in the U.S. This difference in timing needs to be incorporated into the analysis. An illustration follows:

Equipment cost	$1000.00
Term in months	36
Rentals	$35.00

Assuming a 10% VAT on the purchase side, $100 of VAT will be paid up front; on the lease side, $3.50 of VAT will be paid along with each rental for 36 months. Typically a differential cost such as this will not necessarily swing the decision between leasing and buying but will definitely impact the present value numbers.

209. Another example of differential costs?

Another example would be maintenance. On a full-service operating lease, maintenance is most likely built into the rental; on occasion, it may be separately stated. If it is separately stated, the amount of maintenance cost is known; if it is buried in the rentals, it can be imputed. On the other hand, if one were to purchase the asset, one would need to arrive at a reasonable assumption as to what it would cost to maintain the asset. The maintenance cost on a full-service operating lease is likely to be different than what one would have to pay for maintenance if the asset were purchased. The differential numbers have to be factored into the analysis.

210. The last item is the discount rate. What discount rate is used in the lease versus purchase decision?

The answer, the logic and the conclusion will pay for the cost of this publication!

This is one of the more complex assumptions which can have a significant impact on the analysis. After all, the discount rate is merely a number. Take one number and it will give one answer each for the lease and the purchase side. Take another number it will definitely alter the quantitative conclusion; it could even swing the answer.

211. Does this mean that one has a choice in the selection of a discount rate?

The choice of the proper discount rate can make or break the analysis.

Indeed! Starting with larger and/or more sophisticated entities, there are two schools of thought with regard to the choice of a discount rate. One school of thought opts for the cost of capital; the other opts for the after-tax cost of debt.

212. It seems as though the cost of debt is more often used than the cost of capital?
This is true. The main reason it is, in fact, used more often than the cost of capital is that it is easily available! Every entity knows its cost of debt but cost of capital is not a number that is always available or easy to compute.

213. Which of the two is the more appropriate discount rate?
It really depends on the reason as to why the lessee is considering the possibility of leasing. When one compares two financing alternatives—say, either lease versus cash or lease versus loan, the objective in comparing two such financial alternatives can either be interest minimization or liquidity preference.

214. What exactly is meant by each of the two expressions—interest minimization and liquidity preference?
Interest minimization simply means that the entity is seeking that financial alternative with the lowest cost. Liquidity preference, on the other hand, means the entity has a preference for liquidity and within this context is still seeking the lower present value mode of acquisition.

215. An illustration would help—one that would be conclusive as to when does an entity use the cost of debt and when, on the other hand, is cost of capital more appropriate as the discount rate in the lease versus purchase analysis?

Let's use a very simple illustration. Assume an entity is seeking a bank loan for $10,000 and the banker is willing to proceed with the loan at an interest rate of 10%. Further assume that the banker offers the entity two choices as follows:

Plan A			
Loan	Repayment of loan		
	1	2	3
$10,000	$(4,021)	$(4,021)	$(4,021)
Plan B			
Loan	Repayment of loan		
$10,000	$(1,000)	$(1,000)	$(11,000)

Plan A is a 10% loan amortized over three annual payments in arrears at 10%; Plan B is an interest-only loan with principal due as a bullet payment at the end of year three.

216. How does the entity decide which plan is better?

The most appropriate way to arrive at the correct decision is to present value the costs which in this case are the loan repayment costs.

217. What discount rate will be used?

Back to the $64 million question!

This depends on whether the entity is seeking interest minimization or has a liquidity preference. Let's first assume that the entity is pursuing the objective of interest minimization, which means selecting the plan with the lowest cost. In this case the discount rate should be the cost of debt.

Present valuing the two plans at 10% gives us the same answer for each, $10,000. It was made clear in the section on Lease Finance that if the discount rate is equal to the interest rate, present value is equal to principal. The golden rule of finance! This is why the present value of both plans is $10,000. Keystroke computations are unnecessary, but they follow:

PLAN A

> **HP12C**

		f	REG
4,021	CHS	PMT
3		n
10		i
PV		**10,000**

> **HP17BII+**

		☐	CLEAR DATA
4,021	+/-	PMT
3		N
10		I%YR
PV		**10,000**

144 Winning With Leasing!

PLAN B

> HP12C

	f		REG
1,000	g		CFj
2	g		Nj
11,000	g		CFj
10			i
	fNPV		<u>10,000</u>

> HP17BII+

		☐	CLEAR DATA
	0		INPUT
	1,000		INPUT
	2		INPUT
	11,000		INPUT
	1		INPUT
			EXIT
		CALC	
	10		I %
	NPV		<u>10,000</u>

218. So which plan is better?

Based on the process used, the entity is truly indifferent between the two plans as the present value of the costs (the repayment) is the same. From an interest minimization point of view when the cost of debt is used as the discount rate, it makes sense that both plans will have the same present value cost as the cost of debt strips interest out of future cash flows and reduces them to their principal portion.

Another way of putting it is as follows: from an interest minimization point of view, the entity would indeed be indifferent between the two plans as they both have an interest rate of 10%!

219. In the above example, what if the entity has a liquidity preference?

Let's first examine, using the above example, what exactly is meant by this expression. An entity with liquidity preference would prefer Plan B as it has a slower repayment schedule. The premise here is that the entity would prefer to have the extra $3,021 for each of the first two years to reinvest in its business (hopefully at a reinvestment rate greater than 10%, the cost of debt).

220. Using the cost of debt as the discount rate resulted in the entity being indifferent between the two plans. Does this mean the cost of debt, when used as a discount rate, ignores the needs of an entity that has a preference for liquidity?

Yes, this is a critical conclusion. The cost of debt, as can be clearly seen from the above example, definitely ignores liquidity preference. An entity which has liquidity preference and uses the cost of debt in the above simple example will get an incorrect answer. The answer indicates the entity is indifferent; but the entity is not as Plan B provides the needed liquidity preference.

221. What, therefore, is the conclusion to the choice of the most appropriate discount rate in a lease versus purchase analysis?

When an entity has interest minimization as its objective, the most appropriate discount rate is the cost of debt; when an entity has liquidity preference, the most appropriate discount rate is the cost of capital or opportunity cost.

In the author's opinion, most entities in the real world do have a liquidity preference; only those few with true idle cash do not. Yet, unfortunately the cost of debt is used more often; merely because it is easily available! As stated earlier, the choice of an incorrect discount rate will result in an incorrect answer.

Most entities have liquidity preference; opportunity cost, and not the cost of debt should be the discount rate of choice.

222. Let's discount the two financial alternatives at the cost of capital?
The cost of capital or opportunity cost is, and should be, generally higher than the cost of debt. Let's assume, for illustrative purposes, this to be 15%. The computation follows for both plans:

PLAN A

> HP12C

	f	REG
4,021	CHS	PMT
3		n
15		i
PV		**9,181**

Lease Marketing **147**

> HP17BII+

	☐	CLEAR DATA
4,021	+/-	PMT
3		N
15		I%YR
PV		<u>9,181</u>

PLAN B

> HP12C

	f	REG
1,000	g	CFj
2	g	Nj
11,000	g	CFj
15		i
NPV		<u>8,858</u>

> HP17BII+

	☐	CLEAR DATA
0		INPUT
1,000		INPUT
2		INPUT
11,000		INPUT
1		INPUT
		EXIT
	CALC	
15		I %
NPV		8,858

223. So what is the conclusion?

The conclusion is obvious! When the cost of capital or opportunity cost is used to discount the two plans, Plan B has a lower present value cost to it. This clearly shows that the cost of capital or opportunity cost indeed provides the correct answer. Plan B is indeed the correct plan to choose given that the entity has a liquidity preference. Once again, this reinforces that on a lease versus purchase analysis, the cost of debt should not be used as the discount rate when the lessee has a liquidity preference.

224. When it comes to cost of capital perhaps it would help if an example were given?

Let's assume the following hypothetical balance sheet for an entity as of December 31, 200X:

ASSETS		LIABILITIES	
Cash		Debt	$60
Inventory		Equity	40
Fixed Assets			
Total	$100	Total	$100

Let's further assume that the weighted average cost of debt is 8% and the tax rate for the entity is 30%. Lastly, let's assume the targeted return on equity (ROE) is 15%.

Cost of capital is computed as follows:

	Weight		Cost		Tax Adjustment		After-tax Cost
Debt	.60	x	8.00%	x	.70	=	3.36
Equity	.40	x	15.00%	x	N/A	=	6.00
							9.36

9.36% is the weighted average cost of capital, WACC.

225. An embellishment would help?

Let's begin with debt. The weight assigned to debt is .60 which really means that 60% of the total assets are funded through debt with an average cost of 8%. The tax adjustment is necessary as interest on debt is tax deductible. For an entity in the 30% tax bracket every incremental $1 of interest deduction saves the entity 30 cents in taxes. Thus, $1 of interest only costs 70 cents. 3.36% is the weighted average after-tax cost of debt.

226. What about the cost of equity?

First of all, the weight assigned to equity is .40 which obviously means 40% of the total assets are funded through equity with the other 60% from debt—remember the accounting equation: assets = debt + equity! The cost assigned to equity is the same as the targeted ROE. After all,

150 Winning With Leasing!

a simple approach is to state that one person's cost is another person's return.

Thus, if the shareholders expect a return of 15%, using this concept, the cost of equity to the entity is 15% (Yes, there are other far more complicated approaches to arriving at the cost of equity, such as Gordon's Growth Model).

227. Is there no tax adjustment needed for the cost of equity?
No, there is no such adjustment as the incidence of taxation is at the shareholder level.

This concludes the discussion on cost of capital.

228. What if an entity is not sophisticated and does not know or cannot be bothered to compute its cost of capital?
Many entities fall into this category. Such entities would use opportunity cost as a substitute for the cost of capital. More often than not this would be their ROE as this is the closest and perhaps the best approximation of opportunity cost. After all, an entity is in the business to provide returns to their shareholders and the shareholders decide to stay in business if the ROE is equal or better than the opportunity cost elsewhere. Moreover, ROE is easy to compute. It is net income ÷ total shareholder equity.

> *ROE is perhaps the best approximation of opportunity cost.*

229. At this stage it seems like one has a good handle on all the data that needs to be gathered and a good understanding on the assumptions as well. Is it time to go over a complete lease versus purchase illustration?
Here it is! Let's begin with a lease versus cash analysis. The actual numbers provided below are not important; numbers change from country to country and from analysis to analysis. What is important is to understand how lease versus purchase analysis is done, how each of the various numbers are arrived at and what the answers mean.

GENERAL ASSUMPTIONS
- Tax rate, 32.5%
- Cost of capital or opportunity cost (after-tax), 14.05%
- After-tax cost of debt, 8.10% (pretax cost, 12%)
- Inception date, January 1, 200X

FINANCE LEASE ASSUMPTIONS
- Lease payments are $29,932 in advance for 48 months.
- Lessee will purchase the asset at the end of the term for a nominal amount of $2,000; use the asset for one more year and then sell it for $200,000, its assumed salvage value.

PURCHASE ASSUMPTIONS
- Asset cost, $1,000,000
- Tax depreciation, 25% straight line
- Selling price, $200,000, after five years

230. Perhaps some of the data can be embellished?

In the above illustration, the data included both the cost of capital (or opportunity cost) and the after-tax cost of debt (12% x .675). Both rates will be used to discount after-tax cash flows. The lease is a finance lease with a nominal amount of consideration due at the end of lease term for the transfer of ownership. The end of term, useful life and salvage value assumptions are consistent on both the lease and the purchase side. Note that the asset, whether it is leased or purchased, is being used for five years and is being sold for $200,000 at the end of five years. Tax depreciation means the same as capital allowances in some countries.

231. At this stage the numbers can be input into a spreadsheet?

Yes, either a spreadsheet or software. Note for simplicity three assumptions inherent in the spreadsheet:

- The cash flows are being aggregated annually; in the real world, cash flows would be spread monthly.

- Tax timing is being ignored; in the real world any tax savings from say lease rental deductibility would not have an instant benefit as is being assumed in the spreadsheet below. In the real world such tax savings accrue based on the tax installment dates that corporate taxes are due to the government.
- Indirect taxes such as sales tax, GST, or VAT are being left out simply to avoid clutter.

The lease spreadsheet is presented below:

LEASE ALTERNATIVE

	0	1	2	3	4	5
Rentals	$(29,932)	$(329,252)	$(359,184)	$(359,184)	$(359,184)	
Tax Shield	9,728	107,007	116,735	116,735	116,735	
Net Salvage						$135,000
Net Cost	$(20,204)	$(222,245)	$(242,449)	$(242,449)	$(242,449)	$135,000

232. Can the numbers be explained?

The rental in advance is shown at time zero; thereafter, year one shows 11 additional rentals; years two, three and four show 12 rentals each. The tax shield assumes this is a country where the lessee, for income tax purposes, can claim the rentals on a finance lease as a tax deduction (as versus in some countries where the lessee is deemed to be the tax owner and thereby is entitled to claim tax depreciation plus interest expense). The tax savings are 32.5% of the rentals. As indicated before, tax timing is being ignored.

233. Any other tax assumptions being made?

Yes, it is assumed that all tax savings are utilizable.

234. How is the $135,000 salvage value arrived at?
To begin with, one must note that the $2,000 end of term purchase price is being left out for simplicity. If this number was material it would have to be shown as a cash outlay in year four; further, this amount would then become the basis for depreciating an used asset for the fifth year of the analysis.

In the illustration the asset's purchase price is zero (given the above assumption) and it is sold one year later for $200,000. The sale of an asset is a taxable event and the difference between sales price and cost being $200,000, the entire $200,000 is taxable at 32.5%. The resulting tax is $65,000; thus, net salvage is $135,000.

235. Why in the above computation is the corporate tax rate used and not a capital gains tax rate?
Many countries do not have a different rate for the capital gains tax; they use the same corporate tax rate. However, if this is a country where the capital gains tax rate is different than the corporate tax rate then such different rate should be used to arrive at the net salvage value amount.

236. Now that all the numbers have been explained, what is the conclusion on the lease alternative?
There is no conclusion yet. All one has arrived at is the time line which shows the after-tax cash flows for the lease alternative.

237. Thus, one now needs to look at the purchase spreadsheet?
Yes. It is shown below:

PURCHASE ALTERNATIVE (CASH)

	0	1	2	3	4	5
Outlay	$(1,000,000)					
Depreciation		$81,250	$81,250	$81,250	$81,250	
Net Salvage						$135,000
Net Cost	$(1,000,000)	$81,250	$81,250	$81,250	$81,250	$135,000

238. Again can each of the line items be explained?

At time zero the entity pays cash of $1,000,000. Thereafter, there are no further outlays. The purchase of the asset qualifies the entity to claim tax depreciation on it. Given the assumption that the asset is to be depreciated straight line over four years and assuming that the fiscal year is January 1 to December 31, the amount of depreciation claimed as a tax deduction each year is $250,000. At a tax rate of 32.5%, this generates a tax shield of $81,250 (250,000 x .325) each year for four years.

239. What about the salvage value?

The asset has been fully depreciated at the end of four years. At the end of the fifth year it is being sold for $200,000. The entire sales price is taxable. Using 32.5% as the tax rate, the net salvage value is $135,000 as $65,000 is paid in taxes.

240. Why is lost interest on the cash outlay not shown as a cost?

This is a very good question. Lost interest is not shown as the process of present value addresses the opportunity cost or lost interest on the outlay. Present value takes future cash flows and brings them back to time zero, a moment in time. At a moment in time, there is no such thing as lost interest!

241. At this stage one has two time lines—the cost to lease and the cost to purchase. What is the next step?

The next step is to present value the two time lines. This will be done using both the after-tax cost of debt as well as the cost of capital (or opportunity cost) as the discount rates. The computations follow:

LEASE

> HP12C

	f	REG
8.10		i
20,204	CHSg	CFo
222,245	CHSg	CFj
242,449	CHSg	CFj
3	g	Nj
135,000	g	CFj
f NPV		711,297
14.05		i
f NPV		638,231

> HP17BII+

		CLEAR DATA
20,204	+/-	INPUT
222,245	+/-	INPUT
1		INPUT
242,449	+/-	INPUT
3		INPUT
135,000		INPUT
1		INPUT
		EXIT
		CALC
8.10		I%
NPV		<u>711,297</u>
14.05		I%
NPV		<u>638,231</u>

Lease Marketing   **157**

PURCHASE

> HP12C

	f	REG
8.10		i
1,000,000	CHSg	CFo
81,250	g	CFj
4	g	Nj
135,000	g	CFj
	f NPV	640,033
14.05		i
	f NPV	693,542

> HP17BII+

		CLEAR DATA
1,000,000	+/-	INPUT
81,250		INPUT
4		INPUT
135,000		INPUT
1		INPUT
		EXIT
		CALC
8.10		I%
	NPV	640,033
14.05		I%
	NPV	693,542

158 Winning With Leasing!

The answers are summarized below:

Discount rate	Alternative	
	Lease	Purchase
8.10%	$711,297	$640,033
14.05%	$638,231	$693,542

242. So what is the conclusion?

At this stage one can conclude the obvious from the above: that at a discount rate of 8.10%, purchase is cheaper; at a discount rate of 14.05%, leasing is cheaper. If one were to stop here one can conclude that if this were an entity with a preference for liquidity, the appropriate discount rate to be used in the analysis would be the cost of capital (or opportunity cost) and that the entity would choose the lease alternative as it is much cheaper than the buy alternative.

However, one should take the analysis one step further.

243. What is this step?

The next (and last!) step is to ascertain the differential cash flow between the two alternatives. This is presented below:

CASH FLOW DIFFERENTIAL

	0	1	2	3	4	5
Lease	$(20,204)	$(222,245)	$(242,449)	$(242,449)	$(242,449)	$135,000
Purchase	(1,000,000)	81,250	81,250	81,250	81,250	135,000
Differential	$979,796	$(303,495)	$(323,699)	$(323,699)	$(323,699)	0

244. Can the above be explained?

All that has been done is that the differential cash flow has been computed between leasing and purchasing. As an example, at time zero, $979,796 is ($20,204) – ($1,000,000). Remember minus a minus makes it a plus? To put it in words, if the entity were to lease and not purchase, they would have $979,796 cash in hand at time zero. The negative differential numbers thereafter represent the differential cost to service the lease. As an example, in year one, $222,245 is the net cost of the lease to which one needs to add the foregone depreciation tax shield on the purchase $81,250, to arrive at $303,495 as the differential cost for year one.

245. What is the purpose of all this?

There is a purpose to this! The next step is to compute the IRR of the differential cash flow. As is shown below, the IRR is 11.2958%:

LEASE

> HP12C

	f	REG
979,796	g	CFo
303,495	CHSg	CFj
323,699	CHSg	CFj
3	g	Nj
f	irr	11.2958

> HP17BII+

	☐	CLEAR DATA
979,796		INPUT
303,495	+/-	INPUT
1		INPUT
323,699	+/-	INPUT
3		INPUT
		EXIT
		CALC
IRR %		11.2958

160 Winning With Leasing!

Now, let's go back to the answer to QUESTION 241. It was clear that at a discount rate of 8.10% purchase was cheaper; at a discount rate of 14.05% leasing was cheaper. But what had not been stated yet is that there is a number (a certain discount rate) at which the entity is quantitatively indifferent between purchase and lease. In QUESTION 241, it should be visually clear that the number is one between 8.10% and 14.05%. 11.2958% is the number or discount rate at which the entity is quantitatively indifferent.

246. Why is this so?
$979,796 is what the entity has in cash if it were to lease; the other numbers represent the differential cost to lease. Let's take the present value of the cost to service the lease at a discount rate of 11.2958%:

$(303,495) $(323,699) $(323,699) $(323,699)

> HP12C

	f	REG
11.2958		i
303,495	g	CFj
323,699	g	CFj
3	g	Nj
f NPV		979,796

Lease Marketing **161**

> HP17BII+

	☐	CLEAR DATA
	0	INPUT
	303,495	INPUT
	1	INPUT
	323,699	INPUT
	3	INPUT
		EXIT
		CALC
	11.2958	I%
	NPV	979,796

The present value of the cash flow differential from years one through five is a negative $979,796 (remember all the numbers present valued were negative); thus, the NPV of the cash flow differential is zero. In other words, $979,796 is the cash on hand because the entity leased. At 11.2958% the present value of the cost to service the lease is $979,796; the entity is indeed indifferent at 11.2958%.

What this means is that if the lease and the purchase costs were to be discounted at 11.2985%, the two answers would be the same and the lessee would be quantitatively indifferent between the two. Try discounting at 11.2958%!

247. But the chances of an entity's discount rate being exactly equal to 11.2958% is one in a million, is it not?

Perhaps one in ten million!

The whole point is as follows: the entity knows that at 11.2958% it is indifferent between the two financing alternatives. At this stage the last step is for the entity to compare its reinvestment rate/opportunity cost to the break-even IRR and then decide whether to lease or not.

248. How does this work?
If the entity's reinvestment rate/opportunity cost/hurdle rate/cost of capital is greater than 11.2958%, the break-even rate, they will decide to lease; if the rate is less than 11.2958%, they will decide to purchase!

At this stage, it would be a good idea to remember that all of the numbers used were for illustrative purposes only.

249. How can a lessor use this approach in augmenting its sales effort?
Now that is the real question!

When working with quasi-sophisticated and sophisticated entities, a lessor should gather the data contained in QUESTION 194. After the data is gathered, the lessor should do the lease versus purchase analysis on its own spreadsheet or software and solve for the indifference or break-even point.

Note that solving for the indifference rate does not require choosing a discount rate for present value analysis as the indifference or break-even rate is the IRR of the nondiscounted cash flows.

Solving for break-even IRR is a must; it will help win many transactions!

Once the break-even rate has been computed, the lessor now is acutely aware as to what discount rate is needed to have leasing be cheaper than purchase. This is vital information to the lessor.

250. The first lease versus purchase illustration was a finance lease versus a purchase. Perhaps another one showing an operating lease would help?
The following example is one where the lessor has taken a certain residual value on an operating lease:

GENERAL ASSUMPTIONS
- The computer equipment cost is $100,000
- The company's tax rate is 30%
- The company's incremental, weighted average after-tax cost of capital or opportunity cost is 7.30% and its after-tax cost of debt is 5.95% (pretax, 8.5%)
- The equipment is either leased or purchased on January 1

OPERATING LEASE ASSUMPTIONS
- Lease payments are $2,830.19 per month in advance for 36 months
- The lessee expects to return the asset at the end of the lease term.

PURCHASE ASSUMPTIONS:
- The equipment qualifies for 37.5% diminishing value depreciation
- The entity will sell the asset at the end of 36 months for $5,000

The spreadsheet for the lease alternative follows:

LEASE ALTERNATIVE

	0	1	2	3
Rentals	$(2,830)	$(31,132)	$(33,962)	$(33,962)
Tax Shield	849	9,340	10,189	10,189
Net Cost	$(1,981)	$(21,792)	$(23,773)	$(23,773)

251. Can the numbers be explained?

The rental in advance is shown at time zero; thereafter, year one shows 11 additional rentals; years two and three show 12 rentals each. This being an operating lease, the rentals are tax deductible resulting in a tax shield at 30% of the rental amount. Given that at the end of lease term the asset is assumed to be returned there are no other relevant cash flows.

252. Thus, one now needs to look at the purchase spreadsheet?

It is shown below:

PURCHASE ALTERNATIVE (CASH)

	0	1	2	3
Outlay	$(100,000)			
Depreciation		11,250	7,031	4,394
Net Salvage				10,824
Net Cost	$(100,000)	$11,250	$7,031	$15,218

The depreciation line item is computed as follows:

Year	Equipment Basis		Depreciation Percentage		Annual Deduction		Tax Rate	Tax Benefit
1	$100,000	x	37.5%	=	$37,500	x	.30	$11,250
2	$ 62,500	x	37.5%	=	$23,438	x	.30	$ 7,031
3	$ 39,062	x	37.5%	=	$14,648	x	.30	$ 4,394
					$75,586			

The net salvage value is computed as follows:

Selling price	$5,000.00
Less book value	(24,414.00)
Loss	(19,414.00)
x Tax rate	.30
Tax benefit	5,824.00
+ Selling price	5,000.00
Net salvage value	$10,824.00

The book value is $100,000 − $75,586 of accumulated depreciation. The $19,414 loss is deductible and generates a tax savings at 30% equal to $5,824 which when added to the selling price of $5,000 results in net salvage value of $10,824.

253. At this stage, one has two time lines—the cost to lease and the cost to purchase. What is the next step?

The next step is to present value the two time lines. This will be done using both the after-tax cost of debt as well as the cost of capital (or opportunity cost) as the discount rates. The keystrokes follow:

LEASE

> HP12C

	f	REG
5.95		i
1,981	CHSg	CFo
21,792	CHSg	CFj
23,773	CHSg	CFj
2	g	Nj
fNPV		__63,716__
7.30		i
fNPV		__62,182__

> HP17BII+

		☐	CLEAR DATA
1,981	+/-		INPUT
21,792	+/-		INPUT
1			INPUT
23,773	+/-		INPUT
2			INPUT
			EXIT
			CALC
5.95			I%
NPV			__63,716__
7.30			I%
NPV			__62,182__

Lease Marketing **167**

PURCHASE

> HP12C

	f	REG
5.95		i
100,000	CHSg	CF0
11,250	g	CFj
7,031	g	CFj
15,218	g	CFj
fNPV		70,323
7.30		i
fNPV		71,090

> HP17BII+

	☐	CLEAR DATA
100,000	+/−	INPUT
11,250		INPUT
1		INPUT
7,031		INPUT
1		INPUT
15,218		INPUT
1		INPUT
		EXIT
		CALC
5.95		I%
NPV		70,323
7.30		I%
NPV		71,090

The answers are summarized below:

Discount rate	Alternative	
	Lease	Purchase
5.95%	$63,716	$70,323
7.30%	$62,182	$71,090

254. What is the conclusion?

The conclusion is obvious: at both discount rates, leasing is cheaper; yet, the gap between leasing and purchasing narrows as the discount rate becomes smaller.

255. What is the inference from the above?

There is, therefore, a discount rate which is less than 5.95% at which point the entity is indifferent between leasing and purchasing. Once again this rate can be ascertained by arriving at the IRR of the differential cash flows as follows:

CASH FLOW DIFFERENTIAL

	0	1	2	3
Lease	$(1,981)	$(21,792)	$(23,773)	$(23,773)
Purchase	(100,000)	11,250	7,031	15,218
Differential	$98,019	$(33,042)	$(30,804)	$(38,991)

Lease Marketing

The IRR is computed as follows:

> HP12C

	f	REG
98,019	g	CFo
33,042	CHSg	CFj
30,804	CHSg	CFj
38,991	CHSg	CFj
	f IRR	__2.37__

> HP17BII+

		CLEAR DATA
98,019		INPUT
33,042	+/-	INPUT
1		INPUT
30,804	+/-	INPUT
1		INPUT
38,991	+/-	INPUT
1		INPUT
		EXIT
		CALC
IRR%		__2.37__

Thus at a discount rate of 2.37% the entity is quantitatively indifferent between leasing and purchasing. Any discount rate below 2.37% will favor the purchase alternative, whereas any discount rate above 2.37% will favor leasing.

256. Any final conclusions?

Yes, lessors very often lose transactions to cash. Such lost transactions can be salvaged through the use of a lease versus cash analysis. From the author's experience, having been involved in hundreds of real world lease versus cash analyses, the lessee's cost of capital or opportunity cost is generally greater than the break-even rate. This favours leasing!

There is no excuse for losing deals to cash anymore!

> *Paying cash is almost always more expensive than leasing; there is no need to lose to cash anymore.*

257. Now that lease versus cash has been thoroughly discussed, how about lease versus loan?

There are only two differences between lease versus cash and lease versus loan. These are:

- Instead of 100% of equipment cost being paid at time zero, a down payment (if any) is the initial outlay followed by payments, which constitute principal plus interest

- The interest portion of each payment is tax deductible; therefore a corresponding tax shield is created

All other aspects remain the same.

LEASE VERSUS LEASE ANALYSIS

258. Having concluded that leasing is the best choice, what is the next step an entity takes?
As indicated in an earlier subsection, the entity arrives at a short list of lessors.

259. How is this done?
The short list is arrived at based on the attributes or characteristics the entity is seeking.

260. What are these attributes?
Let's first list them and then discuss each sequentially. They include:

- Market rates
- Flexibility
- Responsiveness
- Service
- Diversity of products
- Knowledge
- Integrity and reputation
- Financial strength
- Logistics
- Documentation

Let's begin our discussion with market rates. Lessees are not really looking for "best" rates; they are seeking quotes from lessors who will quote within a narrow range of market rates. If the market rate for a certain credit risk profile is around 10%, lessees want to work with lessors who will quote within a narrow range of this. Rate is not the be all and end all in a lease; yet it is of paramount importance.

Lessees look for more than "best" rates; flexibility, responsiveness and knowledge are sought-after attributes.

261. What are some examples of flexibility?

Flexibility is important to some lessees. One example would be where a lessee may want a lessor to offer a 30-month lease term. Unfortunately, many lessors only know how to multiply by 12 and routinely (and rigidly) only offer say 24-, 36- and 48-month leases. Another example would be where a lessee may want to be invoiced in a manner that the payment due date for each rental is the 20th of each month. Again, many lessors routinely (and rigidly) only invoice in a manner where rentals are always due on the first of each month!

262. What is meant by responsiveness?

Lessees really like lessors to be responsive. The best example of this is the speed with which a lessor processes a lessee's credit application toward either acceptance or rejection.

263. Service is a broad word. Can examples be provided?

Lessees would like a lessor to take a "cradle to grave" approach to service. A lease has three phases: inception, duration and termination. At inception, (which really means preinception) lessees would like a lessor to provide a prompt answer, as indicated above, to a submitted credit application. During the lease, lessees would like lessors to provide reasonable early payoff amounts if the lessee so desires to payoff the remaining rentals. At the termination of the lease, lessees would like an expedient end of term title transfer.

The above are merely examples. Service is indeed a broad word and needs to be translated into a delivery mechanism as often as possible.

264. Why would a lessee like a lessor to have a diversity of products?

Such diversity is important to many lessees. As an example, if a lessee desires off balance sheet financing, the lessor needs to offer an operating lease that qualifies as off balance sheet. As another example, if a lessee desires a synthetic lease (a hybrid lease where the lease is an operating lease for accounting purposes but a purchase for tax purposes), the lessor needs to be in a position to offer this product as well.

This is a good point in time to suggest that all lessees are not seeking all of the attributes enumerated earlier. Some may, at one extreme, simply want market rates; some at another extreme may be seeking a lessor to possess every single attribute.

265. Why should lessors be knowledgeable?
This is an important attribute that many lessees seek in a lessor. Lessors are expected to know more about varied aspects of leasing than the lessee is—after all, the lessor is the service provider, the lessee is the customer.

266. What are examples of knowledge?
One could really list more than 100 items here that could be categorized into product related, accounting, tax, finance and legal. An example of product related would be "what varied end of term options exist on a lease"; an example of accounting would be "what discount rate should a lessee use in the 90% present value test"; an example of finance would be "what is the proper discount rate to be used in a lease versus cash analysis"; an example of tax would be "what is the difference in VAT/GST treatment between a lease on one hand and a loan on the other hand"; lastly, an example of legal would be "what exactly is meant by the quiet enjoyment right a lessee has."

Leasing is complex; lessees expect lessors to know more than they do!

Again, the above are merely examples. The more a lessor knows the better the service the lessee receives.

267. Integrity and reputation are generic expressions. How exactly do they fit into the context of lessor attributes?
Lessees expect impeccable integrity from a lessor. Two examples follow: a lessor may initially quote a rental in arrears; at the last minute when the documentation is about to be signed, the lease rental is shown in advance. When a lessee needs to lease (as versus wants to lease), it becomes difficult for such a lessee to back out at the last minute from doing the transaction.

Another example is where a lease contains a fair market value (FMV) purchase option, the value of which is to be determined by the lessor (sophisticated lessees would never enter into a lease where the lessor is to arrive at the FMV) and at the end of the lease the lessor arrives at an arbitrarily high value knowing the lessee wants to exercise the purchase option.

268. Why is financial strength an issue?

To some lessees this attribute is an important one. After all, the lessor and lessee are partners, so as to say, for the duration of the lease. To take what one may think is an extreme example, but it really is not, let's assume that a lessor declares bankruptcy in the midst of a lease. Though the quiet enjoyment clause is meant to protect a lessee, an administrator in the bankruptcy court may conclude otherwise (this has happened!) and what may be essential production equipment to the lessee may become the subject matter of a court battle.

Thus, sophisticated lessees typically on large-ticket transactions will do the necessary due diligence to assure that the lessor is indeed financially strong.

269. What is meant by logistics?

Some lessees prefer to deal with the lessor face-to-face as versus through telephone and e-mail. Thus, if a lessee is located in an area outside of the head office of a lessor, the lessee would prefer that the lessor have a branch office in the area where the lessee is domiciled.

270. Lastly, why is documentation important?

The quality and quantity of documentation is important to many lessees. Quality has to do with whether the documentation is fair and user friendly; quantity obviously has to do with whether the documentation is unduly cumbersome or whether it is as short and crisp as possible.

271. Now that the attributes of lessors have been discussed, what is the next step?

The next step is that the lessee will create a short list of lessors, based on the attributes each lessee feels is important.

Once the short list is created the lessee will obtain a quote from each of say three or four lessors.

272. How are competing lessor quotes evaluated by the lessee?

It depends on what motivates each lessee. Generally speaking, there are two types of lessees in this context: those that are interest rate focused and those that are cash focused.

273. What is the difference between the two types?

The interest rate focused lessee is obviously looking for the lowest interest rate in the lease. On finance leases most, if not all, lessees can very easily compute the interest rate.

Cash focused lessees are usually looking for the lowest rental (given all other things being equal—such as the term of the lease, the periodicity of the rental and whether the rental is in advance or arrears). However, many lessees are also focused on how much cash each lessor is asking for at the inception of the lease. This would typically be the sum of the advance rental(s), fees (such as documentation or lease management) plus a security deposit, if any.

274. If a lessee is cash focused will it possibly select a lease with a higher interest rate?

Generally yes, as cash is indeed the focus!

275. But can a lease say with a lower monthly rental have a higher interest rate given that lease term is a constant?

A lease with a lower monthly rental can indeed have a higher rate. An example of a finance lease follows:

LEASE A

Equipment cost	$100.00
Term in months	48
Rental in advance	$2.52
IRR (interest rate)	10%

LEASE B

Equipment cost	$100.00
Term in months	48
Rental in advance	$2.39
Security deposit	$10.00
Residual (bullet payment)	$10.00

The security deposit is taken in at time zero and applied to the residual at the end of lease term.

The time line for lease B would look as follows:

```
                        0        1            47      48
                        ─────────────────────────────────
Equipment cost       (100.00)                  10   Residual
Deposit                10.00                  (10)  Deposit refund
Advance rental          2.39
                        ─────                  ───
                       (87.61) ----- 2.39 ------ 0
```

The IRR (interest rate) would be computed as follows:

> HP12C

	f	REG
87.61	CHS	PV
2.39		PMT
47		n
i		1.09
12 x		<u>13.03</u>

Lease Marketing

› HP17BII+

	☐	CLEAR DATA
87.61	+/	PV
2.39		PMT
47		N
I%		**13.03**

Note: to arrive at 13.03%, the calculator must be set at the "end" mode. This is because the first rental has already been incorporated in the $87.61 and the remaining rents, therefore, are in arrears vis-a-vis time zero.

A summary follows:

Lease	Rental	IRR
A	$2.52	10.00%
B	2.39	13.03%

It can be seen from the above that by mixing a number of additional variables even a lower rental caused the lease to have an interest rate higher than the one with a higher rental.

276. Is there any other way of quantitatively comparing one lease to another?

Actually there is! And this is really the best way, but unfortunately not used by too many lessees and not fully understood by all lessors either! The technique very simply is present value. As indicated earlier in the subsection on Lease Versus Purchase Analysis, present value is not understood by unsophisticated lessees and fully understood by the very sophisticated ones. Lessees that are quasi-sophisticated and teachable (and this could be a large category for many a lessor) are the ones where a lessor has the opportunity to help teach this group that present value in fact is the best way to analyze two or more financial alternatives. The comparison between one lease and another is indeed a choice between two financial alternatives.

277. Why is present value the best way to compare two financial alternatives?

There are two ways to analyze competing financial alternatives—IRR (interest rate) and present value. Before one analyzes why present value is the better of the two approaches, one must remember that the objective of the comparison from a lessee's point of view is to select that alternative which maximizes shareholders' wealth. In this context, IRR is a percentage while (net) present value is expressed in terms of dollars. It is easy to understand why present value is better than IRR as dividends (to shareholders) cannot be paid with percentages, they can be paid with dollars!

> *Present value is the best and most sophisticated way to analyze two or more competing leases.*

278. How is present value used to compare two or more competing leases?

It's best to illustrate as follows:

Common parameters to both leases:

Equipment cost	$100.00
Term in months	48
Rental	in advance
IRR	10%

Lease Marketing **179**

LEASE A

    Rental per month $ 2.52

LEASE B
Structured as follows: first 24 rentals are $2.06 and the remaining 24 are $3.08 (later in the Pricing and Structuring Section it will be shown how to structure leases given a certain IRR. Here it should be accepted that rentals of $2.06 and $3.08 indeed give the lessor a 10% IRR).

The present value, say at an internal lessee hurdle rate of 12%, on both leases is computed as follows:

LEASE A

> **HP12C**

	f	REG
12	g	12÷
48		n
2.52	CHS	PMT
	PV	**96.65**

> **HP17BII+**

	☐	CLEAR DATA
2.52	+/-	PMT
48		N
12		I%YR
	PV	**96.65**

LEASE B

> HP12C

	f	REG
12	g	12÷
2.06	g	CFo
2.06	g	CFj
23	g	Nj
3.08	g	CFj
24	g	Nj
fNPV		96.24

> HP17BII+

	☐	CLEAR DATA
2.06		INPUT
2.06		INPUT
23		INPUT
3.08		INPUT
24		INPUT
		EXIT
		CALC
1		I%
NPV		96.24

Lease Marketing **181**

Even though the present value of lease B is slightly less (in this illustration), it goes to show that when two leases have the same interest rate a structured lease can have a lower present value to the lessee.

279. Will any type of structure cause this to happen?
No. The result observed earlier has to do with the theory of interest rate differentials. To fully understand this let's begin by stating that in the narrow context of what one is trying to accomplish here (lowering present value with structure), there are three types of lessees:

- Lessee discount rate is equal to lessor IRR (this will be an extremely rare coincidence);
- Lessee discount rate is lower than lessor IRR;
- Lessee discount rate is higher than lessor IRR.

280. How does this all matter?
In the case of a lessee whose internal discount rate is equal to the lessor IRR, no type of structure will ever lower present value. If the discount rate is equal to the interest rate, present value will always equal principal!

In the example above, the lessee had a discount rate of 12% while the lessor IRR was 10%, a case where the lessee discount rate was higher. The structure that worked was a step-up structure or a low-high structure.

However, had the lessee discount rate been lower than the lessor IRR only a step down or a high-low structure will lower present value.

281. Will this always work?
Always. To summarize:

- If a lessee has a discount rate lower than the lessor IRR, the structure to lower present value should be step down;
- If the lessee has a discount rate higher than the lessor IRR, the structure to lower present value should be step-up.

The author has worked with many real world structures where based on:

- The relative grade between steps and,
- The differential between the lessor IRR and the lessee discount rate

the present value difference between a linear lease and a structured lease can be as high as five percent of equipment cost. This is substantial!

282. A practical conclusion would help?

In the real world, lessors should attempt to structure leases with those lessees who understand present value. The objective of structuring would be two-fold: to teach the lessee to present value as the means of comparing two or more competing leases; but more importantly, to use structure to lower the present value of the lessor's lease as versus what is likely to be a linear lease from a competitor.

| *Structure can win deals!*

283. An overall summary at this stage would help?

There are essentially three ways to analyze two or more competing leases: interest rate, cash and present value. A lessee should prepare the following matrix:

Lease	A	B	C
Interest rate			
Cash			
Periodic rental			
Total rentals			
Amount due upfront			
Present value			

The matrix is helpful in telling the lessee the "whole story" between two or more competing leases and, as an example, even if a lessee is solely motivated by how much cash has to be paid up front, it helps to know the other particulars.

Lessors should use the above matrix not only to show lessees how leases should be properly quantitatively evaluated but more importantly use the matrix to win the deal!

COUNTERING COMMON OBJECTIONS

284. Thus far one has seen (in the subsection on The Benefits of Leasing) that leasing has numerous benefits; also, one has seen (in the subsection on Lease versus Purchase Analysis) that often leasing can be cheaper than purchase. Does this mean leasing is for everyone?
Not at all! Leasing, like any other product, has its share of disadvantages—both real and perceived. Because of these disadvantages many entities prefer to use alternative modes of acquisition.

285. What are some of the common objections to leasing?
Let's first arrive at a list that is as complete as possible and then discuss each objection to gauge whether it is real or perceived. More importantly, lessors should know how to counter each objection keeping in mind that real objections do not really have a counter. One needs to learn how to dance around them!

The list of common objections to leasing includes:

- Leasing is more expensive
- The entity wants to acquire through cash
- Leasing is complex
- The entity believes in ownership
- Noncancelable leases are a concern
- The entity is seeking tax benefits
- Leases lower EBITDA
- The entity wants to control its assets

286. Which is generally the most common objection to leasing?
The most common objection one hears from potential customers is that leasing is more expensive. Unfortunately this expression is almost a "mantra"! When an entity makes this statement they are obviously

comparing the cost to lease to the cost to purchase either through cash or a loan (or in some countries through hire-purchase).

287. How does one counter this frequently encountered objection?

One needs to first find out from the potential customer with what mode of purchase are they comparing leasing. To begin with, let's assume that leasing is being compared to an outright cash purchase.

There are two different counters to this objection depending on how sophisticated the customer is. When one is dealing with a not so sophisticated entity who does not understand present value analysis, the counter would be to state that cash as a component of working capital should not be tied up in the acquisition of an asset and that such acquisition is best procured through medium-term financing (using leasing, of course!); the cash one has today may need to be safeguarded for future use. Another way of expressing this is to state that working capital should be used for operations and not for medium-term financing.

The opportunity cost of tying up cash can make cash more expensive than leasing.

Also, this type of customer should be told that cash has an opportunity cost.

288. What if the potential customer is sophisticated?

Sophisticated, in this case, would simply mean that the entity either understands present value analysis or is teachable. With these types of entities one should convince them to do a lease versus purchase (cash) analysis; better yet, the lessor should do such analysis after gathering the needed data. If the lessor does the analysis there is no scope for error in the choice of the discount rate. As explained in an earlier subsection, the present value after tax analysis is most likely to favour cash—in essence showing the customer that not only does leasing have numerous benefits; it is also cheaper!

289. How about lease versus loan?

If the customer is suggesting that leasing is more expensive compared to a loan, this objection is generally only half the story. In other words, what the customer really means is that the interest rate in a lease is higher than that in a loan—something that is true most of the time.

290. But why is this only half the story?

To meaningfully compare the cost of leasing to the cost of a loan one would have to do a present value analysis on an after-tax basis. Often on a present value after-tax basis, leasing will be less expensive.

291. What factors generally would make leasing less expensive?

On the purchase side if the tax depreciation is over a long fiscal period, this may tend to favour leasing as the tax shield from depreciation is not too generous, or if a large down payment is due on the loan, this too could favour leasing.

292. The next objection to leasing is where an entity states that they prefer to pay cash. How does one counter this objection?

The same as in QUESTION 287 where it was explained that cash should be preserved and that cash has an opportunity cost. Also, as explained earlier, a present value after-tax approach will generally show that cash is the more expensive alternative.

293. Is leasing really complex?

Many potential lessees often use this expression as an excuse to pay cash which they, of course, feel is simpler. Is leasing complex? Perhaps to those who have never leased before.

294. What is a good counter to this objection?

The first thing a lessor needs to do is simply ask a question in response to this expression, the question being "what do you mean by this?" Often a potential lessee is unable to answer this which generally means either the objection is a "mantra" (again!) used by many or an excuse to pay cash. If the customer is really not able to answer the question, the

Lease Marketing   187

lessor needs to assure the customer that if the customer were to provide examples of complexity, the lessor will painstakingly provide needed explanations and answers.

295. Many entities do not wish to lease as they prefer to own. How does one counter this objection?

As most lessors know, this is a very common objection, perhaps as common as the one that states leasing is more expensive. As most lessors also know it is a "psychological" objection. In many countries where leasing is still evolving and where traditionally entities, particularly the small and medium sized ones, have always purchased there is a strong psychological propensity toward ownership.

296. How does one counter this perceived objection?

There are two ways to do so. The first is to explain to the entity that the profitable use of equipment is far more important than ownership. The second, on a finance lease, is to state that if they are really keen on ownership they can, in fact, through a finance lease have legal title be transferred upon termination of the lease for a nominal amount; that this approach is the best of both worlds—they can enjoy profitable usage as well as future ownership of the asset. And, if the subject matter of the transaction is an operating lease, the fact remains that ownership, at the end of lease term, is indeed an option whether stated in the contract or not.

A finance lease is the solution to the common psychological desire for ownership; the lessee can profitably use the asset, have it be financed and eventually own it!

297. Many potential lessees quarrel about the noncancelable aspect of leasing. How can one counter this objection?

First of all it should be explained that lessors seldom, if ever, have an infinite monetary capacity to fund all the transactions they encounter and that when a certain lessee has been funded, the lessor in essence has chosen to invest its funds in a certain transaction with a given maturity to the preclusion of investing in another. The lessor should then state that its funding is tied to the maturity of its leases. Lastly, the lessor should proceed to explain that though leases are generally noncancelable, if a lessee wishes to pay off the remaining balance at a certain point in time this can be discussed and negotiated.

As an unrelated item, it is advised that lessors should not have an early payoff or early settlement formula in the lease agreement. Early payoffs should always be negotiated on a case-by-case basis.

298. Often an entity is seeking to own the asset in order to have the tax benefits incident to ownership. Is this a valid objection to leasing?

It depends on the tax situation in each country. On one hand, as is mostly the case, if the tax depreciable life is longer than the term of the lease and the rentals are deductible, then leasing will be more favourable from a tax point of view. On the other hand, if the tax life is short or if the asset qualifies for substantially accelerated tax depreciation, then ownership is likely to provide faster tax breaks.

If the latter is true and ownership provides a faster write-off then the lessor has to try to convince the potential customer that leasing has many other benefits that will offset any tax disadvantages it may have.

299. Does leasing cause EBITDA to be lower?

To begin with, EBITDA stands for earnings before interest, taxes, depreciation and amortization. It is often used as a measure to arrive at an entity's earnings from operations. If an entity brings this objection to the attention of a lessor, the lessor should explain to the entity that operating leases (that qualify for off balance sheet financing) indeed do adversely affect EBITDA. This is so as rent expense is deducted in arriving at EBITDA; thus, rent expense will lower EBITDA.

However, it is critical to explain to the entity that finance leases do not adversely affect EBITDA. Finance leases are capitalized on the balance sheet; the income statement shows depreciation and interest expense both of which are not deducted in arriving at EBITDA. Thus this objection should be turned around to an opportunity to sell the client a finance lease!

300. The last objection has to do with those who state that they do not want to lease as they seek total control of the asset. Is this a valid objection?

Of all the objections listed this is the only valid one! There is a difference between the desire to own for the sake of owning and the desire to own for the sake of controlling. Entities who seek total control of certain assets should not generally lease such assets. Master lease agreements invariably have clauses that are likely to impinge on the lessee's desire to totally control the asset. As an example most, if not all, lease agreements will have a clause prohibiting the lessee from moving the asset from one location to another without first obtaining written consent from the lessor. Such a clause exists for good reason; yet, it causes complexities/difficulties for those who desire unfettered control of the asset as it forces them to negotiate issues such as these with the lessor.

It is because of this desire to have total control that many entities have a policy that core or strategic assets will be purchased and not leased.

301. Are there any other objections to leasing?

Unquestionably there are. Lessors are advised to put their heads together by discussing this subject with all those who liaise with potential customers. This would include sales, marketing and business development personnel. The focus of such a discussion should be to have the staff bring to the attention of management every single objection that has been raised by potential clients. This list will vary from one lessor to another based on transaction size, equipment type and lessee profile; the list will also vary from country to country based on nuances such as sales tax and VAT. Nonetheless, it is critical for each lessor to arrive at a comprehensive list.

302. Then what?

The next step is even more important. For each objection, particularly the perceived ones, management should arrive at varied counters. The counters to the objections will include the ones discussed above. More importantly, management should enhance the counters. Now imagine a comprehensive list with two columns, one listing objections the other listing counters. Each individual who liaises with potential customers attempting to sell leasing should be armed with this list. The benefit is obvious! Sales staff will be properly equipped with counters and will not have to stumble over objections. This list will indeed help the lessor to win more deals!

> *Making a comprehensive list of commonly encountered objections and arriving at sensible and cohesive responses will help win deals.*

SUMMARY

1. There are two types of lessees—those who want to lease and those who need to lease.

2. The six major reasons for leasing are as follows:

   - Cash flow
   - Financial reporting
   - Financial
   - Technology
   - Tax
   - Convenience

3. The subset for cash flow benefits are as follows:

   - 100% financing
   - 100% plus financing
   - Conservation of working capital
   - Structured leases tailored to meet cash flow needs
   - Lower rentals due to residual and transfer of tax benefits

4. The subset for financial reporting benefits are as follows:

   - Ratio enhancement
   - Possible improvement in earnings
   - Increased performance bonuses to management
   - Avoidance of restrictive financial covenants
   - Avoidance of potential book losses

5. The subset for financial benefits are as follows:

- Availability of medium-term financing
- Often no additional collateral
- Hedge against inflation on fixed-rate leases
- Financial diversification
- Often less expensive
- Availability of financing for marginally creditworthy lessees

6. The subset for technology benefits are as follows:

- Hedge against technology
- Technology refresh during the term of the lease
- Early termination options

7. The subset for tax benefits are as follows:

- Faster tax write-off
- Lower rentals due to tax benefit transfer
- Mitigation of AMT and midquarter (in the U.S.)

8. The subset for convenience benefits are as follows:

- Faster response time than loans
- Faster appropriation from operating budgets
- Master lease agreements
- One stop shopping
- Flexibility from end of term options

9. It is important for lessors to recognize that each lessee is different. Also, lessors should realize that increased awareness and understanding of the benefits of leasing by potential customers will lead to additional business for the lessors.

In light of the above, lessors are advised to prepare a checklist along the following lines:

THE BENEFITS OF LEASING

	──────── Customer Priority ────────		
Benefits:	High	Medium	None

Under the "Benefits" column the lessor should list only those benefits it can deliver in the marketplace. For example, if a lessor does not offer operating leases that lead to off balance sheet financing, then the above list should not contain the financial reporting benefits.

A meeting should be convened of senior, or preferably all, salespeople in the firm so that two things can be accomplished:

- The list from QUESTION 163 should be enhanced based on the lessor's market niche.
- More importantly, all those who liase with potential lessees should be required to use the above list. It helps in two ways:

    1. It forces the lessors to educate their potential customers (very few lessees are knowledgeable about all the benefits of leasing);

    2. It allows the sales person to better understand why a particular entity is interested in leasing. (As an example, one of the benefits in the list will state: 100% financing. This may be a high priority to a certain entity and not to another). Common sense would then suggest that, where possible, the lessor should "tailor" the lease meeting as many of the customer's needs as possible.

10. The "tailoring" mentioned above is generally accomplished as follows:

CUSTOMER NEED	TAILORING
• Cash flow	100% financing Structured lease
• Financial reporting	Off balance sheet financing
• Financial	No additional collateral
• Technology	Operating lease with residual
• Convenience	Fastest response time possible

11. Lessors should be familiar with and be involved in the equipment acquisition process that lessees go through.

12. Lease versus purchase analysis, as a part of the equipment acquisition process, is best done on a present value after-tax basis.

13. The data that is needed for such is shown below:

- Equipment cost
- Lease quote
- Alternative mode of acquisition – cash or loan
- If loan, a loan quote
- Tax rate
- Depreciation details
- Useful life of asset
- End of term assumption (EOT)
- Salvage value
- Differential costs
- Discount rate

The above data should be procured from potential lessees where possible and the lessor should do the analysis on its spreadsheet or software.

14. Though the choice of a discount rate is critical, break-even or IRR analysis which compares the differential cash flows between leasing and purchasing is a better approach to the process.

15. Lessors should adopt a policy of requiring salespeople to use lease versus purchase analysis particularly when the potential lessee is contemplating paying cash. Many a times this will lead to incremental deals!

16. Lessees desire that lessors possess certain attributes. A list follows:

- Market rates
- Flexibility
- Responsiveness
- Service
- Diversity of products
- Knowledge
- Integrity and reputation
- Financial strength
- Logistics
- Documentation

17. A meeting should be convened of senior, or preferably all, salespeople for the purpose of enhancing the above list. After all, salespeople should know what customers are seeking.

18. Once the list is finalized, management should assure that the firm meets all the attributes on the list. Service is more than just an expression; it is a delivery mechanism.

19. Interest conscious customers, wherever possible, should be converted to present value customers. This, too, will help win incremental deals!

20. A list of common objections to leasing includes:

- Leasing is more expensive
- The entity wants to acquire through cash
- Leasing is complex
- The entity believes in ownership
- Noncancelable leases are a concern
- The entity is seeking tax benefits
- Leases lower EBITDA
- The entity wants to control its assets

21. One more meeting should be convened! The objective of this meeting should be to enhance the list and arrive at counters to all listed objections. More importantly, each individual who liaises with potential lessees should be required to use the list in the marketplace.

GLOSSARY

alternative minimum tax
A tax that attempts to assure that every taxpayer pays a certain minimum tax. Referred to as AMT. A corporate entity in the U.S. must pay the higher of its regular tax or AMT.

break-even IRR
The IRR at which an entity is quantitatively indifferent between leasing and purchasing. It is the IRR of the differential cash flows between leasing and purchasing.

capital structure
The debt and equity components of the balance sheet.

cost of capital
The cost of money which has two sources—debt and equity. Properly computed as the weighted average cost of capital, WACC.

current assets
Cash plus those assets, such as receivables, inventory and prepaid expenses, which are generally converted to cash within the normal operating cycle, a period equal to 12 months.

current liabilities
Those liabilities which are generally expected to be paid within the normal operating cycle, a period equal to 12 months.

current ratio
The ratio of current assets to current liabilities; a measure of liquidity.

debt to equity ratio
The ratio of total debt to equity, also known as leverage or gearing. Assets in a firm have only two sources of funding; debt and equity. Thus, the ratio with which total assets are funded.

differential costs
Costs which vary based on whether an entity leases or purchases.

draw down
Subsequent to the signing of a master lease agreement when the lessee needs additional equipment, such is "drawn down" per the master lease agreement. In other words, a new master lease agreement is not needed as draw downs are cross-referenced to the one already signed.

early payoff
An event where the lessee pays off the remaining balance in a lease and obtains title to the equipment.

early termination option
A call option (exercisable at the discretion of the lessee) which allows the lessee to terminate the lease and return the equipment to the lessor.

financial covenants
Terms and conditions generally contained in loan agreements where the lender requires the borrower to meet certain financial criteria such as a minimum debt to equity ratio. Failure to meet these criteria will cause the loan to be in default.

hurdle rate
A discount rate, often the cost of capital, used by entities to arrive at the net present value of benefits and costs associated with projects and/or financing alternatives.

interest minimization
The objective of arriving at the lowest cost when evaluating two financial alternatives.

interest rate differential
The difference between the lessor's IRR in a lease and the lessee's internal discount rate when present valuing the lease.

liquidity preference
The objective to have extra liquidity when selecting one financial alternative over the other.

MACRS
Stands for Modified Accelerated Cost Recovery System—the system used for tax depreciation in the U.S.

master lease agreement
The principal agreement between lessor and lessee which covers any and all of the necessary terms and conditions between the two parties.

match funding
Debt that has the same term (tenor) as leases.

midquarter convention
A convention in the U.S. that reduces the amount of depreciation deductions if an entity purchases more than 40% of its annual purchases in its fourth fiscal quarter.

opportunity cost
The return foregone from the business when money is invested elsewhere.

quiet enjoyment clause
An important clause in a master lease agreement that permits the lessee to have unperturbed use of the asset as long as the lessee is not in default.

return on assets
Net income (or income after taxes) divided by total assets; a measure of profitability.

salvage value
The amount an asset is sold for at the end of its estimated useful life.

tax shield
The tax benefit received on the basis of a deductible expense. Computed as the expense multiplied by the tax rate.

technology refresh
When old equipment that is deemed to be obsolete is replaced during the lease with newer technology.

useful life
The estimated life of an asset in the hands of one user as versus economic life which is useful life in the hands of multiple users.

working capital
Current assets minus current liabilities.

HOMEWORK!

1. What are the six major reasons why lessees lease?

2. What are the formulae for the following ratios and how can off balance sheet financing enhance them: current ratio, return on assets and leverage or gearing?

3. What it the reason that an operating lease as compared to a finance lease is likely to improve lessee earnings?

4. Under what circumstances can a lease provide an income tax benefit to a lessee?

5. What are the four stages to the equipment acquisition process?

6. Why is a lease versus purchase analysis best done on a present value after-tax basis?

7. What data must be gathered in order to do a lease versus purchase analysis?

8. What is the important aspect about the end of term assumption in a lease versus purchase analysis?

9. Which is the most appropriate discount rate to be used in a lease versus purchase analysis?

10. Compute the cost of capital from the following data: debt to equity ratio, 2 : 1; pretax cost of debt, 10%; tax rate 34% and cost of equity 18%.

11. Based on the following prepare a manual spreadsheet for a lease versus cash analysis.

GENERAL ASSUMPTIONS
- Tax rate, 32%
- Cost of capital or opportunity cost (after-tax), 13.71%
- After-tax cost of debt, 9.52% (Pretax cost, 14%)
- Inception date, January 1, 200X

LEASE ASSUMPTIONS
- Lease payments are $27,487 in advance for 48 months.
- Lessee will purchase the asset at the end of the term upon payment of the last rental; use it for one more year and then sell it for $200,000.

PURCHASE ASSUMPTIONS
- Asset cost, $1,000,000
- Depreciation, 20% straight line
- Selling price, $200,000, after five years

12. From the above, compute the present value of both alternatives at 13.71% as well as 9.52%.

13. Compute the cash flow differential and break-even IRR.

14. Why should present value be used in comparing two or more leases?

15. List the five most common objections to leasing.

HOMEWORK ANSWERS

Answer 1

The six major reasons for leasing are as follows:

- Cash flow
- Financial reporting
- Financial
- Technology
- Tax
- Convenience

Answer 2

Current ratio   Current assets ÷ Current liabilities

With off balance sheet financing the debt is not booked; thus, liabilities including current liabilities are lower than otherwise. This being the denominator in the formula causes the current ratio to increase.

Return on assets   Net income ÷ Total assets

Assets not being booked causes the denominator to be lower than otherwise. This causes ROA to increase.

Leverage or Gearing   Debt: Equity

With debt not being booked the debt to equity ratio is decreased.

Answer 3

The impact on the lessee's income treatment is as follows: operating leases will show rent expense while finance leases will show depreciation plus interest expense.

Rent expense typically is a straight line while depreciation plus interest is the sum of a straight line (depreciation) and a downward sloping line (interest).

Due to the slope of the interest expense line, rent expense is generally lower than depreciation plus interest causing the lessee to have higher earnings in the early period of the lease.

Answer 4

A lease will lower a lessee's taxable income when rent expense is deductible over a shorter period than the period over which depreciation would be deducted if the lessee had purchased the asset.

Answer 5

The four stages are as follows:

- Capital expenditure analysis
- Financing decision
- Lessor selection process
- Lease versus lease analysis

Answer 6

Lease versus purchase analysis is best done using present value after-tax for the following reasons: present value is used as the comparison invariably involves two time lines requiring the future cash flows to be present valued to time zero; after-tax is used as the tax consequences of leasing are often different than the tax consequences of a purchase (leasing generally allows the lessee to deduct rent expense, while purchasing causes depreciation to be the deductible item).

Answer 7
The data to be gathered for the lease versus purchase analysis is as follows:

- Equipment cost
- Lease quote
- Alternative mode of acquisition – cash or loan
- If loan, a loan quote
- Tax rate
- Depreciation details
- Useful life of asset
- End of term assumption
- Salvage value
- Differential costs
- Discount rate

Answer 8
The end of term assumptions in a lease versus purchase analysis may never be accurate; they need to be consistent.

Answer 9
If the lessee is seeking interest minimization then the cost of debt is most appropriate; however, if the lessee has a liquidity preference (which most lessees do) then the cost of capital or opportunity cost is the most appropriate discount rate.

Answer 10
Cost of capital is computed as follows:

	Weight		Cost		Tax Adjustment		After-tax Cost
Debt	.6667	x	10.00%	x	.66	=	4.40
Equity	.3333	x	18.00%	x	N/A	=	6.00
							10.40

Answer 11

LEASE ALTERNATIVE

	0	1	2	3	4	5
Rentals	$27,487	$302,357	$329,844	$329,844	$329,844	
Tax Shield	(8,796)	(96,754)	(105,550)	(105,550)	(105,550)	
Salvage Value						(136,000)
Net Cost	$18,691	$205,603	$224,294	$224,294	$224,294	$(136,000)

PURCHASE ALTERNATIVE

	0	1	2	3	4	5
Initial Payment	$1,000,000					
Depreciation		(64,000)	(64,000)	(64,000)	(64,000)	(64,000)
Salvage Value						(136,000)
Net Cost	$1,000,000	$(64,000)	$(64,000)	$(64,000)	(64,000)	$(200,000)

Answer 12

LEASE

> HP12C

	f	REG
9.52		i
18,691	g	CFo
205,603	g	CFj
224,294	g	CFj
3	g	Nj
136,000	CHSg	CFj
f NPV		633,745
13.71		i
f NPV		588,147

LEASE

> HP17BII+

		☐	CLEAR DATA
18,691			INPUT
205,603			INPUT
1			INPUT
224,294			INPUT
3			INPUT
136,000	+/-		INPUT
1			INPUT
			EXIT
			CALC
9.52			I%
NPV			633,745
13.71			I%
NPV			588,147

BUY

BUY

> HP12C

> HP17BII+

	f	REG			CLEAR DATA
9.52		i	1,000,000		INPUT
1,000,000	g	CFo	64,000	+/-	INPUT
64,000	CHSg	CFj	4		INPUT
4	g	Nj	200,000	+/-	INPUT
200,000	CHSg	Nj	1		INPUT
f NPV		668,073			EXIT
13.71		i			CALC
f NPV		707,203	9.52		I%
			NPV		668,073
			13.71		I%
			NPV		707,283

Answer 13

CASH FLOW DIFFERENTIAL

	0	1	2	3	4	5
Lease		$18,691	$205,603	$224,294	$224,294	$224,294	$(136,000)
Cash	1,000,000	(64,000)	(64,000)	(64,000)	(64,000)	(200,000)
Differential	($981,309)	$269,603	$288,294	$288,294	$288,294	$64,000

Lease Marketing   **213**

› HP12C				› HP17BII+		
	f	REG			☐	CLEAR DATA
981,309	CHSg	CFo		981,309	+/-	INPUT
269,603	g	CFj		269,203		INPUT
288,294	g	CFj		1		INPUT
3	g	Nj		288,294		INPUT
64,000	g	CFj		3		INPUT
	f	irr	7.99	64,000		INPUT
				1		INPUT
						EXIT
						CALC
					IRR %	7.99

Answer 14

Present value actually is the most appropriate technique to evaluate two or more competing lease proposals. This is true as the answers are in absolute dollars not in percentages. Under the concept that the objective, in comparing two or more financing alternatives, is to maximize shareholders net worth, dividends to shareholders can be distributed using dollars not percentages.

Answer 15
- Leasing is more expensive
- The entity wants to acquire through cash
- Leasing is complex
- The entity believes in ownership
- Noncancelable leases are a concern

Lease Accounting

Lease Accounting

The Two Types of Leases

The Accounting Impact on Lessees

The Accounting Impact on Lessors

Criteria Distinguishing Finance and Operating Leases

Techniques to Structure Off Balance Sheet Financing

The Future of Lease Accounting

Summary

Glossary

Homework!

Homework Answers

THE TWO TYPES OF LEASES

303. From an accounting point of view, how many types of leases exist?
In the Overview Section, it was stated that there are two types of leases—finance and operating. It is important to note that the discussion had to do with products in the marketplace and not products from an accounting point of view. It is also important to note that the sole distinction between a finance lease and an operating lease from the marketplace point of view has to do with full payout versus nonfull payout.

304. What does all of this have to do from an accounting point of view?
From an accounting point of view, there are also two types of leases—finance leases and operating leases.

305. What is the correlation between the marketplace and accounting?
It is critical to note that marketplace finance leases will always be finance leases from an accounting point of view; marketplace operating leases will either be finance leases or operating leases from an accounting point of view! The logic and detail will be explained later. The following diagram describes the correlation:

The accounting criteria determining whether a lease is a finance or an operating lease are substantially different from the marketplace criteria.

CORRELATION BETWEEN MARKETPLACE AND ACCOUNTING

Party	Marketplace	Accounting
Lessor	Finance Lease → Finance Lease Operating Lease → Operating Lease	
Lessee	Finance Lease → Finance Lease Operating Lease → Operating Lease	

It is important to note from an accounting point of view that a finance lease in the hands of a lessee in the U.S. is referred to as a capital lease.

The diagram below incorporates the subtle difference:

CORRELATION BETWEEN MARKETPLACE AND ACCOUNTING IN THE U.S.

Party	Marketplace	Accounting
Lessor	Finance Lease → Finance Lease Operating Lease → Operating Lease	
Lessee	Finance Lease → Capital Lease Operating Lease → Operating Lease	

Lease Accounting

THE ACCOUNTING IMPACT ON LESSEES

306. What is the impact of each of the two types of leases from a lessee point of view?
The impact needs to be studied as to how these leases appear in the financial statements of the lessee.

307. Why not take one lease at a time?
Let's start with the operating lease. From an accounting point of view, if a lease is classified as an operating lease (criteria are discussed in a subsequent subsection), it is treated as though it is a rental.

308. How exactly does the lessee show this type of a lease in its financial statements?
In the lessee's balance sheet nothing is shown both under the categories of assets and liabilities. The lessee's income statement shows rent expense. Again, just as though the lease is a rental. This is known as off balance sheet financing.

The following diagram summarizes:

IMPACT OF OPERATING LEASE ON LESSEE

Balance Sheet	
Assets	Liabilities
0	0

Income Statement
Rent Expense

309. What about footnotes to financial statements?

Though the operating lease escapes the balance sheet, it is indeed shown in the footnotes. Remember, this is the sole accounting difference between an operating lease and a rental—rentals are off balance sheet and not disclosed in the footnotes.

310. How are operating leases disclosed?

The footnotes inform the reader the total of the future minimum lease payments (this expression, minimum lease payments, will be defined later) under noncancelable operating leases for each of the following periods: a.) not later than one year; b.) later than one year and not later than five years; c.) later than five years.

311. How about a finance lease?

In the lessee's balance sheet the equipment will be shown under the asset side and the corresponding debt will be shown under the liability side. The income statement will show depreciation expense and interest expense—a finance lease is shown as though the lease is a loan.

The following diagram summarizes:

IMPACT OF FINANCE (CAPITAL) LEASE ON LESSEE

Balance Sheet	
Assets	Liabilities
Equipment	Debt

Income Statement
Depreciation + Interest Expense

Lease Accounting   **221**

312. Perhaps an illustration will help?
It will! Let's use a simple one as follows:

Equipment cost	$100.00
Term in months	36
Rental in arrears	$3.23
Residual	$0
Lessor pretargeted IRR	10%

The total rentals amount to $116.28 ($3.23 x 36). It should be obvious that $16.28 is the total interest over 36 months at 10%.

At the inception, the equipment will be debited for $100 and a corresponding liability will be credited for $100. In essence, the equipment is shown at its cost and the liability shows the amount of principal due on the lease obligation.

313. After inception?
Over the term of the lease the asset, just like any other fixed asset, will be written down to zero via depreciation. As an example, if the lessee believes that the useful life of the asset is five years and if straight line depreciation is to be used, then each year the asset will be written down by $20 and simultaneously depreciation expense for $20 will be shown as an expense in the income statement.

Per IAS 17, the depreciation policy for leased assets should be consistent with that for depreciable assets which are owned. However, if there is no reasonable certainty that the lessee will obtain ownership by the end of the lease term, the asset should be fully depreciated over the shorter of the lease term or its useful life.

Per FASB 13, capital leases are amortized (depreciated) in a manner consistent with the lessee's normal depreciation policy for owned assets if the lease meets either or both of the first two criteria distinguishing a capital lease from an operating lease. (These criteria are contained in a subsequent subsection). If either of the two criteria are not met, the leased asset will be amortized in a manner consistent with the lessee's normal depreciation policy except that the period of amortization shall be the lease term.

314. What about the liability?
The liability is amortized at 10% over 36 months; each month the principal portion reduces the liability on the balance sheet, while the interest portion is shown as an expense on the income statement.

315. Can this be further detailed?
Amortization of the lease for the first 12 months provides $8.63 in interest and $30.13 in principal; the unamortized principal balance is $69.87 ($100 -$30.13). The income statement will show $8.63 for the first 12 months as interest expense; the liability (assuming the lease was incepted at the beginning of the accounting year) at the end of the first year will be shown at $69.87.

Of course, as is always done, the liability will be broken out into its current and noncurrent portions.

316. Any disclosure requirements for finance leases?
Notwithstanding the fact that finance leases are shown on the balance sheet, additional disclosure is required in the footnotes to the financial statements per IAS 17. This includes showing the present value of the minimum lease payments. FASB 13 has similar disclosure requirements for each of the following periods: a.) not later than one year; b.) later than one year and not later than five years; c.) later than five years.

THE ACCOUNTING IMPACT ON LESSORS

317. How do operating leases appear in the financial statements of the lessor?
It was learned earlier that operating leases are treated by the lessee as though they are rentals. The same is true with the lessor.

318. So how are they shown?
In the lessor's balance sheet, the equipment appears on the asset side.

319. What about the liability side of the balance sheet?
The liability side is irrelevant for whether a lease is classified as a finance lease or an operating lease any and all debt from funding both types of leases will appear on the liability side.

320. What is the income statement impact?
The equipment (on the asset side) is depreciated giving rise to depreciation expense; also, rent is shown as revenue. The depreciation of leased assets should be on a basis consistent with the lessor's normal depreciation policy for similar assets. Rental income is recognized on a straight line basis over the lease term unless another systematic basis is more representative.

The following diagram summarizes:

IMPACT OF OPERATING LEASE ON LESSOR

Balance Sheet	
Assets	Liabilities
Equipment	N/A

Income Statement
Rent Revenue
—
Depreciation Expense

321. How about finance leases?
Again, it was studied earlier that finance leases are treated by the lessee as though they are loans. The same is true with the lessor.

322. How are finance leases shown in the financial statements of the lessor?
Under the premise that finance leases are treated as though they are loans, the asset side of the lessor's balance sheet will show a receivable, and not the equipment—just like a banker would do on a loan.

323. What about the liability side?
Again, the liability sidé is irrelevant for whether a lease is classified as a finance lease or an operating lease any and all debt from funding both types of leases will appear on the liability side.

324. What about the income statement?
As the receivable is amortized, the principal portion reduces the receivable; the interest portion is shown as interest income on the income statement.

The following diagram summarizes:

IMPACT OF FINANCE LEASE ON LESSOR

Balance Sheet	
Assets	Liabilities
Receivable	N/A

Income Statement
Interest Income

325. An example may help?

Let's use the same example used in the earlier subsection.

Equipment cost	$100.00
Term in months	36
Rental in arrears	$3.23
Residual	$0
Lessor pretargeted IRR	10%

The lessor will show $100 as the receivable. Total rentals amount to $116.28. Obviously, $16.28 is total interest income over 36 months. This will be periodically reflected in the income statement.

326. Can this be further detailed?

As seen in the lessee example in QUESTION 315, amortization of the lease for the first 12 months at 10% results in $8.63 of interest and $30.13 in principal. The unamortized principal balance at the end of the first year is $69.87. Assuming again that the lease was incepted at the beginning of the year, the lessor's income statement will mirror the lessee's income statement and show $8.63 as interest income. The receivable will be shown at $69.87 at the end of the first year.

327. Whereas many lessees prefer operating leases from an accounting point of view as this provides them with the benefits of off balance sheet financing, what do lessors generally prefer from an accounting point of view?

> *Lessors have a strong preference for finance leases as they lead to accelerated income.*

From an accounting point of view, lessors generally prefer finance leases.

328. Why is this so?

This has to do with the focus entities place on earnings. Lessors, like any other entities, prefer to show earnings that are higher than otherwise.

329. Does this mean a finance lease shows higher earnings?

Yes, but only in the early years of the lease. This is because of the following: when a lessor has an operating lease, its income statement shows rental income minus depreciation. Rental income and depreciation expense are almost invariably linear; thus, the net of these two is also almost invariably linear. The "margin" on an operating lease (rental income minus depreciation) is thus a straight line over the lease term.

However, with a finance lease the lessor shows interest income. As in a loan, interest income is higher in the earlier periods and lower subsequently. Thus, the downward slope of the interest income line compared to the straight line from operating leases means higher earnings in the earlier periods.

330. But would this not reverse later?

Yes it would. Yet, for two reasons lessors prefer finance leases: most, if not all, lessors prefer to show higher earnings sooner than later; and secondly, if the portfolio grows, the reversal is deferred.

CRITERIA DISTINGUISHING FINANCE AND OPERATING LEASES

331. From an accounting point of view who determines whether a lease is a finance or an operating lease?
Such determination is made independently by both parties—the lessee and the lessor. Their internal accountants make the determination and if they are audited by an independent external auditor then the final determination, on material transactions, is made by the external auditor.

332. What criteria are used to make the determination?
The criteria are contained in International Accounting Standards Statement #17 (IAS 17). The U.S. uses Financial Accounting Standards Board Statement #13 (FASB 13). IAS 17 is an international accounting pronouncement; most countries have adopted it for domestic application.

FASB 13 is similar to IAS 17. Yet, there are differences. IAS 17 contains five criteria distinguishing the two types of leases; FASB 13 contains four. Also, as will be noted later, FASB 13 provides quantitative guidelines; IAS 17 does not.

333. What exactly are the criteria?
As noted above, IAS 17 provides five guidelines as to what characterizes a finance lease. An operating lease has not been defined; thus, an operating lease is one which is not a finance lease!

334. What then is a finance lease?
A finance lease is a lease that transfers substantially all the risks and rewards incident to the ownership of an asset.

In determining whether a lease is a lease or not, accounting uses the concept of substance over form; structure governs, not the label.

335. What is meant by the expression "transfers substantially all the risks and rewards incident to the ownership"?
This is the concept of substance over form. Under this concept, form (the label of a transaction) is irrelevant; it is the substance (the intent of the two parties) that matters.

336. Can "substance over form" be explained further?
Substance over form follows the economic concept of ownership. Under this concept, if the structure of the transaction points towards ownership or the intent of ownership, then the lease (it is critical to keep in mind that the word "lease" connotes a rental) is really not a lease but a financing transaction akin to a loan. Thus, when the lessor transfers substantially all the risks and rewards incident to ownership, in substance the lease is deemed to be a loan.

337. Are finance leases then akin to loans?
From an accounting point of view, using the concept of economic ownership, finance leases are indeed akin to loans. As seen in a previous subsection, they are treated as though they are loans.

338. But how can one know for sure whether the lessor indeed transferred substantially all of the risks and rewards incident to ownership?
IAS 17 and FASB 13 provide examples or guidelines. However, it will be seen later that often judgment is to be used whether such transfer of risks and rewards is intended to take place or not.

339. What are the guidelines?
There are five examples or guidelines provided by IAS 17. FASB 13 provides the first four of these five. The guidelines are provided as examples of situations which would normally lead to a lease being classified

> *The criteria distinguishing a finance lease from an operating lease are extremely subjective; judgment comes into play so often that two independent auditors could arrive at two different conclusions.*

as a finance lease. Let's take them up one at a time. The first guideline is:

"The lease transfers ownership of the asset to the lessee by the end of the lease term."

This criterion is common to both IAS 17 and FASB 13.

If a lease contains a provision that requires the lessor to transfer title of the leased asset to the lessee during or at the end of the lease, it seems clear that it was the intent of the two parties to enter into a transaction which is a purchase disguised as a lease. Ownership is expressly contemplated in the lease agreement. This would point toward the lease being a financing transaction; and therefore, it would be classified as a finance lease.

340. What is the next guideline?

The next IAS 17 guideline states:

"The lessee has the option to purchase the asset at a price which is expected to be sufficiently lower than the fair value at the date the option becomes exercisable such that, at the inception of the lease, it is reasonably certain that the option will be exercised."

FASB 13 states:

"The lease contains a bargain purchase option."

If a lease has a bargain purchase option, say $1, it seems clear that the intent of the two parties, at the inception of the lease, is for the lessee to definitely be exercising the option at the end of the term. Ownership is implicitly contemplated in the structure of the lease agreement.

A bargain purchase option (BPO) also suggests that the lease is a full payout lease; in essence, a finance lease. Why would a lessor offer a BPO unless the lessor was to be fully paid through rentals? Looking at it from the lessee's point of view, why would a lessee not exercise a BPO after fully paying out the lessor?

Thus, the existence of a BPO suggests that the two parties have entered into a transaction which is a purchase disguised as a lease. This would point toward the lease being a financing transaction; and therefore, it would be classified as a finance lease.

341. How can one determine if the purchase option is a BPO or not?

As IAS 17 states, the option price should be sufficiently lower than the fair value of the asset at the date the option becomes exercisable. The option price should be such that gives one a reasonable degree of certainty, at the inception of the lease, that the lessee will indeed exercise it at the end of the lease—thus it should be a "bargain."

342. How about an example or two?

Earlier, $1 was used – this is clearly a BPO. Let's use another example: assume a 48-month lease of a photocopy machine with a 20% purchase option. 20% of the original equipment cost is not likely to be a BPO on a copier after a few years as this is what the equipment is most likely to be worth. Let's take another example: assume a 48-month lease on a new commercial aircraft with a 20% purchase option. Here, 20% of original equipment cost after four years indeed appears to be a bargain.

Thus, whether the purchase option (if one exists to begin with) is a BPO or not is a case by case situation where one needs to take into account the type of equipment, the lease term and the amount of the purchase option. Often, judgment is needed to conclude whether a purchase option is a BPO or not.

343. What is the third guideline?
The third IAS 17 guideline states:

"The lease term is for the major part of the economic life of the asset even if title is not transferred."

FASB 13 states:

"The lease term is equal to 75% or more of the estimated economic life of the leased property."

344. What is meant by "economic life"?
Economic life is defined as the period over which an asset is expected to be economically usable by one or more users. The key expression is "one or more users."

345. Again, an example or two would be helpful?
Before delving into examples, one must keep in mind that arriving at economic life requires judgment. One should generally not use depreciable lives as prescribed by tax authorities. Let's take two examples. Let's begin with an asset most are familiar with, a motor car. Based on the author's judgment (which itself is based on varied data) the economic life of a new motor car, in the hands of multiple users, given normal repairs and maintenance is approximately 10 to 15 years. Undoubtedly, the economic life depends on the country in question; yet, 10 to 15 is a reasonable range.

346. Does not 10 to 15 years seem too long?
Not at all, keeping in mind again that this is the estimated economic life in the hands of multiple users.

Let's use another example—a new commercial aircraft, say a Boeing 777. Again, based on varied data, the author's judgment indicates that the economic life of this type of an asset is approximately 30 years, again in the hands of multiple users.

347. What is meant by the expression "major part"?

As to what is exactly meant by "major part" once again would be left to judgment. However, most accountants and auditors look to FASB 13. FASB 13, as seen earlier, in lieu of using the expression "major part" uses the expression "equal to 75 percent or more of the estimated economic life."

348. Why would a lease where the term is equal to or greater than 75% of the estimated economic life of the asset be considered to be a finance lease?

Using the motor car example, and assuming that the estimated economic life of the motor car is 12 years, imagine a lease with a term of nine years (not that anyone would write a nine-year lease on a motor car!). The concept here is that the lease term is so long, compared to the economic life of the asset, that the transaction points toward being a financing transaction. Keeping in mind that a "lease" connotes a rental, a nine-year transaction on an asset with an estimated economic life of 12 years by no means can be considered to be a rental! To put it differently, when the lease term is extremely long, asset exhaustion primarily takes place in the hands of the first user and the transaction points toward a purchase disguised as a lease. Ownership is implicitly contemplated in the structure of the lease agreement.

349. Two expressions, "economic life" and "major part" have been explained. What is the exact technical definition of the expression "lease term"?

IAS 17 defines lease term as "the noncancelable period for which the lessee has contracted to lease the asset together with any further terms for which the lessee has the option to continue to lease the asset, with or without further payment, which option at the inception of the lease it is reasonably certain that the lessee will exercise."

FASB 13 defines lease term similarly.

350. Perhaps an example would help?

Assume the following transaction: noncancelable lease term of 48 months with rentals of $100 each month where the lessee has an option to renew the lease for an additional 12 months at $1 per month. It is obvious that it is the intent of both parties for the lessee to indeed renew the lease; in fact, common sense would suggest that no lessor would give a lessee such a bargain renewal option unless the lease to begin with is a full payout lease; in essence a finance lease.

In the above example, for purposes of applying the 75% test, the lease term would be considered to be 60 months and not 48.

351. Are there not two additional guidelines?
The fourth IAS 17 guideline states:

"At the inception of the lease the present value of the minimum lease payments amount to at least substantially all of the present value of the leased asset."

FASB expresses this guideline as follows:

"The present value at the beginning of the lease term of the minimum lease payments equals or exceeds 90% of the fair value of the leased property."

352. It appears to be a fairly complex guideline. Before getting too technical, can it be explained conceptually?
For now assume that the expression "minimum lease payments" (MLPs) means the rentals and that the expression "fair value" means equipment cost. Let's assume a transaction where the equipment cost is $100 and the present value of the rentals is $94. Present value of $94 certainly is at least substantially all of the fair value of the leased asset, $100, and in the case of FASB 13 it is equal to or greater than 90%.

The concept here is that if a lessee pays, in present value terms, an amount that is almost equal to equipment cost, the transaction is a financing transaction and therefore the lease is a finance lease. Ownership is implicitly contemplated in the structure of the lease agreement.

353. What exactly is meant by the expression "at least substantially all of the fair value of the leased asset"?
Just as the expression "major part" (in the third guideline) is open to

interpretation, so also is the above expression. Here, too, accountants and auditors look to FASB 13 which, as seen above, suggests that if the present value of the MLPs is equal to or greater than 90% of the fair value of the equipment, the lease is a finance lease.

This is a good place to note that subsequent to recent (and unfortunately ongoing) corporate accounting irregularities, external independent auditors have tightened up considerably in the entire arena of off balance sheet financing. There was a point in time, a few years ago, that a 89.99% present value lease would qualify for off balance sheet financing—no more! Today it is substance over form; in other words, auditors use more judgment than ever before.

354. Two more expressions need to be fully explained: "minimum lease payments" and "fair value of the leased asset." What is meant by the first expression?

Minimum lease payments are defined by IAS 17 as "the payments over the lease term that the lessee is, or can be required, to make excluding contingent rent, costs for services and taxes to be paid by and reimbursed to the lessor, together with, in the case of the lessee, any amounts guaranteed by the lessee or by a party related to the lessee."

Using different language, the FASB 13 definition is similar.

355. That is a lot of detail. Can it be embellished?

From a lessee's point of view MLPs, keeping in mind that one is looking at what the lessee is likely to pay at the minimum, obviously include the rentals contracted to be paid over the term of the noncancelable lease. Beyond the rentals, a BPO (as it is likely to be paid) and any lessee guaranteed residual are also considered to be MLPs.

356. Why would a lessee guarantee a lessor's residual?

By and large the only reason for this would be to negotiate for a lower rate in the lease. This was explained in the Overview Section under TRAC leases.

357. Why is lessee guaranteed residual considered to be an MLP?

Accountants take the view that if a lessee does guarantee the lessor's residual, it is conceivable that the residual could go all the way down to zero; thus, from a conservative point of view (or in other words, from an accountant's point of view!) the lessee will be obligated to pay the lessor the entire residual.

358. What is excluded from lessee MLPs?

Contingent rents and administrative costs. Let's start with the first. Contingent rents are rents that may trigger in the future, over the term of the lease, based on events that may or may not take place. One example of contingent rent would be on an automobile operating lease where the lessor has assumed a residual position. Let's take a simple example: asset cost, $100; 36-month lease; residual 40% or $40.

359. Would not the residual assumption partly be based on how many miles or kilometers the lessee drives the automobile over the lease term?

That indeed is the reason why the lessor would have contingent rents. Embellishing the above example, the lessor would contractually state that if the lessee drove the automobile say more than 30,000 kilometers each year a contingent rent of 50 cents per kilometer would have to be paid. The excess rent, based on excess usage, compensates the lessor for residual deterioration as the residual will unquestionably go down (all other things being equal) the more the asset is used.

360. Why are contingent rents excluded from lessee MLPs?

The answer is obvious! The decision as to whether a lease is a finance lease or an operating lease is made at the inception of the transaction. At this stage, the contingent rents are not known and are therefore excluded.

361. What are administrative costs?

This expression has to do with items such as maintenance or insurance that the lessor may be providing and bundling such charges as a part of the rentals. It also includes taxes, such as sales tax or VAT that are imposed on lease rentals.

362. Why are administrative costs excluded?

These costs are excluded because they have nothing to do with the basic lease rentals; they are either for additional services provided by the lessor or they are imposed by government.

363. Are lessee MLPs the same as lessor MLPs?

To a very large extent, yes. What the lessee expects to pay at the minimum is what the lessor expects to receive at the minimum.

There is one major difference though. This has to do with any independent third party guaranteeing the lessor's residual.

364. Why would a third party guarantee a lessor's residual?

Often, a supplier or vendor will guarantee a lessor's residual. This happens, as an example, in vendor leasing programs (VLP). A VLP is essentially a joint venture between a lessor and a seller of goods wherein the lessor is typically given, for a certain period of time, a right of first refusal to exclusively finance the seller's goods. The two parties, the lessor and the supplier, often agree that the latter will, on a case by case basis, guarantee the lessor's residual. Without such a guaranty, the lessor often is unwilling to take a residual position sufficiently high enough to have the rentals be low enough for the lessee to fail the 90% test.

365. Why would a lessee want to fail the 90% test?

If the lessee wants an operating lease to avail of off balance sheet financing, none of the guidelines or tests can be met; for even if one is met, the lease is likely to be classified as a finance lease.

366. If a lessor has its residual guaranteed by an independent third party, why would such guaranty amount not be a lessee MLP?

Because it has nothing to do with the lessee. Separately, the lessee generally is unaware of the existence of such a guaranty.

367. Are there any other types of residual guarantees from third parties?

Yes, in those countries where residual insurance is available, lessors often will pay a premium to an insurance company to guarantee a part or all of the residual. Such a residual guaranty is procured either from an economic point of view where the lessor desires to mitigate or eliminate residual risk or from an accounting point of view where the lessor desires to have a finance lease.

368. Why would a lessor seek for the lease to be a finance lease and how can third party guaranteed residual accomplish this?

Two questions in one!

The answer to the first part of the question can be read in QUESTIONS 327 to 330 in the subsection entitled "The Accounting Impact on Lessors."

As to how third party guaranteed residual helps accomplish this goal is simple: with the rentals and the residual both being MLPs, the lease will be a full payout lease (as the present value of the MLPs will equal equipment cost).

369. What is meant by the expression "fair value"?

Fair value means the price at which the lessee could otherwise have purchased the equipment.

The 90% present value test is complex as MLPs can be different in the hands of the two parties and so can the discount rates.

370. A summary of the 90% test, at this stage, would be helpful.

To summarize, one has to present value the MLPs to determine whether the lease is a finance or an operating lease. If the present value is equal to or greater than 90% of the fair value of the asset, the lease is considered to be a financing transaction or a finance lease.

371. The present value process value obviously requires a discount rate. What discount rate do the lessor and lessee use to present value the MLPs?

Let's start with the lessor first. IAS 17 and FASB 13 require that the lessor present value the MLPs using the "interest rate implicit in the lease" ("implicit rate").

372. What is meant by the implicit rate?

IAS 17 defines the implicit rate as "the discount rate that at the inception of the lease causes the aggregate present value of the minimum lease payments and the unguaranteed residual value to be equal to the fair value of the leased asset." FASB 13's definition is basically the same.

373. How about an illustration?

Assume the following:

Equipment cost	$1,000.00
Lease term in months	36
Rentals in advance	$29.03
Unguaranteed residual	$125.00

The IRR in the above lease is 10%. This is computed as follows:

> HP12 C

	f	REG
1,000	CHS	PV
36		n
29.03		PMT
125		FV
	i	.83
12x		10.00

Lease Accounting **239**

> HP17B11+

			CLEAR DATA
			FIN
			TVM
	1,000	+/-	PV
	36		N
	29.03		PMT
	125		FV
	I%YR		__10.00__

10% is the discount rate that equates the present value of the MLPs (the rentals in this case) plus the unguaranteed residual to the fair value of the asset.

374. Is the implicit rate always the IRR in the lease?
Not always, but generally yes. An example where the implicit rate would not be equal to the IRR would be where a lessor has taken a refundable security deposit from the lessee. The security deposit is an integral part of the IRR computation; yet, is not a part of the implicit rate.

375. Why not?
Refundable security deposits are not a part of MLPs. They are shown as liabilities in the books of the lessor and as assets in the books of the lessee.

376. Going back to QUESTION 373, is the lease a finance lease or an operating lease to the lessor?
It is a finance lease in the strict context of the 90% test as the present value of the MLPs using 10% is $907.17, an amount greater than 90% of the fair value of the asset. Note that the present value calculation shown below only includes the rentals as the MLPs; the unguaranteed residual is not a component of MLPs as it is unguaranteed.

Thus, unguaranteed residual is a part of the implicit rate calculation but not a part of the present value calculation.

> HP12 C

		f	REG
	29.03	CHS	PMT
	10	g	12÷
	36		n
	PV		907.17

> HP17B11+

		☐	CLEAR DATA
			FIN
			TVM
	29.03	+/-	PMT
	10		I%YR
	36		N
	PV		907.17

377. What discount rate does the lessee use for the 90% test?

IAS 17 and FASB 13 require the lessee to present value the MLPs using the implicit rate, if known. However, as seen earlier, unguaranteed residual is an integral part of the implicit rate calculation and lessees almost invariably do not know what the residual position of the lessor is. Thus, lessees cannot generally calculate the lessor's implicit rate.

378. What discount rate is then used by the lessee?
Recognizing that the lessee generally cannot determine the lessor's implicit rate, IAS 17 and FASB 13 state that if it is not possible to determine the implicit rate, the lessee must use its incremental borrowing rate.

379. Can this expression be embellished?
The lessee's incremental borrowing rate is the rate of interest the lessee would have to pay on a loan with a similar term and with similar security.

380. How about an illustration?
Let's use the same illustration from QUESTION 373, but further assume that the lessee's incremental borrowing rate is 12%. The present value of the MLPs is $882.76 as seen below:

> HP12 C

	f	REG
12	g	12÷
29.03	CHS	PMT
36		n
	PV	882.76

242 Winning With Leasing!

> HP17B11+

	☐	CLEAR DATA
		FIN
		TVM
29.03	+/-	PMT
36		N
12		I%YR
PV		**882.76**

Thus, within the narrow context of the 90% test, the lease is an operating lease to the lessee as the 90% test has not been met.

At this stage, it is easy to understand why marketplace finance leases will always be classified as finance leases from an accounting point of view. Full payout finance leases when present valued at the interest rate in the lease (as the lessee can always compute the lessor's implicit rate in a finance lease as this type of a lease has no residual) will result in a present value of 100% of equipment cost. (Remember the golden rule of finance: when the discount rate in a transaction is equal to the interest rate in the transaction, the present value will equal principal).

Thus, the accounting criteria are only applied to marketplace operating leases (with residual) to gauge if these are either finance or operating leases from an accounting point of view.

381. The same lease turned out to be a finance lease to the lessor and an operating lease to the lessee?

This is not uncommon. Remember, earlier, it was stated that the determination whether a lease is a finance lease or an operating lease is made independently by the two parties.

382. Whereas using different discount rates can, on occasion, cause the same lease to have a different character in the hands of the two parties, can any other factor have the same consequence?

Yes, if the lessor has its residual guaranteed by a third party this would cause the lessor's MLPs to be greater than the lessee's MLPs possibly causing the lessor to meet the 90% test and have a finance lease and the lessee to fail the 90% test and have an operating lease.

383. Are we ready to move to the fifth guideline now?

Not yet! It is best to state at this stage that the guidelines are merely guidelines. Independent auditors can and do exercise judgment. As an example, let's assume that the present value of the MLPs to a lessee is 88.3%. This does not automatically mean that the lease is an operating lease. 88.3% is so close to 90% that, in material transactions, the auditor is most likely to consider other facts and circumstances as well.

384. Such as?

Let's assume that this particular lessee has, in the past, a history of entering into net leases with present value close to but less than 90% and has always, at the expiration of the lease term, purchased the asset either through the exercise of a purchase option or through negotiations. It is possible that an auditor may conclude that the 88.3% lease is a finance lease.

385. And now, the fifth and last guideline?

Only IAS 17 has a fifth guideline. It states:

"The leased assets are of a specialized nature such that only the lessee can use them without major modifications being made."

This guideline suggests that specialized assets are unlikely to be operating leases as lessors would be highly averse to taking any residual positions on such assets and as such the lease would be a full payout lease; in other words a finance lease.

386. A summary of the accounting criteria would be helpful?

IAS 17 has five criteria; FASB 13 has the first four. These are:

- Automatic ownership transfer
- Bargain purchase option
- Lease term equal to or greater than 75% of the asset's economic life
- Present value of minimum lease payments equal to or greater than 90% of equipment cost
- Special purpose equipment

The criteria are provided as guidelines to determine if substantially all of the risks and benefits in a lease are transferred to a lessee. Generally speaking, if one or more of the criteria is met, the lease will point toward one that is implied to be a loan and will therefore be classified as a finance lease. Judgment is required in applying many of the criteria.

If a lease does not meet any of the above criteria it is most likely to be classified as an operating lease.

387. What is the best way to assure that a lessee indeed can have off balance sheet financing?

The most difficult of all tests to fail is the present value test as "equal to or greater than 90%" has lost its significance.

On large transactions, it is best that the lessee's auditors are brought into the picture sooner than later; they need to "bless" the structure that leads to off balance sheet financing. This way, there will be no surprises—unless, the lessee has a change in auditors!

TECHNIQUES TO STRUCTURE OFF BALANCE SHEET FINANCING

388. If a lessee insists on off balance sheet financing, how easy is it to satisfy the lessee's desire?
For a lease to qualify as an operating lease from an accounting point of view, it should not meet any of the five (four for FASB 13) IAS 17 criteria.

Though summarized at the end of the last subsection, the five criteria are:

- Automatic ownership transfer
- Bargain purchase option
- Lease term equal to or greater than 75% of the asset's economic life
- Present value of minimum lease payments equal to or greater than 90% of equipment cost
- Special purpose equipment

389. How can one fail all of the above criteria?
Let's take them one at the time. The first criterion states that if a lease contractually provides for a transfer of the asset to the lessee by the end of the lease term, the lease will be a finance lease.

The above criterion is easy to fail; all one has to do is not provide for any transfer of ownership in the contract.

390. What about an option to purchase?
Many lessors are erroneously of the opinion that the mere existence of a purchase option will cause a lease to be a finance lease. This is not the case as the existence of a purchase option is not a contractual transfer of ownership. Perhaps the confusion has to do with tax rules in some countries where the existence of a purchase option can cause a lease

to be considered to be a nontax lease from a tax point of view.

391. How about the existence of a bargain purchase option?

Now, that is indeed the second criterion which states that if a lease agreement contains a bargain purchase option, the lease will be a finance lease.

> *The existence of a purchase option does not cause a lease to be a finance lease; it is the existence of a bargain purchase option that does.*

392. How can one fail this criterion?

This criterion is easy to fail as well. In attempting to fail it, there are degrees of assurance one can gain in descending order as follows:

- No purchase option. If a lease does not contain a purchase option at all, how could it ever be concluded that it has a bargain purchase option? If the lessee later on wishes to purchase the asset, the lessor and the lessee can arrive at a mutually acceptable transfer price
- A fair market value purchase option. This is a common approach used by lessors
- A fixed purchase option. This would work so long as the amount is not deemed to be a bargain. In this case, judgment may have to be used and therefore the assurance is not as high that there is indeed no bargain purchase option

393. What about the third criterion?

The third criterion states that the lease term should not be equal to or greater that 75% of the estimated economic life of the asset.

394. How does one definitely fail this test?

Before any conclusions as to how to fail this test, one needs to revisit two expressions, lease term and economic life. The objective is for the lease term not to be so long that it is equal to or greater than 75% of the asset's economic life.

Lease term is the noncancelable term of the lease plus any periods covered by bargain renewal options. Given that the goal is to not have the lease term be too long, one simply does not provide for bargain renewal options. Either there should be no renewal options or fair market value renewal options. This way, the lease term will simply be the firm term or the noncancelable term.

395. What about economic life?

Economic life is the life in the hands of multiple users given normal repairs, upkeep and maintenance. Obviously, judgment is to be used in arriving at this number. With long-lived assets, such as automobiles and airplanes, there should be no concern at all as the lease term will invariably, by marketplace practice, be much less than 75% of the estimated economic life.

> *Estimated economic life is not the life in the hands of the user; it is the life in the hands of multiple users.*

As examples: Whereas the estimated economic life of a new automobile is say 10 years; the marketplace never sees 8-year automobile leases. Similarly, whereas the estimated economic life of a new commercial aircraft is say 30 years; the marketplace never sees 24-year aircraft leases. Thus, with long-lived assets, the third criterion is not met simply due to the extremely long estimated economic life of these types of assets.

396. What about short-lived assets?

This is where one needs to exercise caution. Let's take IT equipment, say a personal computer. Given the rapid technological changes in such an asset, it is not that easy to arrive at its estimated economic life; also, two independent auditors may have two different opinions.

Thus, on these types of assets it is best that the independent auditor be asked its opinion before finalizing the lease term.

In conclusion, the third criterion is easy to fail as well. With respect to long-lived assets, the criterion is not an issue; with respect to short-lived ones, one simply assures up front that the lease term is not equal to or greater than 75% of the estimated economic life.

It should be noted here that the 75% test is borrowed from FASB 13. The author has experienced that some independent auditors do not blindly adopt that which FASB 13 states. Thus, 75% is not necessarily the universal threshold.

397. How about the fourth criterion?

This is the one that can lead to ulcers! The criterion states that if the present value of the minimum lease payments at the inception of the lease is equal to or greater than 90% of the fair value of the equipment, the lease will be classified as a finance lease.

Given that this is a quantitative test it needs to be illustrated. Prior to an illustration though, one needs to review certain definitions but only from a lessee point of view as one is seeking to give the client off balance sheet financing; in this subsection, whether the lessor desires an operating lease or a finance lease from an accounting point of view is not the issue.

398. What lessee items need to be reviewed?

To begin with, one needs to fully understand what discount rate the lessee is to use.

In present valuing the minimum lease payments (MLPs), the lessee generally uses its incremental borrowing rate. This is true because more often than not the lessee does not know the lessor's implicit rate as this rate is computed by the lessor by including in its computation the unguaranteed residual which amount the lessee is unaware of.

However if a lease has a fixed purchase option, then the lessee can compute the lessor's implicit rate in which case the implicit rate should be used.

It should be noted that there is a difference between IAS 17 and FASB 13 in this area. IAS 17 states that the implicit rate should be used if known;

FASB 13 states that the implicit rate should be used if it is known and if it is less than the lessee's incremental borrowing rate.

399. How exactly is the lessee's incremental borrowing rate defined?

The incremental borrowing rate is that rate which the lessee would have to pay on a secured loan with a term equal to the lease being considered.

400. Any other aspects that have to be reviewed?

Now that it has been clearly understood what discount rate the lessee uses, one needs to shift to what is being present valued. It is the minimum lease payments (MLPs) that are being present valued. MLPs from a lessee's point of view constitute the following:

- Noncancelable rents
- Any bargain purchase option
- Any lessee (or related party) guaranteed residual

One needs to remember that the following are excluded from MLPs:

- Contingent rents
- Executory or administrative costs

401. The present value of the MLPs is compared to the fair value of the leased asset. What is meant by "fair value?"

Fair value means that amount which the lessee would have otherwise paid had the equipment been purchased in an arm's length transaction.

402. Now that all the necessary expressions have been reviewed and embellished, perhaps it is time to look at an illustration?

Let's look at the following:

Equipment cost (fair value)	$100,000.00
Lease term in months	36
Rentals in arrears	$3,189.47
Residual (unguaranteed)	$12,500.00
Lessor IRR (implicit rate)	15.00%
Lessee incremental borrowing rate	14.00%

From the lessee's point of view, the implicit rate is not known as the lessee is unaware of the lessor's residual position. Thus, the lessee will present value the MLPs (in this case, just the 36 rentals) at 14%:

> HP12 C

			f	REG
	3,189.47		CHS	PMT
	36			n
	14		g	12 ÷
	PV			93,320.40

> HP17B11+

			☐	CLEAR DATA
				FIN
				TVM
	3,189.47		+/−	PMT
	36			N
	14			I %YR
	PV			93,320.40

Lease Accounting

Ignoring all of the other criteria, the lease is a finance lease to the lessee.

403. But the lessee wants off balance sheet financing?

The task is now to convert the finance lease into an operating lease. This needs to be done without impairing the lessor's IRR; otherwise, it would be too simple (and foolish!): all one would do is lower the IRR which would then result in a lower rental which in turn would result in a lower present value to the lessee.

The goal, at least for purposes of this publication, is to lower the present value to $89,000 without impairing the lessor's IRR of 15%.

404. How can this be done?

There are many techniques that can be used. This publication will deal with those that will generally not be frowned upon by the lessee's independent auditor!

Let's first list them:

- Higher discount rate
- Lower rental with higher residual
- Inclusion of a refundable security deposit
- Early termination option
- Structuring the lease
- Shorter lease term
- Vendor arrangements

405. How can one justify the use of a higher discount rate?

First of all, it is important to note the universal rule in the world of finance: higher the discount rate, lower the present value. In suggesting that a higher discount rate be used, the real issue here is to assure that the lessee is indeed using its incremental cost of debt and not a lower rate. Often large lessees use certain rates given to them by their trea-

Lessees often use incorrect discount rates in the context of the 90% test.

sury department and if this rate is lower than their incremental borrowing rate, the present value of the MLPs will be higher than it needs to be.

406. Will a lessor take a higher residual to accommodate a lower rental?

Let's first go through the quantitative part. To achieve a present value of $89,000, the lower rental amount is computed as follows:

> HP12 C

	f	REG
89,000	CHS	PV
36		n
14	g	12 ÷
PMT		3,041.81

> HP17B11+

	☐	CLEAR DATA
		FIN
		TVM
89,000	+/-	PV
36		N
14		I %YR
PMT		3,041.81

In essence, if the rental were to be reduced to $3,041.81 (from the existing rental of $3,189.47), the lessee would achieve a present value of $89,000 and thus have the transaction qualify for off balance sheet financing.

407. Would this not cause the lessor to have an IRR lower than 15%?

Yes, it would; which is why one needs to solve for a higher residual to compensate for the impaired IRR:

> HP12 C

	f	REG
100,000.00	CHS	PV
3,041.81		PMT
15	g	12 ÷
36		n
FV		<u>19,161.59</u>

> HP17B11+

	☐	CLEAR DATA
		FIN
		TVM
100,000.00	+/-	PV
3,041.81		PMT
15		I %YR
36		N
FV		<u>19,161.59</u>

The residual needs to be increased from the original $12,500 to $19,161.59 to accommodate a lower rental and yet preserve the lessor's 15% IRR.

408. But will the lessor take a higher residual risk?

That is entirely up to the lessor. The important point here is to compute the break-even residual amount that accommodates a lower rental. Let's say the lessor is willing to increase its residual risk to $14,000. At this stage, the lessor could approach the vendor to ascertain if the vendor would be willing to take a first net loss risk of approximately $5,200.

409. Why would the vendor do this?

The vendor would take such a risk only if it felt the exposure was worth the benefit; the benefit being giving its customer off balance sheet financing.

Vendors will only take such risks if they are motivated to do so. This could be on a large transaction where the combined lessor and vendor residual risk is not high enough causing the transaction to not qualify as off balance sheet financing, where the customer may then not consummate what otherwise would be a sale for the vendor. Another example would be within the realm of a vendor leasing program where the vendor, on certain occasions, may decide to absorb some residual risk.

410. Are there any adverse consequences to the vendor?

Besides the economic exposure, it is possible that the vendor may not be allowed, as per accounting standards, to book the sale.

411. Why is this so?

This is because if the seller of goods is contingently materially exposed on the transaction, accounting rules require that the transaction may not qualify as a sale. In such case, the vendor would be reluctant to provide a residual guaranty.

412. With regards to the third technique what is meant by a "refundable security deposit"?

A refundable security deposit is often used as a credit mitigation technique. If the credit risk in a transaction needs to be shored up; lessors, in lieu of or in addition to additional collateral and/or a personal guaranty, will often take a refundable security deposit.

413. How does this work?

It is best illustrated. Let's assume a $100 transaction on a 48-month lease with a refundable security deposit of $10. The time line would look as follows:

```
0                                              48
_____

(100)
  10                                          (10)
_____                                        _____
 (90)                                          (10)
```

At time zero, the lessor pays the vendor $100 and receives $10 as the deposit. The deposit is refunded to the lessee at the end of the lease if the lessee has not defaulted.

The security deposit provides the lessor with a cash cushion that mitigates credit risk.

414. How can a refundable security deposit be used in the context of achieving off balance sheet financing?

To begin with, a refundable security deposit is not an MLP. It is an asset in the books of the lessee and a liability in the books of the lessor.

Secondly, under the premise that most refundable security deposits are noninterest bearing, the lessor is able to reduce the rental on the lease given the fact that it will earn interest on such deposit for the entire duration of the lease.

415. Can this be illustrated?

Let's continue to use the same illustration from QUESTION 402 where the initial rental was $3,189.47 and QUESTION 406 where the reduced rental of $3,041.81 converted the finance lease to an operating lease.

In reducing the rental by $147.66 each month, the lessor has lost $4,259.59 in present value terms. This is computed below:

> HP12 C

	f	REG
147.66	CHS	PMT
36		n
15	g	12 ÷
PV		4,259.59

> HP17B11+

	☐	CLEAR DATA
		FIN
		TVM
147.66	+/−	PMT
36		N
15		I %YR
PV		4,259.59

The present value loss of $4,259.59 needs to be offset with the noninterest bearing refundable security deposit.

416. How is such amount arrived at?

Let's assume a security deposit of $1; further, let's assume the lessor can earn say 10% on this deposit (remember, the IRR in the lease is 15%). Based on this:

> HP12 C

	f	REG
10	g	12 ÷
1	g	Cfo
0	g	Cfj
35	g	Nj
1	CHSg	Cfj
fNPV		.258260

> HP17B11+

	☐	CLEAR DATA
1		INPUT
0		INPUT
35		INPUT
1	+/-	INPUT
		EXIT
		CALC
10÷12		I%
NPV		.258260

For every $1 of security deposit that comes in at the inception of the lease and is refunded at the end of the lease, the lessor earns .258260. But the lessor needs to recover the present value amount lost through the reduction of rentals, $4,259.59.

The amount of the security deposit is, therefore, computed as follows:

Amount earned		Security deposit
.258260		$1
$4,259.59		x
x	=	4,259.59 ÷ .258260
	=	$16,493.42

Thus, if the lessor took a refundable security deposit of $16,493.42, its IRR would be preserved and the lessee would avail of off balance sheet financing.

417. Is not $16,493.42 too high a deposit?

Yes it is. Generally in the marketplace, deposits are less than 16% of equipment cost. This, therefore, is a good time to conclude that often in the real world a combination of techniques will have to be used to reduce present value to the lessee. Based on what has been discussed so far, one could take a slightly higher residual and a lower security deposit which in combination would make up the present value loss of the reduced rentals.

418. How can early termination options help?

Early termination options (ETOs) provide the lessee with flexibility in deciding at a point in time during the lease (or at various points in time) whether to exercise the option of paying an ETO fee to terminate the lease and return the equipment to the lessor.

419. How can an ETO help in reducing the present value of MLPs?

This is best illustrated using the base case. Let's assume that the lessee has an ETO at months 33 (after paying 33 of the 36 rentals). Further, let's assume the ETO fee is $2,500.

Accountants generally take the posture that if the ETO fee is "reasonable" (yes, judgment is needed to conclude whether it is reasonable or not), then the lessee is likely to terminate the lease. In this case, the MLPs in the illustration would be 33 rentals plus the ETO fee.

420. Why is the ETO fee an MLP?

For the last three rentals not to be a part of MLPs, the lessee must pay the ETO fee. Anything the lessee must pay, or is likely to pay, is an MLP!

421. So what is the present value of the MLPs?

The computation follows:

> HP12 C

		f	REG
3,189.47			PMT
33			n
14		g	12 ÷
2,500			FV
PV			-88,649.31

> HP17B11+

		☐	CLEAR DATA
			FIN
			TVM
3,189.47			PMT
33			N
2,500			FV
14			I %YR
PV			-88,649.31

The ETO facilitates a reduction in the present value to $88,649.31.

422. Would ETOs be questioned by the independent auditor?

This is a good point in time to discuss this, not just from the ETO point of view. Independent auditors are likely, on material transactions, to review all the nuances of a deal. Whereas, quantitatively it has been seen that one can very easily reduce the present value of MLPs; in the real world, the auditors would have to be convinced that the techniques used are not being used merely to reduce present value but that there are compelling reasons for such structure.

Both the security deposit and ETO fall into this category of auditor scrutiny and questioning. Thus, on material transactions it is best that any structure that attempts to achieve off balance sheet financing be blessed by the auditors up-front before the transaction is consummated.

423. How can structuring the lease lower present value?

Structuring a lease means arriving at a nonlinear rental stream; generally step-up or step-down. As will be seen in the Pricing and Structuring Section, lessors can structure leases at any IRR. Thus, let's assume that through structure the 15% IRR can be preserved.

The real issue is: can structure lower the lessee's present value—and the answer is an absolute yes! After all, the lessee is using its internal discount rate (in this case 14%) to present value the MLPs. It is only when the interest rate (the IRR) in a lease is the same as the discount rate in the lease that present value will always equal principal—the golden rule of finance!

424. The real question then is what type of structure will lower present value?

The detail to this is contained in QUESTIONS 278 to 282. However, a quick answer follows:

- When the lessee discount rate is less than the lessor IRR, a step-down structure will lower present value
- When the lessee discount rate is greater than the lessor IRR, a step-up structure will lower present value

Proper structure will lower present value; the key is to know whether such is to be a step-up or step-down structure.

In this illustration, the lessee discount rate (14%) is less than the lessor IRR; thus, a step-down structure is needed.

At this point, structure is not being illustrated as it has been substantially discussed in the Pricing and Structuring Section. The lessor would have to, on a trial and error basis, arrive at the appropriate structure that reduces the present value to $89,000.

Here too, the auditor may need to be convinced that the structure has economic merit and is not merely being used to achieve off balance sheet financing.

425. The next technique is shortening the lease term. How does this work?
This technique is very simple to understand. If the present value of 36 rents is in excess of 90% of the fair value, then the present value of say 30 rents is likely to be less than $89,000. Of course, this depends on the new rental amount, which in turn depends on what the lessor's residual value will be at the end of 30 months. Let's assume it is $18,000.

The lessor will arrive at the new rental as follows:

> HP12 C

	f	REG
100,000	CHS	PV
30		n
18,000		FV
15	g	12 ÷
PMT		3,519.64

> HP17B11+

	☐	CLEAR DATA
		FIN
		TVM
100,000	+/-	PV
30		N
18,000		FV
15		I %YR
PMT		3,519.64

The present value of 30 rentals in arrears discounted at 14% is $88,659.58. Try it!

Thus, the lease will qualify as off balance sheet financing.

426. What type of vendor arrangements can be arrived at to lower present value?

It was explained in detail in QUESTION 408 that if a vendor is willing to guarantee a part of the lessor's residual, the lessor can lower the rental to arrive at a lower present value.

Another technique is to arrive at extended payment terms to the vendor. This enables the lessor, in present value terms, to price the lease at an amount lower than $100,000 thereby allowing for the rentals to be lower. Just as it was explained in QUESTION 409, one needs a vendor who is motivated to agree to such a plan.

Lastly, a blind discount can possibly be negotiated with the vendor.

427. What is a blind discount?

Once again, this may work with a motivated vendor either if the transaction is large or if it is within the realm of a vendor leasing program.

A blind discount is where the lessor is able to purchase the equipment at a discount without the lessee being aware of such discount; the lessee is blind to the discount. If a lessor is indeed able to purchase the equipment at a discount, this allows the lessor to reduce the rental to the lessee. The lessee will then present value the reduced rentals; but in doing so will compare it to the fair value of the leased asset which would be the amount the lessee would otherwise have to pay if it purchased the asset.

There is undoubtedly a double benefit. Not only are the rentals lower but the base to which the present value of the rentals is being compared is not the reduced/discounted price that the lessor is paying.

428. That concludes all the techniques to convert a finance lease to an operating lease without impairing the lessor's IRR?

Yes, for purposes of this publication it does. In the real world there are other techniques the author has seen; these, in the author's opinion, are a bit too "flaky" to be presented here!

429. How can the last criterion be failed?

The fifth and the last criterion is only contained in IAS 17 and not in FASB 13. It states that if the leased assets are of a specialized nature such that only the lessee can use them without major modifications being made, the lease will be deemed to be a finance lease.

In the real world this criterion is very easy to fail. Why would a lessor even dream of taking a residual position on special purpose assets; the point being, this criterion is academic as only full payout finance leases are done on these types of assets.

430. How about a summary?

In summary, the most important thing to remember is that a fair amount of judgment is used in determining whether a transaction qualifies for off balance sheet financing. Different independent auditors arrive at different conclusions. As only one example, but a very important one, though the 90% test has been used in this publication (as it is so stated in FASB 13); in the real world, the author has seen independent auditors often use 85% or even 80%!

Thus, if one wanted 100% assurance that a certain transaction will indeed qualify as off balance sheet financing, it is imperative that the lessee's auditors review it prior to it being "signed, sealed and delivered."

> *There is only one way to absolutely assure that a transaction qualifies for off balance sheet financing—the lessee's independent auditor needs to be brought into the picture before the deal is consummated.*

THE FUTURE OF LEASE ACCOUNTING

431. Are any changes anticipated in the area of lease accounting?
In July 1996, Warren McGregor, the then Executive Director of the Australian Accounting Research Foundation wrote a paper entitled "Accounting for Leases: A New Approach, Recognition by Lessees of Assets and Liabilities Arising under Lease Contracts."

432. What does the paper propose?
As noted in an earlier subsection, the essence of the distinction between a finance lease and an operating lease has to do with the transfer from the lessor to the lessee of substantially all the risks and rewards incident to the ownership of the leased asset. This approach, used for decades, has been called the risk-reward approach.

433. Is a new approach being proposed?
The new approach is called the asset-liability approach.

434. Why is a new approach being proposed?
McGregor and others feel that current lease accounting standards are unsatisfactory, at least with respect to accounting by lessees. The most frequently noted concern relates to the fact that the standards do not require rights and obligations arising under operating leases to be recognized as assets and liabilities in the lessee's financial statements.

435. But if a lease fails to meet the five criteria studied earlier, should the lease not be properly classified as an operating lease?
Under current accounting standards if a lease does not meet any of the five finance lease criteria, the lease is classified as an operating lease. However, the paper written by McGregor states that current standards have promoted the structuring of financial arrangements so as to meet the conditions for classification as an operating lease.

436. Can this be embellished?

As indicated in the earlier subsection, the most difficult test to fail is the present value test. It is easy to fail the others as follows:

- The lease contract should not provide for transfer of ownership
- If a purchase option is required, it should be at fair market value
- The definition of economic life (life in the hands of multiple users) itself will generally preclude the third test from being met
- Not to do an operating lease on assets of a specialized nature (who would anyway?!).

437. But with the present value test, can the lessor not simply have the present value of the minimum lease payments be less than 90% of the fair value of the asset?

That is exactly what McGregor means when he states that current standards have promoted the structuring of financial arrangements so as to meet the conditions for classification as an operating lease. It is not at all difficult to lower the present value of minimum lease payments through a variety of techniques deliberately designed to give the lessee an operating lease. In fact, varied techniques were discussed in the earlier subsection.

438. How would the new approach prevent such maneuvering?

The new approach discards the risk-reward approach and embraces what is known as the asset-liability approach.

439. How does this work?

Under the asset-liability approach it is recommended that all lease contracts with a duration greater than one year be recognized in the financial statements at their present value.

The details as to exactly how such recognition is to be accomplished are being debated by some accounting bodies throughout the world.

Off balance sheet financing, as we know it today, may disappear in a few years.

440. So what does this all mean?

What it means is that the International Accounting Standards Board (IASB) in the U.K. is currently discussing and debating switching from the risk-reward approach to the asset-liability approach.

As of the publication date of this book, it appears that the asset-liability approach may be implemented sometime in the future with many of the details having to be worked out.

441. Will this basically kill off balance sheet financing?

Lessors will continue to be creative!

SUMMARY

1. From an accounting point of view there are two types of leases: finance and operating.

2. Finance leases in the hands of a lessee in the U.S. are known as capital leases.

3. Marketplace finance leases are always accounting finance leases; this is because the full payout nature will invariably cause the present value of the MLPs to be equal to 100% of equipment cost.

4. Marketplace operating leases are either finance leases or operating leases from an accounting point of view. Setting aside the other criteria but focusing on the 90% present value criterion, the present value of the MLPs will either be less than 90% or equal to or more than 90% of the equipment cost based on the residual position assumed by the lessor. The residual needs to be high enough for the rents (MLPs) to be low enough to not meet the 90% test if the lessee is seeking off balance sheet financing.

5. Finance leases are shown by the lessee and lessor in their financial statements as though they are loans. The lessee books the equipment and the corresponding debt onto the balance sheet; the income statement shows depreciation and interest expense. The lessor books receivables on the balance sheet; the income statement shows interest income.

6. Operating leases are shown by the lessee and the lessor in their financial statements as though they are rentals. No asset or liability is booked by the lessee in its balance sheet; the income statement shows rent expense. The lessor shows the equipment on the balance sheet; the income statement shows rent revenue minus depreciation.

7. It is not uncommon for the same lease to have a different character in the hands of the lessee and the lessor. The most desirable permutation combination is for the same lease to be an operating lease for the lessee giving rise to off balance sheet financing, and for it to be a finance lease for the lessor allowing the lessor to accelerate income owing to the downward sloping interest income.

8. The same lease can be an operating lease to the lessee and a finance lease to the lessor based on one or both of the following as it applies to the 90% test:

- Different discount rates used by the two parties
- The lessor having a part of its residual guaranteed by an independent third party

9. IAS 17 is the international accounting standard; FASB 13 is used in the U.S. The former lists five criteria distinguishing a finance from an operating lease; the latter lists four.

10. If one or more of the criteria is met the lease is likely to be classified as a finance lease under the premise that there has been a substantial transfer of risks and rewards in the lease.

11. An operating lease has not been defined from an accounting point of view. An operating lease, therefore, is one which is not a finance lease.

12. The accounting criteria distinguishing the two types of leases are listed below:

- Automatic ownership transfer
- Bargain purchase option
- Lease term equal to or greater than 75% of the asset's economic life
- Present value of minimum lease payments equal to or greater than 90% of equipment cost
- Special purpose equipment (IAS 17 only)

13. It is essentially the 90% test that determinates whether a lease is a finance lease or an operating lease. Again, marketplace finance leases will always meet the 90% test and therefore be classified as finance leases. Marketplace operating leases will either meet the 90% test or not depending, by and large, on the amount of residual.

14. In the 90% test the discount rate for the lessor is its implicit rate; the discount rate for the lessee is generally its incremental cost of debt.

15. MLPs for the lessee generally constitute rentals plus any bargain purchase option and any lessee guaranteed residual; MLPs for the lessor constitute the same three plus any independent third party guaranteed residual.

16. Contingent rents and administrative costs are excluded from MLPs by both parties.

17. If a lessee is seeking off balance sheet financing, all five accounting criteria should not be met. Four of them are easy not to meet as follows:

- The lease contract should not have a clause providing for automatic ownership transfer
- The lease contract should either not have a purchase option or if a purchase option is necessary, it should be at FMV
- The definition of economic life, being life in the hands of multiple users, is generally long enough for most leases not to have a lease term equal to or greater than 75% of such economic life
- The subject matter of the lease should not be a special purpose asset

18. There are many techniques to fail the 90% present value test; but, at the onset one must remember that substantial judgment is used in applying this criterion. Also, some independent auditors have recently lowered the 90% down to 85% or 80%. Thus, on large transactions, it is imperative that the auditor be brought into the picture up-front.

19. Techniques to fail the 90% test include:

- Higher discount rate
- Lower rental with higher residual
- Inclusion of a refundable security deposit
- Early termination option
- Structuring the lease
- Shorter lease term
- Vendor arrangements

20. Off balance sheet financing will be done away with if IAS 17 is to take the asset-liability approach as versus the current risk-reward approach.

GLOSSARY

bargain purchase option
An option that exists in a lease where the exercise price is substantially lower than the fair market value of the asset, at the time that the option becomes exercisable, creating the likelihood that the lessee will exercise the option. As to exactly what is meant by "bargain" at times, is left to judgment.

blind discount
A discount in purchase price made available to the lessor that the lessee is unaware of. Generally seen in vendor leasing programs.

capital lease
An expression used in the U.S. to describe a finance lease in the hands of a lessee.

contingent rent
Rent contingent on excess usage (as typically seen in operating leases of motor cars and copy machines).

economic life
Life in the hands of multiple users given normal repairs and maintenance.

executory cost
Costs such as sales tax, VAT, maintenance and insurance that have nothing to do with the base rental but are added on either because they are imposed upon by government or because additional services are included in the lease.

fair value
The amount the lessee would pay for the equipment, in an arm's length transaction, had it been purchased.

FASB 13
Financial Accounting Standards Board Statement #13 which is U.S. GAAP (Generally Accepted Accounting Principles). A convergence between FASB and IAS is expected soon.

finance lease
A lease that transfers substantially all the risks and rewards incident to the ownership of an asset.

first net loss
From the top down.

IAS 17
International Accounting Standards Statement #17 entitled "Leases"; a standard that has been adopted by a vast majority of the countries in the world. Now known as IFRS or International Financial Reporting Standard.

implicit rate
The rate used by the lessor to ascertain if the present value test has been met or not. This rate is generally the same as the IRR in the lease. It is the rate that equates the present value of the minimum lease payments plus any unguaranteed residual to the fair value of the leased asset.

incremental borrowing rate
The rate the lessee would pay on a loan with a similar term and similar security.

lease term
The base noncancelable period of the lease plus the period over which the lessee has a bargain renewal option.

minimum lease payments
That which the lessee is likely to pay the lessor at the minimum. From a lessee's point of view, this would generally mean the rents contracted for over the noncancelable term of the lease plus any lessee (or related party) guaranteed residual. From a lessors point of view, minimum lease payments generally mean that which the lessee is likely to pay (as just described) plus any third party (such as vendor or insurance company) guaranteed residual.

off balance sheet financing
The impact of an operating lease on the lessee's balance sheet where neither the asset nor the liability is recorded.

operating lease
A lease which is not a finance lease.

HOMEWORK!

1. Why will marketplace finance leases always be classified as finance leases from an accounting point of view?

2. What are the five criteria (four for FASB13) that distinguish a finance lease from an operating lease?

3. What is the definition of an operating lease from an accounting point of view?

4. How are finance leases recorded by the lessee?

5. How are operating leases recorded by the lessee?

6. How are finance leases recorded by the lessor?

7. How are operating leases recorded by the lessor?

8. Why do lessors generally prefer finance leases from an accounting point of view?

9. For purposes of the third criterion, how is economic life defined?

10. For purposes of the third criterion, how is lease term defined?

11. What does the 90% present value test state?

12. What discount rates are used by the two parties in the 90% test?

13. Given the following data solve for the implicit rate in the lease.

Equipment cost	$100,000.00
Term in months	36
Rental in arrears	$3,189.47
Unguaranteed residual	$12,500.00
Monthly maintenance	$500.00

14. Given the same data above and with a discount rate of 14%, compute the present value of the MLPs to the lessee.

15. What constitute MLPs for the lessee and the lessor?

16. How does one fail the following two criteria: automatic ownership transfer and bargain purchase option?

17. What are the varied techniques that can be used to fail the 90% test?

18. The following is an illustration of a lease which is a finance lease to the lessee as the present value of the MLPs is greater than 90% of equipment cost:

Equipment cost	$200,000.00
Lease term in months	36
Rental in arrears	$6,378.94
Residual (unguaranteed)	$25,000.00
Lessee discount rate	14.00%

Solve for the lower rent and higher residual to arrive at a present value equal to 89% of equipment cost.

19. What structure is used to lower present value when the lessee discount rate is less than the lessor IRR?

20. What structure is used to lower present value when the lessee discount rate is higher than the lessor IRR?

HOMEWORK ANSWERS

Answer 1
Marketplace finance leases will always be classified as finance leases from an accounting point of view as the full payout nature of such leases will always cause the 90% present value test to be met; in fact, the present value of the MLPs (the rentals) will always be equal to 100% of equipment cost. This is true given that when the discount rate (in the present value test) is equal to the interest rate (in the lease), the present value will equal principal.

Answer 2
These are:

- Automatic ownership transfer
- Bargain purchase option
- Lease term equal to or greater than 75% of the asset's economic life
- Present value of minimum lease payments equal to or greater than 90% of equipment cost
- Special purpose equipment (IAS 17 only)

Answer 3
Operating leases have not been defined from an accounting point of view. Those leases which do not meet any of the finance lease criteria will generally be operating leases. In other words, an operating lease is one which is not a finance lease.

Answer 4
Finance leases are recorded by the lessee as though they are loans. The lessee will book the equipment and the debt onto the balance sheet; the income statement will show depreciation plus interest expense.

Answer 5
Operating leases are recorded by the lessee as though they are rentals. Neither the asset nor the corresponding debt will be booked onto the balance sheet; the income statement will record rent expense.

Answer 6
Finance leases are recorded by the lessor as though they are loans. The lessor's balance sheet will show the lease receivables while the income statement will show interest income.

Answer 7
Operating leases are recorded by the lessor as though they are rentals. The leased equipment will be shown as an asset in the lessor's balance sheet while the income statement will record rent revenue minus depreciation.

Answer 8
Lessors generally prefer finance leases, as versus operating leases, from an accounting point of view as such leases show higher earnings in the early periods of the lease. This is because interest income is a downward sloping line with more interest in the early periods and less in the latter. This downward sloping line when compared to the straight line margin (rent minus depreciation) on operating leases causes earnings to be higher in the early periods.

Answer 9
Economic life is the life in the hands of multiple users given normal repairs and maintenance.

Answer 10
Lease term is the noncancelable term plus any renewal term based on a bargain renewal clause in the lease.

Answer 11
The present value of the minimum lease payments is equal to or greater than 90% of the fair value of the asset.

Answer 12

The lessor uses its implicit rate; the lessee uses the implicit rate if known; if not, the lessee uses its incremental cost of debt. Generally the lessee will not know the lessor's implicit rate as unguaranteed residual is a part of its computation.

Answer 13

> HP12C

		f	REG
100,000		CHS	PV
36			n
3,189.47			PMT
12,500			FV
		i	1.25
12 x			<u>15.00</u>

> HP17BII+

		☐	CLEAR DATA
			FIN
			TVM
100,000		+/−	PV
36			N
3,189.47			PMT
12,500			FV
I%YR		=	<u>15.00</u>

Note: Monthly maintenance is not an MLP.

Lease Accounting **285**

Answer 14

> HP12C

	f	REG
36		n
14		12 ÷
3,189.47	CHS	PMT
		PV
		<u>93,320.40</u>

> HP17BII+

	☐	CLEAR DATA
		FIN
		TVM
36		N
14		I%YR
3,189.47	+/-	PMT
		PV
		<u>93,320.40</u>

Answer 15

Lessee MLPs include noncancelable rentals, plus any bargain option and any lessee guaranteed residual; lessor MLPs include these three items plus any third party guaranteed residual.

Answer 16

The automatic ownership transfer criterion is failed by not providing for any transfer of leased asset provisions in the lease agreement.

The bargain purchase option criterion is failed by either having no purchase option or a FMV purchase option.

Answer 17

The techniques follow:

- Higher discount rate
- Lower rental with higher residual
- Inclusion of a refundable security deposit
- Early termination option
- Structuring the lease
- Shorter lease term
- Vendor arrangements

Answer 18

Solve for lower rental:

> HP12 C

	f	REG
178,000	CHS	PV
36		n
14	g	12÷
PMT		6,083.62

> HP17B11+

	☐	CLEAR DATA
		FIN
		TVM
178,000	+/-	PV
36		N
14		I%YR
PMT		6,083.62

Solve for higher residual:

> HP12 C

	f	REG
200,000	CHS	PV
6,083.62		PMT
15	g	12÷
36		n
FV		38,323.17

288 Winning With Leasing!

> HP17B11+

	☐	CLEAR DATA
		FIN
		TVM
200,000	+/-	PV
6,083.62		PMT
15		I%YR
36		N
FV		<u>38,323.17</u>

Answer 19
Step-down

Answer 20
Step-up

Lease Taxation

Lease Taxation

Defining a Lease

Depreciation and its Value

U.S. Tax Nuances

Summary

Glossary

Homework!

Homework Answers

DEFINING A LEASE

442. From a tax point of view, how many types of leases are there?

Basically two. A lease is either a tax lease (often known as a true lease as in the U.S.) or a nontax lease. A tax lease is one which qualifies as a lease for tax purposes; on the other hand, a nontax lease is one which is considered to be a loan for tax purposes.

443. What is the distinction between these two types of leases?

It depends in which country the question is being asked. Many countries provide guidelines which distinguish between the two types of leases. Countries which distinguish between the two types of leases by providing guidelines are referred to as "substance" countries. In such countries, the tax authorities are keen on looking at the substance of the transaction and not the form (form means the label). Substance is gauged by looking at the intent of the two parties (the lessor and the lessee) and intent in turn is best determined by reviewing the economic structure of the transaction.

444. What are some of the guidelines?

The guidelines vary substantially from country to country and the reader is advised to seek tax counsel, if necessary, in the country in question. However, three of the guidelines are common to many countries and are discussed here merely to provide a flavour as to the type of items the tax authorities consider in determining whether a lease indeed qualifies as a lease for tax purposes or whether it should be treated as a loan.

Tax practices, defining exactly what a lease is, vary from one country to another.

445. What are the three guidelines?

Before discussing the guidelines, it should be noted that tax authorities in substance countries generally believe that if a transaction contains certain characteristics that point toward ownership, then the lease will not be treated as a lease from an income tax point of view. It will be treated as though it is a purchase/loan.

The first guideline has to do with the existence of a nominal purchase option. In countries such as the U.S., the existence of a nominal or a bargain purchase option is deemed to be an indicator pointing towards a lease transaction being a purchase. The thought process here is obvious. Such an option clearly demonstrates that the two parties intended from the very beginning for the lessee to definitely end up as the legal owner and; therefore, the lease is not considered to be a true lease for tax purposes.

446. Another guideline?

Another guideline has to do with the mere existence of a purchase option, whether bargain or not. In countries such as Australia and the U.K., the mere existence of an option will generally cause a lease to be accorded nonlease status. The tax authorities in these countries believe that a true lease should be akin to a rental agreement and should not have an option at all. Options, tax authorities conclude, indicate a purchase mode.

447. Yet another?

The third and the last one to be provided here has to do with maximum lease term. In countries such as Japan, the tax authorities have established maximum lease terms. If the lease exceeds such maximum terms, the authorities consider it to be too lengthy a transaction to be accorded rental (lease) treatment and therefore it is considered to be a purchase/loan.

448. What about countries which do not distinguish between the two types of leases?

These are known as "form" countries. Form, as indicated before, has to do with the label or title given to the lease agreement. In a large number of countries if an agreement is labeled a lease, it is considered to be a lease for tax purposes. The economic structure of the transaction is not a consideration. As an example, if a lease contains a nominal purchase option, though in substance it is clear that the parties intended for it to be a purchase, the tax authorities in a form country would consider it to be a true lease.

449. Why so?
The form type of countries, in their tax policies, believe that leasing should be incentivised to grow. As will be explained later in the subsection entitled "Depreciation and its Value," lessors generally prefer true leases over loans as depreciation provides them with tax benefits. Governments in form countries believe "a lease is a lease" thereby enabling lessors to claim such tax benefits and be motivated to do more leases.

450. What about the U.S.?
In the U.S. the tax code (the statute) has not defined a lease. It is thus left to the interpretation of the Internal Revenue Service (IRS). Over the past several decades the IRS has put out various guidelines and rulings as to what constitutes a lease from a tax point of view. Unfortunately, and as one would suspect, these guidelines and rulings are vague and ambiguous not to mention ancient!

Thus as to what constitutes a tax lease (also known as a true lease) in the U.S. is eventually left to the discretion of an IRS agent who is involved in any tax audit. If the lessor wishes to dispute the tax agent's determination then such has to be contested in tax court on a case by case basis. One court ruling does not necessarily set a precedent (A precedent; by the way, means one bad judgment follows another!).

U.S. tax law does not define a lease. Whether a transaction qualifies as a lease is left to the interpretation of the IRS.

Nonetheless, the essence of many rulings have to do with one crucial issue: for a lease to qualify as a tax lease in the U.S. it should impose a reasonable amount of asset risk on the lessor. Credit risk alone will generally cause the IRS to conclude that the transaction is akin to a loan and should therefore be accorded loan treatment. Unfortunately, the exact magnitude of asset risk has not been spelled out as different courts have ruled differently.

451. What is the difference in impact between substance and form?

Let's start with form. In a form country, as stated earlier, all leases are considered to be leases by the tax authorities. What this really means is that for tax purposes all leases are accorded rental treatment.

452. And what is the impact?

This means that for tax purposes all leases are treated as though they are operating leases whereby the lessor claims rental or lease income as revenue offset by tax depreciation as an expense and the lessee claims the rent expense or lease expense as a deduction. This is shown below:

IMPACT OF TAX LEASE

Lessor
Rental Income
–
Depreciation Expense

Lessee
Rent Expense

453. What about in a substance country?

In substance countries, as stated earlier, there are two types of leases: leases that are considered to be leases for tax purposes and leases that are not. The former are accorded rental treatment; the latter, purchase or loan treatment.

454. An embellishment would help?

Drawing a parallel to the world of accounting, leases considered to be leases are treated as though they are operating leases; those that are not considered to be leases are treated as though they are finance leases.

455. And the impact on the two parties?

With leases considered to be leases, the lessor as discussed earlier, in a form country claims rental or lease income as revenue offset by tax depreciation as an expense and the lessee (again as in form countries) claims the rent expense or lease expense as a deduction.

On the other hand, in substance countries with leases not considered to be leases, the lessor claims interest income. This is because the lease is considered to be a loan and the "rent" received is deemed to be comprised of principal and interest. The lessee, under the premise that the lease is considered to be a loan, claims depreciation plus interest expense as though the asset had been purchased. This is shown below:

IMPACT OF NONTAX LEASE

Lessor
Interest Income

Lessee
Depreciation Expense + Interest Expense

456. What is the correlation between the marketplace and taxation?

Just as much as this was addressed in the Accounting Section from an accounting point of view, here it will be addressed solely from a tax point of view. The correlation is different for form and substance countries.

457. Let's start with form?

The following describes the correlation:

Party	Marketplace	Tax
Lessor	Finance Lease	Tax Lease
	Operating Lease	
Lessee	Finance Lease	Tax Lease
	Operating Lease	

The summary is simple: both types of marketplace leases are treated as tax leases from a tax point of view.

458. And in substance countries?

The following diagram describes the correlation:

Party	Marketplace	Tax
Lessor	Finance Lease	Nontax Lease
	Operating Lease	Tax Lease
Lessee	Finance Lease	Nontax Lease
	Operating Lease	Tax Lease

Here the correlation is complex: depending on the guidelines in the country in question, it is possible in some countries for some finance leases to considered to be tax leases; on the other hand, all finance leases in some other countries would be treated as nontax leases! Marketplace operating leases will generally be considered to be tax leases almost always; not always! As indicated before, it is best to seek tax counsel when needed!

459. Additional country examples would help?
The danger in providing country specific examples is obvious. Tax laws are dynamic, not static. Nevertheless, examples are being provided along the lines of which party in a finance lease generally claims the tax depreciation. The examples go beyond form and substance.

A sampling follows:

GLOBAL LEASE TAXATION PRACTICES
Who Claims Depreciation on Marketplace Finance Leases

Country	Lessor	Lessee
Argentina	✓	
Australia	✓	
Bangladesh	✓	
Brazil	✓	
Chile	✓	
China		✓
Costa Rica		✓
Czech Republic	✓	
Germany		✓
Ghana		✓
India	✓	
Italy	✓	
Japan	✓	
Korea		✓
Mexico		✓
New Zealand		✓
Nigeria		✓
Pakistan	✓	
Sri Lanka	✓	
Taiwan		✓
Thailand	✓	
United Kingdom	✓	
United States		✓

It should be noted that when the lessor claims the tax depreciation, the lessee deducts rent or lease expense and when the lessee claims the tax depreciation, the lessor shows interest income.

Tax laws are often vague and invariably dynamic. Seeking tax counsel is, therefore, always a good idea!

It should also be noted from the above that in those countries where the lessor claims the tax depreciation on a finance lease, the lease is being considered to be a lease for tax purposes either because tax guidelines have been met or because the country is a form country where all leases are tax leases!

460. What about operating leases?

Throughout the world, as stated in earlier, operating leases are almost invariably considered to be tax leases whereby the lessor claims the tax depreciation and the lessee deducts rent expense.

DEPRECIATION AND ITS VALUE

461. Why does tax depreciation (known as capital allowances in some countries) have a value to the lessor?
There are two ways of looking at the value of depreciation from an income tax point of view. The first way is to look at deprecation as it shelters revenue causing the lessor to defer its tax liability.

462. Can this be embellished?
This is best done through an illustration using a single lease; however, one needs to imagine that the illustration is an entire portfolio:

Equipment cost	$1,000.00
Term in months	36
Rental in advance	$29.44
Residual	$150.00
Lessor pretargeted IRR	12%
Inception date	January 1

Let's assume that the lessor's fiscal year ends on December 31 and that the lease is a U.S. lease with the asset qualifying for a five-year depreciation schedule.

The first year's tax liability (ignoring all expenses of doing business) will be computed as follows:

Rental income ($29.44 x 12)	$353.28
Depreciation	(200.00)
Taxable income	$153.28

The next subsection will explain, to the U.S. reader, how the $200 of depreciation was arrived at, but what is clear from the above is that the lessor will have taxable income of $153.28 and will have to pay taxes.

463. What happened to tax deferral?

Let's change the inception date to December 31 based on which the tax liability will be computed as follows:

Rental income	$29.44
Depreciation	(200.00)
Taxable loss	($170.56)

Only one rental is picked up as income on December 31 as the lease is in advance; yet, depreciation is a constant. The consequence is obvious: no tax is due this year and the $170.56 loss will be carried forward to subsequent fiscal years.

464. What happens thereafter?

This can be gauged by looking at the tax returns for the second, third and fourth fiscal years. There are four fiscal years as the three-year lease with an inception date of December 31 spans four periods. The tax returns are shown below including for the first year as seen above.

Year	1	2	3	4
Rental revenue	$29.44	$353.28	$353.28	$323.84
Depreciation	(200.00)	(320.00)	(192.00)	(115.20)
Taxable income/loss	$(170.56)	$33.28	$161.28	$208.64
Loss carry forward		(170.56)	(137.28)	0
Taxable income or loss	$(170.56)	$(137.28)	$24.00	$208.64

The second year shows taxable income of $33.28 but with the loss carry forward from year one, no tax will be paid. In fact, there remains a tax loss carry forward of $137.28.

The third year shows taxable income of $161.28 but only $24.00 in reality after the remaining tax loss is carried forward.

In essence, the lessor is deferring taxes to the third and fourth year. Deferral of tax has a true cash value to the lessor from a present value point of view. It should be noted that in the above lease it was assumed the asset was returned to the leasing company after 36 months.

465. Thus taxes can be deferred with accelerated depreciation?
Not only with accelerated depreciation but in some countries with timing the inception date of leases.

466. Can this be embellished?
In many countries, such as in the U.S., the amount of depreciation in the first year is a constant regardless of when a lease is incepted. As was seen earlier, whether the lease was incepted on January 1 or December 31, the amount of depreciation was a constant. Lessors are able to take advantage of this nuance.

467. Do not deferred taxes turn around or reverse in latter periods?
Generally yes; however, if a lessor keeps adding portfolio then it is possible to defer taxes for a long period of time.

468. Is tax deferral a good thing?
Surprisingly the answer is both yes and no!

Yes, as deferred taxes cause the present value of the tax liability paid to be a lower amount, and there is nothing wrong with paying such lower amount within the realm of tax planning.

No, if the lessor's strategy is merely based on deferred taxes. Leasing merely based on tax deferral can cause problems down the road—problems such as those caused by inability to add portfolio, changes in tax law such as increased tax rates or slower depreciation, as well as poor quality transactions being incepted merely to continue to defer taxes.

> *Lessors reap many benefits from leasing; generally spread or margin is the primary benefit, depreciation a secondary one.*

469. What is the second way of looking at the value of depreciation?

The second way is on a lease by lease basis by comparing the value of depreciation to the recovery of principal on a loan.

470. Can this be embellished?

It is best illustrated as follows:

Equipment cost	$100,000.00
Term in months	48
Rental in arrears	$2,633.38
Residual	0
Lessor pretargeted IRR	12%
Inception date	October 31

Let's assume the lessor's fiscal year end is December 31 and that the above finance lease is in a country where the lessor is able to claim the tax depreciation. Let's further assume that the depreciation will be claimed on a straight line basis over four years; yet, the first year's depreciation will not be adversely affected by the fact that the inception date is late in the year.

Now let's compare the above lease to a four-year loan with the following terms:

Principal	$100,000.00
Term in months	48
Payment in arrears	$2,633.38
Interest rate	12%
Inception date	October 31

The lease and loan are identical other than the tax consequences.

471. What is the difference from a tax point of view?

The lease rentals will be taxable to the lessor offset by deprecation. With regard to the loan interest income is taxable; interest income means the loan payment minus the principal portion.

It is important to conclude from the above that depreciation is synonymous to principal.

472. How so?

In a lease, rent minus depreciation equals margin or profit; in a loan, payment minus principal equals margin or profit. This shows that depreciation and principal "shelter" the rental or payment from taxation. In other words, they represent the nontaxed portion of gross cash flow.

473. Come again?

Let's take the illustration forward starting with the lease:

Year	Rental	Depreciation	Taxable income
1	$5,267	$25,000	($19,733)
2	31,601	25,000	6,601
3	31,600	25,000	6,600
4	31,600	25,000	6,600
5	26,334	0	26,334
Total	$126,402	$100,000	$26,402

The 48 lease rentals span five fiscal years owing to the October 31 inception date. Depreciation is linear each year. The last column is nothing more than rentals minus depreciation.

Year one only has two rentals for November 30 and December 31; year five has 10 rentals.

Looking at the total line it should be clear that the total rentals of $126,402 ($2,633.38 x 48) minus total depreciation of $100,000 shows total taxable income of $26,402.

474. How about the loan?

The loan analysis follows:

Year	Payment	Principal	Taxable income
1	$5,267	$3,283	$1,984
2	31,601	21,132	10,469
3	31,600	23,811	7,789
4	31,600	26,832	4,768
5	26,334	24,942	1,392
Total	$126,402	$100,000	$26,402

The 48 loan payments add up to $126,402 with $100,000 being principal and the balance of $26,402 being interest. The principal and interest columns were arrived at through an amortization of the loan.

It should be noted that the overall tax consequence of both transactions is the same; over the five year period taxable income for both is $26,402, the essential difference is the timing of taxable income.

It is important to note that depreciation under the lease and principal under the loan both add up to $100,000. Both depreciation and principal represent the recovery of cost, the nontaxed portion of cash flow; hence they are synonymous to each other.

475. Can this be explained again?

Yes, the two columns, depreciation and principal, "shelter" pretax cash flow. Using year one as an example under the lease, the pretax cash flow is $5,267 (the two rentals); depreciation shelters it and given that depreciation is in excess of the rentals, there is no taxable income in year one. On the loan the pretax cash flow for year one is also $5,267.

Here the principal is $3,283. $3,283 of principal shelters $5,267 of the pretax cash flow and thus only the difference, $1,984, is subject to tax.

Thus both columns, depreciation on a lease and principal on a loan, represent benefits given that they shelter cash flow from being taxed.

476. What next?

To compare the advantage that one transaction has over another one must present value the two columns representing depreciation and principal respectively. Let's assume that the internal hurdle rate or cost of capital for the firm is 15%. The present value of depreciation and principal are shown below:

Depreciation

> HP12 C

		f	REG
15			i
25,000	g		Cfo
25,000	g		Cfj
3	g		Nj
fNPV			82,081

Lease Taxation 309

> HP17B11+

		CLEAR DATA
25,000		INPUT
25,000		INPUT
3		INPUT
		EXIT
		CALC
15		I %
NPV		<u>82,081</u>

Principal:

> HP12 C

	f	REG
15		i
3,283	g	Cfo
21,132	g	Cfj
23,811	g	Cfj
26,832	g	Cfj
24,942	g	Cfj
fNPV		<u>71,566</u>

> HP17B11+

	☐	CLEAR DATA
3,283		INPUT
21,132		INPUT
1		INPUT
23,811		INPUT
1		INPUT
26,832		INPUT
1		INPUT
24,942		INPUT
1		INPUT
		EXIT
		CALC
15		I %
NPV		71,566

The present value advantage of depreciation on the lease over the principal on the loan is $82,081 - $71,566 = $10,515. This is the incremental pretax benefit a lease has over a loan given that the two columns being compared are benefits as explained earlier.

Assuming a 30% tax rate, the after-tax benefit advantage the lease has over a loan is $10,515 x .30 = $3,155.

The same conclusion can be arrived at by present valuing taxable income under both alternatives as follows:

Lease:

> HP12 C

	f	REG
15		i
19,733	CHSg	Cfo
6,601	g	Cfj
6,600	g	Cfj
2	g	Nj
26,334	g	Cfj
fNPV		<u>10,394</u>

> HP17B11+

		CLEAR DATA
19,733	+/-	INPUT
6,601		INPUT
1		INPUT
6,600		INPUT
2		INPUT
26,334		INPUT
1		INPUT
		EXIT
		CALC
15		I %
NPV		<u>10,394</u>

Loan:

> HP12 C

	f	REG
15		i
1,984	g	Cfo
10,469	g	Cfj
7,789	g	Cfj
4,768	g	Cfj
1,392	g	Cfj
fNPV		<u>20,908</u>

> HP17B11+

	☐	CLEAR DATA
1,984		INPUT
10,469		INPUT
1		INPUT
7,789		INPUT
1		INPUT
4,768		INPUT
1		INPUT
1,392		INPUT
1		INPUT
		EXIT
		CALC
15		I %
NPV		<u>20,908</u>

The difference in present value between the two is $10,514 ($20,908 - $10,394), which is the advantage the lease has over the loan, as income is taxed slower (given the large negative in year one). Using 30% as the tax rate, the advantage the lease has over the loan is $10,514 x 30% = $3,154.

Depreciation on a lease is generally faster than principal on a loan; all other things being equal, lessors therefore prefer to do tax leases as versus nontax leases.

Setting aside rounding, this is the same answer as arrived earlier.

477. A summary?

The $3,154 represents the after-tax cash flow advantage the lease has over the loan given that less taxes are due in the first three years on the lease compared to the loan. Though there is a reversal later on, the $3,154 represents the present value savings in the lease over the loan.

478. What does the lessor do with the $3,154?

One must remember that the $3,154 in the above example is the up-front benefit the lease has over the loan. It is as though on October 31 when the lease was written that the tax authorities stepped into the lessor's office and handed it a cheque for $3,154! There are two things the lessor can do with this in pricing the lease. The lease can be priced as before in which case the lessor is not passing on any of the value of depreciation to the lessee; or the lease can be priced at an amount lower than $100,000 in which case the rentals will drop from $2,633.38 to a lower number. This is how the value of depreciation is often passed on to lessees in highly competitive markets.

479. In the real world what influences the value of depreciation?

The following items influence the value of depreciation:

- Depreciable life of the leased asset
- Method of depreciation
- Inception date of transaction
- Tax rate
- Discount rate at which analysis takes place

To embellish, using the same example, if the inception date were to be December 31, the depreciation column will remain the same, $25,000 if it is a country where the first year's depreciation is not affected by the inception date. However, the first year's principal column will be zero as the loan will have been written on the last day of the fiscal year. This will cause the difference between depreciation and principal to become more favourable toward depreciation, thereby increasing the present value advantage of depreciation over principal.

480. A final summary?

Tax depreciation has a value to the lessor either from the point of view of it enabling the lessor to defer taxable income or from the point of view as it is compared to another product, loan. In either case it is a benefit.

U.S. TAX NUANCES

This section is for the benefit of the U.S. reader only; however, others will gain perspective on tax nuances, vis-a-vis leasing, in the most mature leasing market in the world.

481. What are the various tax aspects that one needs to understand in the context of leasing?

There are three items that need to be discussed in the important context of lessors gaining an understanding of the tax nuances involved in the selling of leases:

- Depreciation
- Alternative minimum tax
- Section 179 of the Internal Revenue Code (IRC)

482. What is the nuance having to do with tax depreciation?

The nuance is referred to as the midquarter convention.

483. What exactly is the midquarter convention?

To really understand this, one has to gain a quick understanding about the system of tax depreciation. Tax depreciation in the U.S. is known as Modified Accelerated Cost Recovery System (MACRS). MACRS was introduced effective January 1, 1987; prior to this it was known as ACRS—the "M" stands for certain modifications that were made.

484. How are assets depreciated under MACRS?

Under MACRS there are six classes of personal (as contrasted with real property, meaning real estate) property. Various types of assets fall into each of these six classes. The detail, as to which types of assets fall under which class, is best ascertained by reviewing IRS Publication 946. The six classes are 3, 5, 7, 10, 15 and 20 years.

485. How exactly is MACRS calculated under each class?

Cost recovery (or depreciation) for the 3-, 5-, 7- and 10-year classes is calculated using the 200% declining balance method using the half-year convention with a crossover to straight line at the optimal point.

486. Wow, that is a mouthful! Can it be embellished?

It is best embellished with an illustration. Let's use the 5-year class and a $100 asset.

To begin with, 200% declining balance means double declining balance or twice the otherwise straight line rate. The straight line rate for a 5-year asset would be 100 ÷ 5 or 20%; thus, twice the straight line rate would mean 40%. The 40% is applied to the undepreciated balance each year to determine the amount of cost recovery (or depreciation) for that year.

487. How does the half-year convention work?

The half-year convention is to make compliance easier. Setting the convention aside and using a December 31 fiscal year as an example, if property were purchased say on March 20, it would have to be depreciated for 287 days; property say purchased on November 17, for 45 days and so on. The half-year convention simplifies such daily proration.

Regardless of when property is purchased, in the year of acquisition the amount of cost recovery is one-half of the otherwise full amount. Thus, using the five-year illustration from above, the first year's cost recovery will be $100 x 40% x .50 = $20.

488. What about the next several years?

This is shown below:

Year	Undepreciated Amount	Factor	Cost Recovery
1	$100.00	.40 x .50	$20.00
2	80.00	.40	32.00
3	48.00	.40	19.20
4	28.80	.40	11.52
5	17.28	Crossover	11.52
6	5.76		5.76
Total			$100.00

The explanation follows: in year one, $100 was multiplied by the declining balance factor of 40% and further multiplied by 1/2 owing to the half-year convention. In years two, three and four the undepreciated balance was simply multiplied by 40% to get each year's cost recovery.

Year five is where the "crossover to straight line at the optimal point" takes place. If double declining balance were continued to be used, the cost recovery for year five would be: $17.28 x 40% = $6.91. However, if one crossed over (switched) to straight line, cost recovery would be computed as follows: at this stage cost recovery for three and a half years has been computed, one and a half years remain. Thus the remaining balance of $17.28 divided by the remaining life of 1.5 = $11.52. One crosses over to straight line in the year in which straight line is greater than the otherwise double declining balance amount.

489. But how does one know the crossover takes place in the fifth year?

Having done this example 1,000 times before, the author knows this!

490. Let's continue?

The sixth year remains: here it is quite simple. The undepreciated amount is $5.76 and the entire amount is the cost recovery for the sixth year; or it could be computed as follows: if $11.52 is the straight line cost recovery for one year, half of this amount, $5.76, is the cost recovery for the half-year that remains.

491. What about the other classes?

Whereas 200% declining balance applies to the first four classes, 150% declining balance applies to the last two classes, the 15-and the 20-year classes.

Using the same approach as explained in detail, the cost recovery for each class can be computed. The varied MACRS percentages for each class are shown below:

MACRS Table

	3-years	5-years	7-years	10-years	15-years	20-years
			CLASS LIFE			
1	33.33	20.00	14.29	10.00	5.00	3.750
2	44.45	32.00	24.49	18.00	9.50	7.219
3	14.81	19.20	17.49	14.40	8.55	6.677
4	7.41	11.52	12.49	11.52	7.70	6.177
5		11.52	8.93	9.22	6.93	5.713
6		5.76	8.92	7.37	6.23	5.285
7			8.93	6.55	5.90	4.888
8			4.46	6.55	5.90	4.522
9				6.56	5.91	4.462
10				6.55	5.90	4.461
11				3.28	5.91	4.462
12					5.90	4.461
13					5.91	4.462
14					5.90	4.461
15					5.91	4.462
16					2.95	4.461
17						4.462
18						4.461
19						4.462
20						4.461
21						2.231

It should be noted that for each of the six classes, the cost recovery is claimed over the respective class life plus one extra year owing to the half-year convention. In other words, in the year of acquisition only half a year's cost recovery is claimed; in the last year the remaining half year is claimed.

492. Is MACRS the only available method?

Other methods are available. They are typically slower than MACRS. Thus, most taxpayers use MACRS.

493. Now that MACRS has been understood what about the midquarter convention?

The midquarter convention applies to taxpayers who have purchased in their fourth fiscal quarter more than 40% of the total purchased during the entire fiscal year.

494. Can this be embellished?

Yes. First it should be noted that the midquarter convention only applies to personal property and not to real property. Secondly, as indicated above, it applies on a fiscal year basis. An illustration follows:

A taxpayer has a fiscal year of March 31. During the entire fiscal year the taxpayer has purchased $100 of personal property, equipment such as plant and machinery, computers and vehicles. Of the $100, $41 was purchased in the fourth fiscal quarter, January 1 to March 31. It can be clearly seen from this example that the 40% rule has been triggered as more than 40% was indeed purchased in the fourth fiscal period.

495. What is the consequence of the midquarter convention?

When the 40% rule is triggered the half-year convention cannot be used; it is replaced with the midquarter convention. The midquarter convention has the following impact:

Quarter	Midpoint	Months in Service	Fraction
1st	May 15	10.5	$\dfrac{10.5}{12} = \dfrac{7}{8}$
2nd	Aug. 15	7.5	$\dfrac{7.5}{12} = \dfrac{5}{8}$
3rd	Nov. 15	4.5	$\dfrac{4.5}{12} = \dfrac{3}{8}$
4th	Feb. 15	1.5	$\dfrac{1.5}{12} = \dfrac{1}{8}$

496. Can the above be embellished?

The first column represents the four fiscal quarters. The second column represents the midpoint of each of the four fiscal quarters. The third column is the number of months the equipment is in service from the midpoint of each quarter to the end of the fiscal year. For example: in the first fiscal quarter ending June 30, the midpoint is May 15 and the number of months from May 15 to March 31 (the end of the fiscal year) is 10½ months.

The last column is the fraction arrived at by taking the number of months in service as the numerator and 12 (the number of months in the year) as the denominator.

497. What is the significance of the four fractions?

The four fractions 7/8, 5/8, 3/8 and 1/8 replace the single fraction under the half year convention, 1/2.

498. Can this be further explained?

Yes. With the following illustration:

Assume that a taxpayer has a fiscal year the same as the calendar year, December 31. Further assume the following personal property acquisitions:

1st Quarter	$50,000
2nd Quarter	50,000
3rd Quarter	50,000
4th Quarter	100,000
Total	$250,000

Note that the fourth quarter acquisitions, $100,000, exactly equal 40% of the total acquisitions, $250,000; the taxpayer therefore has not triggered the 40% rule. Thus the midquarter convention does not apply. The half-year convention is still to be used.

499. What is the total cost recovery (depreciation) under the half-year convention?

The total depreciation, assuming all the assets fall in the 5-year MACRS class, is computed as follows:

$250,000 x 40% x .50 = $50,000

500. What next?

Let's use the same illustration again but assume that one is looking at it on November 17. Let's further assume the taxpayer is contemplating acquiring $20,000 of equipment on November 17. If the acquisition mode is a purchase the total for the year will be as follows:

1st, 2nd and 3rd Quarter	$150,000
4th Quarter	120,000
Total	$270,000

As versus in the previous illustration where the taxpayer did not trigger the 40% rule, here the taxpayer clearly has done so as $120,000 is greater than 40% of $270,000. The taxpayer must now use the midquarter convention.

Lease Taxation 323

501. What therefore is the impact of the midquarter convention?

It is seen below:

1st quarter	$50,000	x	.40	x	7/8	=	$17,500
2nd quarter	$50,000	x	.40	x	5/8	=	12,500
3rd quarter	$50,000	x	.40	x	3/8	=	7,500
4th quarter	$120,000	x	.40	x	1/8	=	6,000
Total							$43,500

Note that each quarter's acquisitions are impacted by the four different fractions.

502. What is the consequence of the midquarter convention to the taxpayer?

The consequence is best understood if one compares the midquarter convention to the half-year convention. Had the November 17 acquisition been a true (tax) lease, the total purchases for the fourth quarter would have remained at $100,000 and the total for the year would have remained at $250,000. Using the half-year convention, the total depreciation for the year would have been $250,000 x .40 x .50 = $50,000.

With midquarter, the amount of total depreciation decreased to $43,500; using a 34% tax rate, this translates into additional taxes of $6,500 x 34% = $2,210.

In other words, had the taxpayer entered into a true (tax) lease, $2,210 could have been saved. (In reality, one also needs to consider the tax savings from the rental deductibility from the $20,000 lease entered into on November 17).

503. What is the logic behind the midquarter convention?

Does revenue enhancement to the government ever need any logic??

504. But?

Well, the logic is as follows: the half-year convention, as seen earlier, is a compliance convenience. However, a taxpayer could use this convention and deliberately purchase, say on an exaggerated basis, all of its annual acquisitions on the last day of its fiscal year and still get one half of the otherwise full year's depreciation. Of course, with the 40% rule, the taxpayer would then be trapped under midquarter!

505. It is only through true (tax) leases that midquarter can be avoided?

Yes. This is very important to understand. A lease that is not considered to be a true (tax) lease will be deemed to be a purchase by the IRS. Thus, nontax leases do not come to the rescue of the midquarter convention.

506. Any other aspects of the midquarter convention that need to be discussed?

Yes. Let's assume in the above illustration the taxpayer inadvertently (a polite word for "foolishly"!) triggered midquarter. A lessor can help the entity remedy this by doing a sale leaseback transaction, so long as the lease is indeed a true (tax) lease. The sale leaseback must be done by the last day of the fiscal year, in this case December 31.

507. A summary?

True (tax) leases are of substantial benefit to taxpayers whose intended acquisitions in the fourth fiscal quarter are likely to trigger the midquarter convention.

The convention is a powerful sales tool for true leases in the fourth fiscal quarter.

508. Moving on to the second tax nuance, the alternative minimum tax?

Yes, the alternative minimum tax (AMT) is another tax nuance that is actually helpful in selling true (tax) leases to customers.

509. What exactly is the AMT?

Ready for a mild headache? The AMT was introduced into the Internal Revenue Code as early as 1969. Its objective is an attempt to assure that every business (in the context of this publication, a business is meant to be a corporate taxpayer) pays a certain minimum amount of taxes. Given all the deductions, breaks and loopholes that existed (and still do), it was (and is) conceivable for businesses to have considerable accounting profit and yet not pay any taxes, based on the deductions, breaks and loopholes.

Note: Many countries have a simplified version of the AMT. As an example, a certain country has corporate tax laws that state an entity will pay the higher of 30% of taxable income or 2% of total assets. It can be clearly seen that even if entities end up with zero or negative taxable income, they will be trapped under the percentage of assets tax!

510. How does the AMT attempt to create a minimum tax base for business?

The thought process behind the AMT is simple, yet clever. Tax law identifies many "preferences." Preferences are certain deductions such as depreciation; mining exploration and development costs; and deductions for pollution control facilities. The more deductions a taxpayer claims, all other things being equal, the smaller will be the tax base; conceivably, even a negative tax base such that there is no tax liability.

511. How then does the minimum tax come into play?

From now on let's assume that the only preference item (remember, a preference generally is simply a deduction) is depreciation. With a large amount of (accelerated) depreciation, it is possible for a business to substantially reduce its taxable income. The AMT comes into play as follows: every business must compute its tax liability twice; once under the "regular" method, and again under AMT.

512. What is the difference between the two?

This is best illustrated. Assume a corporate taxpayer has $1,000,000 of taxable income (taxable revenue minus deductions; the deductions include $800,000 of depreciation). The taxpayer will compute its tax liability as follows:

| *AMT is a tax on a deduction!*

	Regular		AMT
Taxable income	$1,000,000		$1,000,000
Preferences			800,000
Total/AMT	$1,000,000		$1,800,000
Tax rate	x .34	x	.20
Tax liability	$340,000		$360,000

In the above computations, note the following:

- The regular corporate tax rate is 34%
- The regular tax liability is $340,000
- Under AMT, the preferences (depreciation) are added back to taxable income
- The corporate AMT rate is 20%
- The AMT tax liability is $360,000

Essentially, under AMT the preferences are added back and the base ($1,800,000) is taxed at 20%. Conceptually, the AMT is a tax on a deduction! On one hand the taxpayer deducted depreciation in arriving at its regular taxable income of $1,000,000; on the other hand, the depreciation deduction was taxed at 20%. Very clever!

513. Which of the two amounts does the taxpayer pay?

What a silly question! The taxpayer pays the larger of the two amounts, which is how the AMT assures that a certain amount of tax will be paid if the regular tax liability is zero. In this case, $360,000 is due and payable to the IRS.

From the above, it should be clear that the AMT is not only a minimum tax, it is a penalty tax. In the illustration, the taxpayer paid $20,000 more than its regular tax liability (remember, the taxpayer will always pay the larger of the two amounts). AMT thus causes bracket creep; the taxpayer in the illustration is no longer in the 34% bracket; it is in the 36% tax bracket.

514. How can AMT be avoided?

Read on! Excess preference items (remember in this illustration the taxpayer had $800,000 of preferences which were assumed to be just one category of a deduction—depreciation) cause a taxpayer to trigger AMT. This is easy to demonstrate. Let's take another illustration for another taxpayer:

	Regular		AMT
Taxable income	$1,000,000		$1,000,000
Preferences			700,000
Total/AMT	$1,000,000		$1,700,000
Tax rate x	.34	x	.20
Tax liability	$340,000		$340,000

The only difference, as can be clearly seen with the second taxpayer, is that the preferences (again let's assume that these are entirely comprised of depreciation) are $700,000 and not $800,000. Having managed its preferences, this taxpayer has not triggered AMT as its regular taxable liability is exactly equal to its AMT liability.

515. How can preferences be managed?

Preferences can be managed through a very simple rule. Note in the above example that the total of the preferences are exactly equal to 70% of taxable income. By keeping total preferences equal to or less than 70% of taxable income, AMT can generally be avoided if the preferences are deductions (A few preferences such as tax exempt interest income are not deductions).

516. Can the 70% rule be embellished?

Let's do this through another illustration for yet another taxpayer:

	Regular	AMT
Taxable income	$1,000,000	$1,000,000
Preferences		700,001
Total/AMT	$1,000,000	$1,700,001
Tax rate	x .34	x .20
Tax liability	$340,000	$340,000.20

Note by adding $1 of a preference, this taxpayer has fallen into AMT as the total preferences are not equal to or less than 70% of taxable income.

517. What does all of this have to do with leasing?

One of the more common preferences is depreciation. All other things being equal, the more equipment an entity purchases, the more depreciation it will have to a point where many an entity will violate the 70% rule and fall into AMT.

This is where leasing comes into the picture! Instead of purchasing equipment, if the entity were to enter into true (tax) leases, in lieu of depreciation the rental amount would be deductible thereby allowing the taxpayer to manage the amount of depreciation deduction, so as not to fall into AMT.

The key thing to remember is whereas depreciation expense is a preference item, rent expense is not.

518. The leases have to be true (tax) leases?

AMT is a tax nightmare; yet an opportunity to sell true leases.

Just as much in managing the mid-quarter convention, the leases have to be true (tax) leases as nontax leases are deemed to be purchases from a tax point of view. Nontax leases would generate depreciation expense—aggravating the situation, not mitigating or eliminating it.

519. Will true (tax) leases always keep taxpayers out of AMT?

Not always. Remember that though depreciation is one of the most common preference items, there are other preference items (it would behoove the reader to get a list of the most current preference items).

520. Does AMT apply to all corporate taxpayers?

No, small corporations are AMT exempt. The general rules for the exemption are that AMT will not apply:

- In the first taxable year (for all corporations)
- When the average "gross receipts" for the first three-year period is not greater than $5 million
- When the average "gross receipts" for subsequent periods is not greater than $7.5 million

The above rules, though complex in their implementation, are meant to provide AMT relief to small entities.

521. Any other nuances to AMT?

Just one important one. Up to now, the reader was given the impression that the entire amount of depreciation expense is a preference item.

This is not true, it was done for simplicity purposes. In reality, the depreciation preference for the most common MACRS classes (3, 5, 7 and 10) is the difference between 200% declining balance and 150% declining balance.

522. Can this be illustrated?

Let's use a five-year asset with a $100,000 cost. As can be seen below, the depreciation preference is the difference between 200% MACRS and 150% declining balance:

Year	200%	150%	Preference
1	$20,000	$15,000	$5,000
2	$32,000	$25,500	$6,500
3	$19,200	$17,850	$1,350
4	$11,520	$16,660	$(5,140)
5	$11,520	$16,660	$(5,140)
6	$ 5,760	$ 8,330	$(2,570)
	$100,000	$100,000	0

It is important to note that the previous three illustrations, where the preferences were $800,000, $700,000 and $700,001, respectively, the depreciation preference was not the entire amount of depreciation expense actually claimed but the difference between 200% and 150% declining balance.

The impact is not changed, though. Excess depreciation, regardless of how the preference is computed, can trigger AMT and true (tax) leases are indeed the solution to potentially stay out of AMT.

523. In the above example, the preference reverses. Is AMT therefore a timing tax?

Good observation! In isolation, on a single transaction, AMT does reverse or turnaround. In the aggregate too, it can. Any AMT paid can be used as a credit against regular tax liability; thus, at least in theory, it is a timing tax. The varied preferences and other complexities are such that in practice, taxpayers may not see perfect reversals.

524. Anything more?

No, other than the conclusion that AMT offers a tremendous selling opportunity for true (tax) leases.

525. To move onto the last tax nuance, Section 179?

Section 179 of the IRC allows taxpayers to treat the cost of any tangible personal property (and certain computer software) as an expense in the year in which such property is placed in service.

526. All tangible personal property?

Not at all! For taxable years before 2006, the aggregate cost which may be written off entirely as an expense is limited to $100,000; thereafter, it reverts to $25,000. In other words, for taxable years through 2005, a taxpayer may write off the first $100,000 of equipment cost in lieu of depreciating such equipment.

527. Is the $100,000 write off available to all taxpayers?

Yes it is, but through another limitation it can quickly disappear. If a taxpayer has placed in service tangible personal property in excess of $400,000 in any taxable year before 2006 ($200,000 thereafter), the $100,000 write-off ($25,000 for taxable years after 2006), for that taxable year is reduced by $1 for every dollar in excess of the $400,000.

528. An embellishment?

Let's assume a taxpayer in fiscal 2005 places in service tangible personal property amounting to $460,000. The $100,000 limitation is reduced by $60,000, thus only $40,000 is eligible for the first year write-off.

Section 179 is an opportunity to sell nontax and tax leases.

Taking this one step forward, if a taxpayer has placed in service tangible personal property amounting to $500,000 the entire $100,000 first year write-off is lost.

For fiscal years after 2005, is should be noted again that the threshold is $200,000 and not $400,000 and the write-off is $25,000 and not $100,000.

529. What does all of this have to do with leasing?

Just as much as in the midquarter convention and AMT true (tax) leases came to the rescue, here too, true (tax) leases are the solution in not losing the first year write-off.

530. How so?

A smaller taxpayer (this advice does not apply to very large companies to whom losing $100,000 of the first year write-off is immensely insignificant) should plan as follows:

- The first $100,000 of acquisitions should be purchases so as to qualify for the write-off. Of course as a lessor, one should try to sell the client nontax leases as these will be deemed to be purchases
- The first $100,000 of acquisitions should preferably be those asset types which fall into the longest MACRS category; this way, equipment which otherwise would be depreciated over a long (say seven- year MACRS) period can be written-off in the year of acquisition
- Beyond the first $100,000 the entity should do true (tax) leases thereby not losing a single dollar of the write-off

531. Well, it seems like true (tax) leases are a product of substantial benefit?

Yes they are as they can provide substantial tax relief as follows:

- Prevent damage from the midquarter convention
- Avoid the AMT penalty tax
- Preserve the Section 179 first year write-off

SUMMARY

1. In some countries all leases are considered to be leases from a tax point of view; in some other countries, some leases are nontax leases and the others are tax leases.

2. As to whether a lease qualifies to be a lease is a country by country situation.

3. The tax code in the U.S. does not define a lease; it is left to the interpretation of the IRS.

4. On a tax lease, the lessor claims rental income which is offset by tax depreciation; the lessee deducts the rental payments.

5. On a nontax lease, the lessor claims interest income; the lessee deducts depreciation plus interest expense.

6. Operating leases are almost always tax leases.

7. Depreciation is a benefit; it shelters revenue and defers taxes.

8. Depreciation on a lease is synonymous to principal on a loan; they both represent the recovery of cost, the nontaxed portion of cash flow.

9. Generally, depreciation on a lease is more advantageous than principal on a loan.

10. The value from depreciation is either retained by the lessor or passed on to the lessee; if passed on, it is done through a reduction in the rental payment.

11. The system of tax depreciation used in the U.S. is known as MACRS.

12. Under MACRS there are six classes of personal property—3, 5, 7, 10, 15 and 20 years.

13. For the first four classes, MACRS is computed using the 200% declining balance method using the half-year convention with a crossover to straight line at the optimal point.

14. The midquarter convention applies to those taxpayers who purchase in their fourth fiscal quarter more than 40% of the total purchased during the entire fiscal year.

15. The midquarter convention only applies to personal property.

16. Under midquarter there are four placed in service dates; under half-year, there is only one.

17. Unless a taxpayer purchases 59.9% in the first quarter and 40.1% in the fourth, midquarter is a damper on depreciation and results in a larger amount of tax being paid.

18. True leases in the fourth quarter can help avoid the midquarter penalty.

19. A sale leaseback can undo the damage done by midquarter so long as the transaction is completed by the end of the fiscal year.

20. AMT is a tax on a deduction.

21. Preferences are certain deductions; depreciation is one of the more common preferences.

22. Preferences lead to AMT.

23. A taxpayer pays the larger of its regular or AMT tax liability.

24. When total preferences are less than or equal to 70% of taxable income, the taxpayer will generally not be in AMT.

25. True leases will help a taxpayer potentially stay out of AMT as rent expense is not a preference item.

26. Section 179 of the tax code allows taxpayers to fully expense the first $25,000 of tangible personal property purchased in 2006.

27. The $25,000 expense benefit is entirely lost if a taxpayer purchases tangible personal property equal to or greater than $225,000.

28. Lessors should advise clients to get into nontax leases for the first $25,000 of equipment as such leases will qualify as purchases.

29. After the first $25,000 of nontax leases, lessors should advise their clients to enter into true leases so as never to lose the $25,000 write-off.

30. True leases or tax leases help in three different ways:

- Prevent damage from the midquarter convention
- Avoid the AMT penalty tax
- Preserve the Section 179 first year write-off

GLOSSARY

alternative minimum tax
A tax designed to prevent taxpayers in the U.S. from claiming excess deductions to reduce their tax liability.

form country
A country where all leases are considered to be leases from a tax point of view. In such countries the "form" (the label) governs; thus, regardless of the economic substance that establishes intent (such as a bargain purchase option), a lease is considered to be a lease from a tax point of view.

half-year convention
Used in the U.S. where in the year of acquisition, regardless of the date of acquisition the asset is placed in service, the taxpayer is entitled to one-half of the full year's depreciation.

internal revenue code
The tax statute in the U.S.

MACRS
The expression used for tax depreciation in the U.S. MACRS stands for Modified Accelerated Cost Recovery System. It has been in place since January 1987.

midquarter convention
A depreciation convention in the U.S. that replaces the half-year convention. The midquarter convention applies when a taxpayer purchases more than 40% of its total annual personal property in its fourth fiscal quarter.

nontax lease
A lease that is not considered to be a lease for tax purposes and is therefore considered to be a loan whereby the lessor claims interest income and the lessee deducts depreciation plus interest expense.

personal property
All property other than real property.

preference
The expression used for certain deductions (and other items) which can trigger the alternative minimum tax in the U.S.

real property
Immovable property, generally land and buildings.

Section 179
A section in the Internal Revenue Code that allows taxpayers in the U.S. to write-off a certain amount of purchased personal property in the year of acquisition.

substance country
A country where tax authorities consider the economic substance in lease transactions in determining whether a lease is to be treated as a lease (rental) or as a purchase (loan) for tax purposes.

tax lease
A lease that is considered to be a lease from a tax point of view whereby the lessor claims rental income offset by depreciation and the lessee deducts the rental expense. Also referred to as a true lease in the U.S.

true lease
A lease that is considered to be a lease from a tax point of view whereby the lessor claims rental income offset by depreciation and the lessee deducts the rental expense. Also referred to as a tax lease.

HOMEWORK!

1. How many types of leases are there from a tax point of view?

2. What is meant as a "substance" country?

3. What is meant as a "form" country?

4. What is the tax treatment of a nontax lease in the hands of the two parties?

5. What is the tax treatment of a tax lease in the hands of the two parties?

6. Why does tax depreciation have value to a lessor?

7. Why is depreciation synonymous to principal?

8. What are the six class lives under MACRS?

9. How is MACRS claimed on a 5-year asset?

10. What is meant by the half-year convention?

11. When does a taxpayer trigger the midquarter convention?

12. An illustration follows:

- $100,000 asset
- 5-year MACRS
- Acquired in the fourth fiscal quarter

What would MACRS be if the taxpayer did not trigger the midquarter convention? What would MACRS be if the taxpayer did trigger midquarter?

13. What is meant by a "preference"?

14. How is the depreciation preference computed?

15. Why does a true (tax) lease not trigger a preference?

16. How can a taxpayer avoid AMT?

HOMEWORK ANSWERS

1. There are two types of leases from a tax point of view: tax leases or true leases and nontax leases.

2. A "substance" country is one where a distinction is made between tax leases and nontax leases. Such distinction is based on looking at the economic substance or the structure of the transaction.

3. A "form" country is one where all leases are considered to be tax leases. In such countries, the form or label governs; not the substance.

4. A nontax lease is treated as though it is a purchase/sale. The lessee claims depreciation and interest expense; the lessor claims interest income.

5. A tax lease is treated as though it is a rental. The lessee claims rental expense; the lessor claims rental revenue offset by depreciation.

6. Tax depreciation has value to a lessor as it defers the lessor's tax liability. Separately, the value of depreciation stems from the fact that generally its value is greater than the value of principal on a loan.

7. Depreciation and principal both represent the recovery of cost and as such the nontaxed portion of cash flow. Another way of expressing this is as follows: on a tax lease, rent minus depreciation equals margin; on a loan, the payment minus principal equals margin.

8. 3, 5, 7, 10, 15 and 20 years.

9. On a 5-year asset MACRS is computed using 200% declining balance using the half-year convention with a crossover to straight line at the optimal point.

10. Under the half-year convention, all property purchased is considered to be purchased at the midpoint of the year; thus, in the year of acquisition the taxpayer gets one-half of the otherwise full year's depreciation.

11. Midquarter is triggered when a taxpayer purchases in its fourth fiscal quarter more than 40% of the total personal property purchased during the entire fiscal year.

12. Under the half-year convention:

$100,000 x 40% x .5 = $20,000

Under the midquarter convention:

$100,000 x 40% x 1/8 = $5,000

Note: The answer is not $100,000 ÷ 8 = $12,500.

13. A preference is a certain deduction which could lead to AMT.

14. The depreciation preference is the difference between 200% declining balance and 150% declining balance.

15. A true (tax) lease will not trigger AMT as rent expense is not a preference item.

16. A taxpayer can possibly avoid AMT if the sum of the preferences is equal to or less than 70% of taxable income.

Pricing and Structuring

Pricing and Structuring

Difference Between Pricing and Structuring

Arriving at Lessor IRR

Lease Pricing

Lease Structuring

Summary

Glossary

Homework!

Homework Answers

DIFFERENCE BETWEEN PRICING AND STRUCTURING

532. What is the difference between pricing a lease and structuring a lease?
In pricing a lease, a lessor uses its pretargeted IRR (interest rate in the lease) to arrive at a rental amount which is linear (straight line) over the term of lease. In structuring a lease, a lessor considers varied lessee needs.

533. What types of needs?
Most of the needs are from a lessee's cash flow point of view. For example, if a lessee's credit is acceptable to the lessor; yet, the lessee say is a developer who has received a contract from the government to build a highway and the cash flow is such that the lessee has to expend a fair amount of cash in the earlier months of the contract, whereas the cash inflow will be coming a bit later, the lessee may prefer a step-up or a low-high lease as follows:

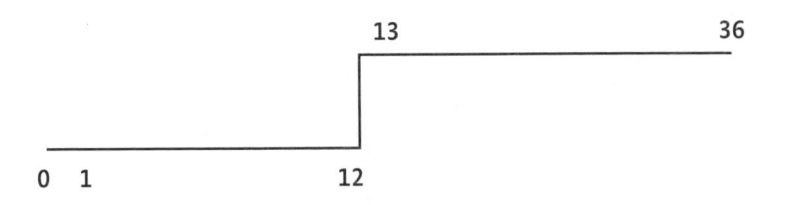

```
                     13                    36
                     ┌─────────────────────
                     │
─────────────────────┘
0   1                12
```

The above structure clearly shows that the rentals in the first 12 months are lower than the rentals in the last 24 months. Of course, the lessor is likely to mitigate any adverse credit risk the structure may pose by taking additional collateral.

534. What other types of cash flow needs do lessees have?
Another lessee may wish to make larger rental payments say in the first 18 months of a 36-month lease given the fact that the lessee, through

short-term cash forecasting, concludes that they have the extra cash to "buy down the rate" later in the lease.

The structure would be as follows:

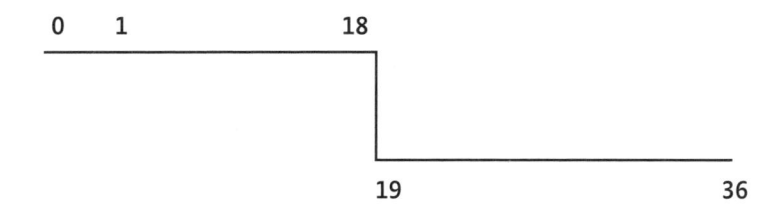

```
     0   1              18
     ┌───────────────────┐
                         │
                         │
                         └───────────────────
                         19                36
```

The above represents a step-down or a high-low structure.

Yet another lessee may be in a seasonal business. This lessee, say in the agricultural industry, may have close to zero cash flow in certain dry months and therefore would like a skip payment lease as follows:

```
    ─────────      ─────────       ─────────
    0                                      36
```

It is obvious from the above time line that in certain months there are no rentals at all. Of course, the other rentals would be higher than what a nonskip payment lease would show.

535. Are there any other structures the types of which accommodate lessee cash flow?

There can be, and are, an infinite number of structures. As another example, a lessee who has budgetary issues toward the end of the budget year may request for a grace period lease where there are no payments from the inception date until the start of the next budgetary cycle. This is how such a lease would look:

```
    - - - - - ───────────────────────────────
    0     3                                36
```

Pricing and Structuring   **351**

The gap shows the period (say from October 1 until December 31) with no cash flows.

The infinite number of structures comes from permutation combinations and grades. As one example, a lease may have three steps with a 10% increase as follows:

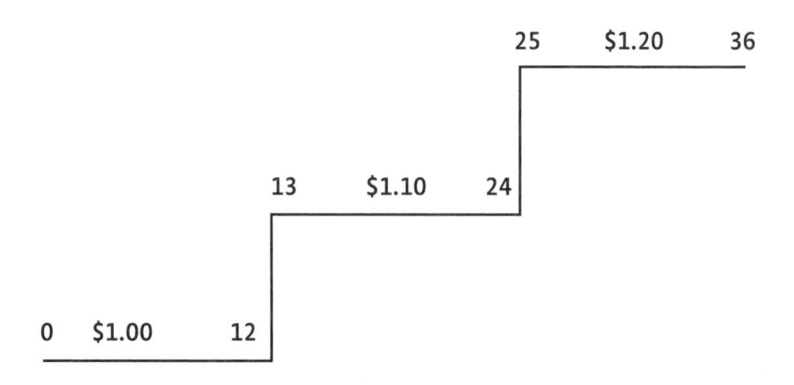

```
                                    25      $1.20      36
                                    ┌──────────────────
                      13    $1.10   24
                      ┌─────────────┘
    0    $1.00    12
    ┌─────────────┘
```

The rentals in the second period are 10% more than in the first; in the third period, they are 20% more than in the first.

Or another 36-month step-up lease may have one step with a 10% increase but skip payments integrated into both periods as follows:

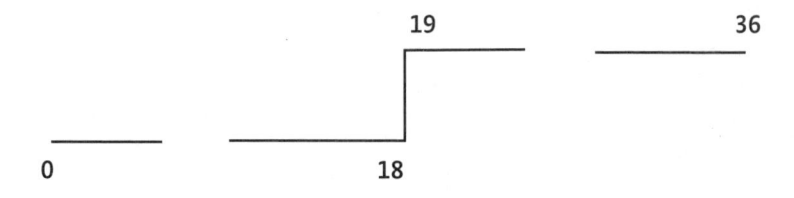

```
                          19                        36
                          ┌─────────    ─────────────
    ─────    ─────────────┘
    0                     18
```

352 Winning With Leasing!

536. Other than cash flow, do lessees have any other types of needs in the context of structured leases?

Some lessees are tax motivated and as such they would prefer step-down or high-low leases.

537. Why so?

In the step-down or high–low structure, the rentals in the earlier part of the lease are higher than the rentals in the latter part of the lease as follows:

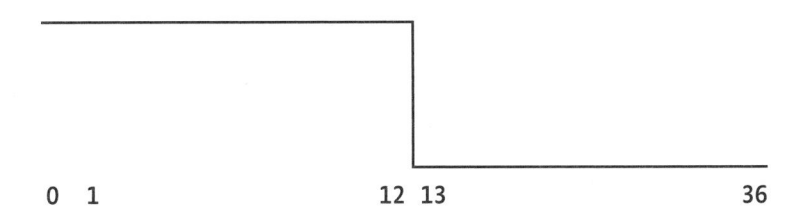

```
            |‾‾‾‾‾‾‾‾‾‾‾‾‾‾|
            |              |
            |              |_____
            |                                      |
 0    1                  12  13                    36
```

In the above 36-month lease, it should be clear that with higher lease rentals in the first 12 months, the lessee is able to claim a larger tax deduction in the first 12 months as compared to a linear lease.

Of course, the above presupposes that the lease is being done in a country where lease rentals are properly claimed as a deduction, or that the lease is an operating lease for income tax purposes (remember, operating lease rentals are deductible regardless of which country one is talking about).

538. In the above lease the cash outflow in the earlier part of the lease is greater than otherwise. Does this not cause a cash flow problem for the lessee?

Good point! What one needs to keep in mind is that lessees have different needs. A tax motivated lessee may not be too concerned about cash flow, or the benefit from taxation more than makes up the fact that a larger amount of cash has to be paid sooner.

Pricing and Structuring 353

539. Do tax authorities allow the above type of structure?

Given that tax laws vary from country to country, it is best to seek appropriate tax counsel.

540. How does the lessor benefit from structuring a lease to meet lessee needs?

Well, to begin with, the lessor wins the deal! Had the lessor not accommodated the lessee needs, the lessee would have done the transaction elsewhere.

There is another major benefit to structuring leases. In many countries in the world a large number of lessees are interest rate conscious. They shop for the "best" interest rate (best means lowest!). If a lessor is able to address a lessee's cash flow needs (and all lessors are not willing to do this), it is likely that the lessee will not focus on interest rates. What this means is that structuring a lease provides the lessor with an opportunity to actually increase the IRR from an otherwise linear lease to the same customer.

> *Structuring allows the lessor to possibly increase the IRR as the focus is shifted from rate to cash flow.*

ARRIVING AT LESSOR IRR

541. How does a lessor arrive at the interest rate in a lease?
A lessor has two objectives in arriving at interest rates in its leases: to be competitive and to assure that the portfolio of leases has an adequate return to enable the lessor to cover all its cost and provide an appropriate return to its shareholders.

542. How does the lessor assure it is competitive in the marketplace?
In every country lessors always keep abreast of market rates. Rates vary with transaction sizes. Using the U.S. as an example, the industry has four transaction categories by size as follows:

SIZE	$ RANGE
Micro	$0 - $25,000
Small	$25,001 - $250,000
Medium	$250,001 - $5,000,000
Large	> $5,000,000

Lessors often specialize within a category or two of transaction sizes; this, of course, makes it easier to keep a good eye on market rates. Given that lessors will always know the range of IRRs in each transaction size category, they then attempt to stay within that range.

543. An example?
Let's assume in a certain country the range of IRRs in the small-ticket market is 14%-16% for a "quality" credit. The lessor pricing a small-ticket transaction would be well advised to stay within the range unless there was a compelling reason not to do so.

544. In arriving at the IRR in a lease, how does the lessor assure that it will indeed cover all costs and provide an adequate return to its shareholders?

It better! Otherwise the shareholders will exit the industry. There are two ways this can be done. The first approach is more commonly used.

545. How does it work?

The lessor takes its average cost of debt, adds the needed spread to stay competitive and hopes that the spread will indeed cover all costs and keep the shareholders satisfied!

A finer tuned approach is where the lessor, through a budget, arrives at the cost of doing business for the year in question as it pertains to new originations. The cost is then converted to a percentage of new volume that is to be priced in the current year. This in turn is then added to the average cost of debt—the total, therefore, covers all costs.

546. Then what?

Then a spread is added which is the return to the shareholders. History hopefully shows that this spread has kept the firm profitable in the past to the satisfaction of the shareholders.

547. What is the second approach?

The second approach is more sophisticated and even more finely tuned than the one discussed above.

Money is the raw material for the lessor—given this, the lessor computes its cost of capital.

548. What exactly is the cost of capital?

Capital (money) comes from two sources and two sources only: debt and equity. Let's go over a simple illustration. Assume that the year-end balance sheet of the lessor is as follows:

Assets		Liabilities & Equity	
Assets	$100	Liabilities	$60
		Equity	40
Total	$100		$100

It is clear from the above that the total assets of $100 have been funded through $60 of debt and $40 of equity. Remember the accounting equation: assets = liabilities + equity? Equity includes initial equity plus retained earnings.

549. What next?
One now proceeds to compute the weighted average cost of capital (WACC) as follows:

	Weight
Debt	.60
Equity	.40

From the balance sheet it is clear that the weight assigned to the two components of money is 60 : 40. Each of the two components of capital has a cost associated with it.

550. What exactly is the cost of debt given that the lessor generally borrows from multiple sources and, that too, at different rates?
The cost of debt is the weighted average cost of debt.

551. Can this be embellished?
Assume the lessor borrows the $60 from two sources as follows:

Amount Borrowed	Interest Rate
$40	10%
$20	12%
$60	

One now computes the weighted average cost of debt as follows:

Amount Borrowed	Interest Rate	Aggregate
$40	10%	400
$20	12%	240
$60		$640

$ 640 ÷ $60=10.67;
thus, 10.67% is the weighted average cost of debt.

552. What about any tax consequences?

Interest on debt is invariably tax deductible. Let's assume the lessor's tax rate is 30%. Thus for every $1 of interest, the lessor saves 30 cents in taxes which means that the cost of debt (interest) only costs 70 cents for every $1 of interest. Thus to continue with WACC:

	Weight	x	Cost	x	Tax Adjustment	=	Total
Debt	.60	x	10.67%	x	.70	=	4.48
Equity	.40						

4.48% is the after-tax cost of the debt component of WACC.

358 Winning With Leasing!

553. What about the cost of equity?
Generally the cost of equity is greater than the cost of debt.

554. Why is this so?
Equity is riskier. Both on a going concern basis as well as in bankruptcy, the shareholders are paid last. Obviously lenders have a priority over shareholders; this makes equity riskier. Given the simple financial concept of risk/reward, equity is therefore costlier than debt.

555. How does one arrive at the cost of equity?
There are some extremely sophisticated models such as the Gordon's Growth model which provide varied answers. (And in the process deliver a mild headache, at the least!)

556. Is there a simpler yet accurate method to arrive at the cost of equity?
One takes the approach that one person's cost is another person's return. Under this simple approach if the shareholders are targeting a return on equity (ROE) of say 15%, this 15% becomes the cost of equity to the firm.

557. But how does one arrive at say 15%?
Based on history, forecasts and industry averages. Let's now plug in the 15% into WACC as follows:

	Weight	x	Cost	x	Tax Adjustment	=	Total
Debt	.60	x	10.67%	x	.70	=	4.48
Equity	.40	x	15.00%				

Pricing and Structuring **359**

558. Does the cost of equity have to be tax adjusted?

No, as the incidence of taxation is at the shareholder level. To complete WACC:

	Weight	x	Cost	x	Tax Adjustment	=	Total
Debt	.60	x	10.67%	x	.70	=	4.48
Equity	.40	x	15.00%	x	1.00	=	6.00
					WACC		10.48

The entity's WACC is 10.48%. In other words, the weighted average after-tax cost of capital (money) is 10.48%.

559. What next?

Going back to the purpose of computing WACC—to help in arriving at the interest rate in the lease—one should understand that the 10.48% computed above is an after-tax number. As will be explained later, leases are generally priced with pretax interest rates. Thus the 10.48% has to be converted to its pretax equivalent.

560. How is this done?

Simply by dividing it by one minus the tax rate (or .70) as follows: 10:48 ÷ .70 = 14.97%. Ignoring any expenses of doing business (which must be computed and added to the 14.97%), if leases on an average are priced at 14.97%, the shareholders will receive an ROE of 15%.

561. How so?

Because the 10.48% was arrived at by using two cost components: 10.67% for debt and 15% for equity. When leases are priced at 14.97% (10.67% converted to its pretax equivalent of 14.97%), this means that the interest rate in the lease is precisely sufficient to pay the lenders at 10.67% and return 15% to the shareholders.

562. But every company cannot compute its WACC?

Why not? No one should be in the money business unless they know the cost of raw material, money!

> *Money is the lessor's raw material; cost of capital means the same as cost of money.*

563. A summary could be helpful?

WACC provides management with a pricing floor. Again, assuming there are no expenses of doing business, leases (using the above example) should not be priced below 14.97% on an average if shareholders are targeted to receive 15% on their equity. The above model correlates IRR to ROE, an important correlation.

564. Are all leases priced at the same rate?

Not at all!

As seen earlier, rates vary based on transaction size. Generally, the smaller the transaction size the higher the rate. Also other adjustments are made based on the lessor's credit due diligence of each customer.

565. Can this be embellished?

Most, if not all, lessors have an internal system of grading each credit application say from "A" to "E", "A" being prime credits, "E" being the worst. The grading is based on numerous internal criteria used such as a review of key ratios, cash flow, number of years in business, etc.

566. Then what?

"A" leases are priced below average ("C" leases) and "E" leases are priced above average—the risk/reward approach.

LEASE PRICING

567. How exactly are leases priced?
Leases are priced either on a pretax or an after-tax basis.

568. What is the difference between the two approaches?
Pretax pricing essentially ignores taxation and prices a lease as though it is a loan; whereas, after-tax pricing includes all aspects of taxation (such as the tax rate, depreciation details, etc.) and prices a lease with much greater precision.

> *Pretax pricing is far more pervasive than after-tax pricing.*

569. When does one use pretax pricing?
Pretax pricing is commonly used to price mostly all leases in emerging lease markets. In mature markets, such as the U.S., pretax pricing is typically used to price micro, small and middle-market transactions unless the middle-market transaction is on the high end and is a tax lease (as versus a nontax lease).

570. When does one use after-tax pricing?
After-tax pricing is used to price large transactions which qualify as tax leases where the lessor is entitled to claim the tax depreciation.

In this subsection, only pretax pricing will be discussed as after-tax pricing, as explained above, is rarely used and is complex enough to warrant the use of pricing software.

571. What tools are needed to price leases?
Leases can be priced on a pretax basis either with a calculator, a spreadsheet or pricing software.

572. What are the quantitative variables that enter into the pricing of a lease?

There are many input variables. These are input into the calculator, spreadsheet or computer. The only output is the amount of the rental.

Let's first list all the quantitative input variables and then discuss them one at a time. The variables are:

- Equipment cost
- Initial direct costs
- Lease term
- Frequency of payment
- Mode of payment
- Up-front fees
- Residual value
- Lessor IRR

573. When does the lessor pay the cost of the equipment to the supplier?

Equipment cost (plus sales tax or VAT, if applicable) is typically paid by the lessor to the supplier within a very short period after the lessee signs a Delivery and Acceptance Certificate (D&A) certifying that the equipment received is indeed the equipment ordered and that it is in proper functioning condition.

Let's assume a D&A certificate has been signed on the 10th of December and that the lease is for 36 months. Let's further assume that the commencement date of the lease (the date the first lease payment begins) is January 1. The time line would look as follows:

The practice of interim rents is logical as the lessee is using the leased asset during this period.

```
Dec 10                 Jan 1, 200X                 Dec 31, 200Y
```

574. What about the period between December 10 and January 1—does the lessor receive any rent or consideration for this period given that the lessee has begun using the equipment?

Prorated rents or interim rents are typically paid by the lessee—in this example for 21 days.

575. How are interim rents calculated?

To begin with (as will be seen later), the lease will be priced on December 10 for 36 months—not 36 months + 21 days. Once the lessor arrives at the monthly rental, this monthly rental will be prorated for 21 days. Thereafter 36 rentals will be due beginning January 1, 200X.

From now on, for simplicity, all subsequent illustrations will ignore the time gap between the inception date (date D&A is received and lease is priced) and the commencement date (the date the payments begin). The illustrations will assume that the two dates are the same and that they take place on January 1, 200X. It will also be assumed that the lessor pays for equipment cost on January 1, 200X as well.

576. What is meant by the expression "Initial Direct Costs"?

Some leases have certain direct costs associated with them. The word direct is obviously the opposite of indirect; the latter includes all of the selling, general and administrative costs of doing business.

577. Perhaps an example or two of a direct cost would be helpful?

One common direct cost is when a lease broker or agent originates the transaction for the lessor and is paid a commission or a fee for such origination. Another example would be when a certain large lease transaction requires the drafting of a new lease agreement as the lessee is not willing to accept the lessor's standard documentation; outside legal counsel is paid a fee for the legal work.

Both of the above examples are costs directly related to a specific lease transaction and are typically added to the cost of the equipment for purposes of pricing the lease. In essence, the impact of this is that the lessee pays for the initial direct costs as such costs cause the computed rental to be higher than otherwise.

578. Is lease term typically a certain number of months?
Not necessarily. The lease term and the frequency of payments are connected. Frequency of payments is typically monthly whereby the term is a certain number of months. However the payments sometimes can be, and are, made quarterly in which case the lease term would be so many quarters.

579. Are semi-annual or annual payments common?
Semi-annual or annual payments are not too common.

580. What is meant by mode of payment?
As studied in the section on Lease Finance, mode of payment refers to either advance or arrears.

581. Are up-front fees common in leasing?
Up-front fees are extremely common in the world of leasing. In the small to middle-market transactions they range from one-half of one percent of equipment cost to as high as three percent of equipment cost.

582. What are they typically called?
They take many different themes and variations. They are called one of the following: closing fees, documentation fees, management fees, administration fees, establishment fees and the like.

583. How are these fees treated?
There are two common ways to treat the fees. Either the fees are "pocketed" which means that the interest rate in the lease eventually is higher than the IRR the lessor is seeking, or the fees are added to equipment cost which means that the rental is higher than otherwise as the fees are financed.

> *Up-front fees are extremely common; they are an IRR kicker!*

584. Can the above two approaches be illustrated?
Illustrations will follow shortly.

585. Does not residual value pertain only to operating leases?
Generally yes; however, any balloon or bullet payment due at the end of a finance lease is synonymous to residual in the context of pricing. Balloon or bullet payments on finance leases are increasingly more common than before as such payment, essentially the last rental, causes the periodic rental to be lower than otherwise.

586. Lastly the lessor IRR?
The earlier subsection explained in detail how a lessor arrives at the IRR or the interest rate in the lease.

587. Now that all the quantitative input variables have been explained, perhaps an illustration will help?

Let's start with an illustration that will then be used throughout this subsection as well as in the subsequent subsection on structuring.

The illustration follows:

Equipment cost	$100,000
Term in months	36
Rentals	arrears
Up-front fees	$1,000
Residual	0
Lessor pretargeted IRR	12%

588. Is the lease a finance lease as residual is zero?
It is. In the real world the lessee would typically pay a nominal transfer fee at the end of the lease as legal consideration for the transfer of title. This fee could, as an example, be either $1 or one percent of equipment cost.

In either event the nominal transfer fee is not generally a part of the pricing input which means (other than when it is $1) it slightly increases the lessor's interest rate in the lease.

589. Since the illustration has up-front fees, can the two approaches of treating such fees be illustrated?

Let's first illustrate the approach where the fees are "pocketed." This means that the fees will not be input into the calculator as an input variable. The time line will be as follows:

0	36
(100,000)	0

The rental will be computed as follows:

> HP12 C

	f	REG
100,000	CHS	PV
36		n
12	g	12÷
	PMT	**3,321.43**

> HP17B11+

	☐	CLEAR DATA
100,000	+/-	PV
36		N
12		I%YR
	PMT	**3,321.43**

Pricing and Structuring

590. What was meant earlier that when fees are pocketed the interest rate to the lessee is higher than otherwise?

Let's look at the time line first:

```
    0        1                                           36
    _____

(100,000)
  1,000
 (99,000)    --------------    3,321.43    --------------
```

In reality the lessor has paid the supplier the $100,000 at time zero and has received the $1,000 in fees at the same time. The net cash outflow at time zero is $99,000 and not $100,000. Based on this, let's compute the interest in the lease as follows:

> HP12 C

	f	REG
99,000	CHS	PV
36		n
3,321.43		PMT
	i	1.06
12x		<u>12.70</u>

> HP17B11+

	☐	CLEAR DATA
99,000	+/-	PV
36		N
3,321.43		PMT
	I%YR	<u>12.70</u>

It can be seen from the above that though the lease was priced at 12%, the "pocketed" fees caused the lessor IRR and the lessee interest rate to increase to 12.70%.

591. What about the second approach?

In the second approach, which is not as common as the first approach, the fee is financed and the time line will look as follows:

```
0        1                                          36
─────────────────────────────────────────────────────
(100,000)
 (1,000)
(101,000)
```

Financing the fee entails adding the fee to the equipment cost and thus the rental is computed on $101,000 and not on $100,000 as follows:

> HP12 C

	f	REG
101,000	CHS	PV
36		n
12	g	12÷
PMT		3,354.65

> HP17B11+

			CLEAR DATA
101,000	+/-		PV
	36		N
	12		I%YR
	PMT		**3,354.65**

592. What about the IRR?

Here, too, the lessor's IRR is higher than 12%. In computing the IRR, the amount at time zero is shown, as can be seen below, at $100,000 as the lessor is paying this amount to the supplier.

```
0    1                              36
─────────────────────────────────────
(100,000) ---------------  3,354.65  ---------------
```

The IRR is computed as follows:

> HP12 C

	f		REG
100,000	CHS		PV
	36		n
3,354.65			PMT
	i		1.06
	12x		**12.69**

> HP17B11+

		CLEAR DATA
100,000	+/-	PV
36		N
3,354.65		PMT
I%YR		12.69

593. Can the next illustration be a lease with residual?

Using the same data in the earlier illustration, but without confusing the issue with fees, the next illustration follows:

Equipment cost	$100,000
Term in months	36
Payment	arrears
Residual	$20,000
IRR	12%

The monthly rental drops from $3,321.43 (see QUESTION 589) to $2,857.14 merely because of the residual. See computation below:

> HP12 C

	f	REG
100,000	CHS	PV
36		n
12	g	12÷
20,000		FV
PMT		2,857.14

Pricing and Structuring

> HP17B11+

	☐	CLEAR DATA
100,000	+/-	PV
36		N
12		I%YR
20,000		FV
PMT		2,857.14

594. It is almost too easy to push keystrokes on a calculator and obtain instant answers. Can pricing be explained more analytically?

A lease is a time line. Pricing is always done at time zero. Equipment cost is assumed to be paid to the supplier at time zero and, of course, the equipment cost is known. The other cash flow known in the above illustration is the residual of $20,000 (residual is considered to be cash flow even if the lessee, on an operating lease, returns the equipment). The time line at this stage looks as follows:

```
0                                                              36
───────────────────────────────────────────────────────────────
(100,000)                                                  20,000
```

> *It behooves a lessor to go beyond the mechanics of lease pricing; understanding it analytically adds a dimension.*

Using the concept of the time value of money which states that one dollar today is not equal to one dollar tomorrow, the $20,000 of residual is present valued to time zero such that all known cash flows are brought to a common denominator, time zero.

595. At what discount rate is the residual present valued?

The residual is present valued using the IRR as the discount rate as follows:

> HP12C

			f	REG
	36			n
	12		g	12÷
	20,000			FV
	PV			-13,978.50

> HP17B11+

			☐	CLEAR DATA
	36			N
	12			I%YR
	20,000			FV
	PV			-13,978.50

596. What next?

The time line now looks as follows:

```
0                                          36
_____

(100,000.00)
  13,978.50
 (86,021.50)
```

Analytically, the investment in the lease is not $100,000 but $86,021.50 as analytically the present value of the residual offsets the amount paid to the supplier.

The next step is to assume that the monthly rental is $1 and to ascertain the present value of a stream of hypothetical $1 rentals as follows:

> HP12C

	f	REG
1	g	CFj
36	g	NJ
1		i
f NPV		30.107505

> HP17B11+

	CLEAR DATA
	FIN
	CFLO
0	INPUT
1	INPUT
36	INPUT
	EXIT
	CALC
1	I%
NPV	<u>30.107505</u>

597. What does $30.107505 signify?

$30.107505 is the present value of a stream of hypothetical $1 rentals being received in arrears over 36 months discounted at the IRR in the lease, 12%.

All pricing, as mentioned earlier, takes place at time zero which is present value. If the investment in a lease were to be $30.107505 where the lease is in arrears over 36 months at 12%, the monthly rental would be $1.

598. Can this be explained again?

Starting with a $1 rental, one gets present value of $30.107505. Going the other direction, if the present value is $30.107505, the rental is $1. But the present value is not $30.107505. The present value is $86,021.50.

Thus assuming the rental to be $x and solving for $x:

$$\$x = \frac{86{,}021.50}{30.107505}$$
$$= \underline{\$2{,}857.14}$$

Which is exactly the same answer in QUESTION 593!

599. Does one need to understand the above analytical approach to price leases in the real world?

Not for pricing leases; however, if leases are to be structured using a calculator in lieu of spreadsheets or software, the above approach is indispensable.

LEASE STRUCTURING

600. What exactly is meant by the expression "lease structuring"?

As noted in an earlier subsection, lease structuring entails tailoring the lease to meet lessee cash flow and, occasionally, lessee tax needs. It also, at times, can mitigate lessor credit risk. Lease structuring also helps in defocusing the interest rate in the lease as focus is shifted to achieving and delivering specific lessee needs.

601. What type of lease structures exist?

Leases can be structured in many different ways. To summarize what was indicated in an earlier subsection, leases can be:

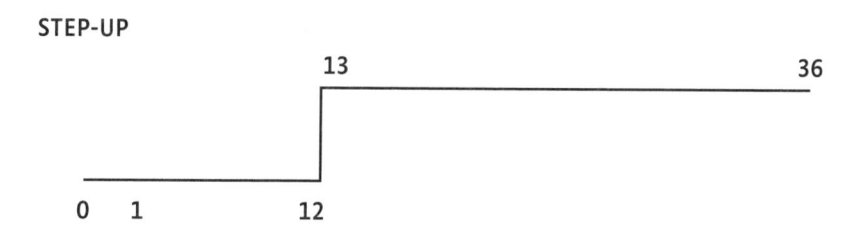

STEP-UP

```
                  13                              36
                   _____
                  |
         _____|
         0   1   12
```

STEP-DOWN

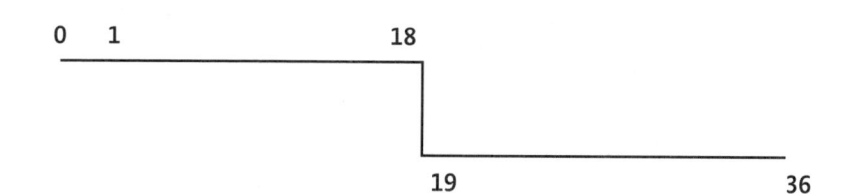

```
         0   1            18
         _____
                          |
                          |_____
                         19                        36
```

Pricing and Structuring   377

SKIP

0 _____ _____ _____ _____ 36

GRACE PERIOD

0   6 _____ 36

> *Structuring permutation combinations are indeed infinite.*

The permutation combinations are infinite: as an example, a step-up lease can have three steps with varied grades, a step-down lease in its first 18 months can have a period where payments are skipped, etc.

Whereas in pricing, the rentals are linear (straight line); in structuring they are not.

602. Is it difficult to structure a lease?

Spreadsheets and software can structure leases in a heartbeat! However, the analytical approach to pricing illustrated in QUESTION 594 onwards in the earlier subsection can be used to structure leases with a calculator. This approach should enable a salesperson to structure a lease on a dynamic basis while sitting across the desk from a customer at the customer's office!

603. Perhaps a few illustrations will help?

To begin with, the illustration will borrow from the one used in the Lease Pricing subsection. Let's start with a simple structure as follows:

Equipment cost	$100,000
Term in months	36
Rentals	2 in advance, 34 remaining
Residual	$20,000
Lessor pretargeted IRR	12%

Taking two advance rents up-front is an example of lease structuring as the cash flows in the lease are not even (where one rental equals all other rentals). The first rental is twice that of all other rentals.

604. How is this done?

As simple as the illustration appears it cannot be done on the calculator without using the analytical approach studied earlier.

605. Why so?

Given that the rental is not known, the two advance rentals are also not known. This creates a simultaneous equation with two unknowns. The investment in the lease (or the amount to be priced) is unknown as the two advance rentals offset the equipment cost. Thus, both the investment in the lease and the rentals are unknown—this, indeed, is a simultaneous equation!

606. But simultaneous equations are not difficult to solve?

They are when combined with the time value of money!

607. How is the simultaneous equation then solved?

As indicated earlier, using the analytical approach.

To begin with, given that this is the same illustration as in QUESTION 593 onwards from the Lease Pricing subsection, the first part of computing at the present value of all known cash flows has already been solved to arrive at $86,021.50.

The next step is to, as before, assume that the monthly rental is $1 and to ascertain the present value of a stream of hypothetical rentals as follows:

› HP12C

	f	REG
2	g	CFo
1	g	CFj
34	g	Nj
12	g	12÷
f NPV		30.702666

› HP17B11+

	☐	CLEAR DATA
2		INPUT
1		INPUT
34		INPUT
		EXIT
		CALC
12 ÷ 12	=	I%
NPV		30.702666

Given that there are two rentals taken in advance, the cash flow at time zero is shown at $2 and the remaining 34 rentals at $1. $30.702666 is the present value of a stream of hypothetical $1 rentals over 36 months with two in advance and 34 remaining discounted at the IRR in the lease, 12%.

608. What next?

As before, if the investment in the lease or the amount to be priced is $30.702666, each rental is equal to $1. However, the investment in the lease is not $30.702666, it is $86,021.50. Thus, assuming each rental to be $x and solving for $x:

$$\$x = \frac{86{,}021.50}{30.702666}$$

$$= \$2{,}801.76$$

Thus the lessor will collect $5,603.52 in advance ($2,801.76 x 2) and the 34 remaining rentals will be $2,801.76.

609. A time line may help?

The time line follows:

0	1		34	35	36
(100,000.00)					20,000
5,603.52					
(94,396.48)	2,801.76			0	20,000

Note that at point 35 there is a zero. This is because the last two rentals have been collected in advance. There is no rental at point 36 either, just the residual of $20,000.

It helps to do a quick proof to assure that the answer arrived at is correct. The proof follows:

› HP12C

	f	REG
94,396.48	CHSg	CFo
2,801.76	g	CFj
34	g	Nj
0	g	CFj
20,000	g	CFj
f IRR		1.00
12x		12.00

› HP17B11+

	☐	CLEAR DATA
94,396.48	+/-	INPUT
2,801.76		INPUT
34		INPUT
0		INPUT
1		INPUT
20,000		INPUT
1		INPUT
		EXIT
		CALC
IRR%		1.00
x12	=	12.00

610. Another illustration?

Continuing to use the same illustration last seen in QUESTION 603:

Equipment cost	$100,000
Term in months	36
Rentals in arrears	3 steps with 10% increase from base first year rentals
Residual	$20,000
Lessor pretargeted IRR	12%

In the above illustration, to embellish, the 36-month lease has three 12-month steps where the second set of rentals are 10% greater than the first set and the third set of rentals are 20% greater than the first set.

Once again, given that this is basically the same illustration, the first step of arriving at the present value of all known cash flows has already been computed to be $86,021.50.

611. What is the next step?

The next step, as before, is to assume that the initial set of rentals is $1; thus, the second set of rentals will be $1.10 and the third set will be $1.20. The present value of a hypothetical stream of rentals will be as follows:

› HP12C

	f	REG
1	g	CFj
12	g	Nj
1.10	g	CFj
12	g	Nj
1.20	g	CFj
12	g	Nj
12	g	12÷
f NPV		__32.879160__

› HP17B11+

	☐	CLEAR DATA
0		INPUT
1		INPUT
12		INPUT
1.10		INPUT
12		INPUT
1.20		INPUT
12		INPUT
		EXIT
		CALC
12 ÷ 12		I%
NPV		__32.879160__

Again, as before, solving for $x:

$$\$x = \frac{\$86{,}021.50}{32.879160}$$

$$= \underline{\underline{\$2{,}616.29}}$$

Complex structuring with a calculator can, and should, be done on a live basis with the client.

612. Is $2,616.29 the first set of rentals?

Yes. The other two sets are simple to compute as follows:

| Second set | = | $2,616.29 | × | 1.10 | = | $2,877.92 |
| Third set | = | $2,616.29 | × | 1.20 | = | $3,139.55 |

613. Is a proof necessary?

When a complex computation is done on the calculator, a proof helps confirm that the answer is correct. The proof follows:

> HP12C

	f	REG
100,000	CHSg	CFo
2,616.29	g	CFj
12	g	Nj
2,877.92	g	CFj
12	g	Nj
3,139.55	g	CFj
11	g	Nj
23,139.55	g	CFj
fIRR		1.00
12x		<u>12.00</u>

Pricing and Structuring

> HP17B11+

		CLEAR DATA
100,000	+/-	INPUT
2,616.29		INPUT
12		INPUT
2,877.92		INPUT
12		INPUT
3,139.55		INPUT
11		INPUT
23,139.55		INPUT
1		INPUT
		EXIT
		CALC
IRR%		1.00
x12	=	<u>12.00</u>

614. How about one last illustration?

Before doing this, let's go over the three standard steps in structuring leases:

1. Compute the present value of all known cash flows. (For cross reference, this would be the $86,021.50 in all the previous illustrations.)
2. Assume the initial rent to be $1 and give the lease its pattern (such as the previous illustration where the pattern was $1, $1.10 and $1.20). Compute the present value of the hypothetical stream of rentals (for cross reference, this would be the 32.879160 from the previous illustration).

3. Solve for $x (initial rental) by dividing step one by step two (for cross reference this would be $86,021.50 ÷ 32.879160 = $2,616.29).

615. Can the above three steps be used to structure any type of lease?

Yes. The essence lies in step two. This step permits infinite permutation combinations for structure. As an example, if a lease is a step-down or a high-low lease, once one knows the number of steps and the relationship between the first set of rentals and the remaining rentals, it is easy to perform step number two.

For example; if the step–down or high-low lease has three equal steps with the second set of rentals being 20% less than the first and the third set being 30% less than the first, the three hypothetical sets of rentals will be $1, $0.80 and $0.70.

If a lease is a skip payment lease, the pattern will simply mean a few $1 rentals followed by zeros in those months where the payment is skipped.

616. At this stage how about one last illustration?

For the last time using the same data again:

Equipment cost	$100,000
Term in months	36
Rentals	arrears
First 12 rentals	$3,000
Residual	$20,000
Lessor pretargeted IRR	12%

In this example the lessee desires to pay $3,000 as each of the first 12 rentals. The lessor now needs to solve for a lease with the following structure:

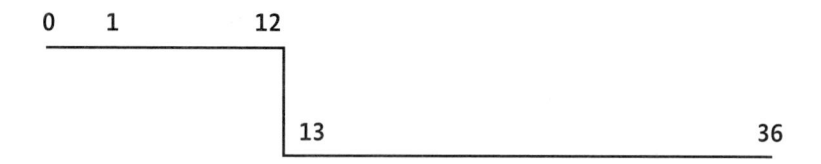

```
0    1         12
┌─────────────┐
              │
              │   13                              36
              └──────────────────────────────────┘
```

The lessor knows the structure will be step-down or high-low as the lessor is aware that if the lease were to be a level payment lease each rental would be $2,857.14 (as per QUESTION 593 in the Lease Pricing subsection).

Thus, the lessor needs to solve for the remaining 24 rentals.

617. What next?

Keeping in mind step #1 from the three steps studied in QUESTION 614, one must first compute the present value of all known cash flows.

At this stage it is necessary to first compute the present value of the known rentals as follows:

> HP12C

	f	REG
3,000	g	CFj
12	g	Nj
12	g	12÷
f NPV		33,765.23

388 Winning With Leasing!

> HP17B11+

	☐	CLEAR DATA
0		INPUT
3,000		INPUT
12		INPUT
		EXIT
		CALC
12 ÷ 12	=	I%
NPV		<u>33,765.23</u>

The time line now looks as follows:

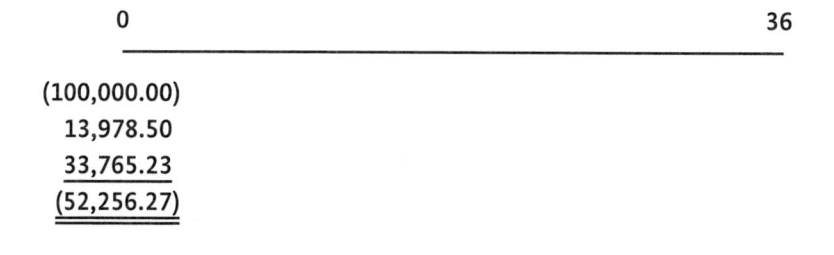

```
0                                                          36
─────────────────────────────────────────────────────────────
(100,000.00)
  13,978.50
  33,765.23
 (52,256.27)
```

$13,978.50 is the present value of the $20,000 residual as seen in previous illustrations. $33,765.23 is the present value of the 12 known rentals. Both the $13,978.50 and the $33,765.23 analytically offset the equipment cost of $100,000 resulting in a net investment of $52,256.27 at time zero.

618. In computing the present value of the hypothetical stream of rentals what is done with the first 12 rentals of $3,000 each?

The computation below addresses this issue:

> HP12C

	f	REG
0	g	CFj
12	g	Nj
1	g	CFj
24	g	Nj
12	g	12÷
fNPV	g	<u>18.852428</u>

> HP17B11+

		CLEAR DATA
0		INPUT
0		INPUT
12		INPUT
1		INPUT
24		INPUT
		EXIT
		CALC
12 ÷ 12		I%
NPV		<u>18.852428</u>

Note that the first 12 rentals have been shown at zero. The reason is obvious: the first 12 rentals have already been accounted for; if they were to be shown at $1 in the above computation, there would be a double counting of such rentals.

The remaining 24 rentals are assumed to be $1 each and $18.852428 is the present value of a stream of rentals where the first 12 rentals are zero and the remaining 24 rentals are $1 each.

The last step is as before:

$$\$x = \frac{\$52{,}256.27}{18.852428}$$
$$= \$2{,}771.86$$

Thus, the remaining 24 rentals are $2,771.86 each.

619. And the proof?
It follows:

> HP12C

	f	REG
100,000	CHSg	CFo
3,000	g	CFj
12	g	Nj
2,771.86	g	CFj
23	g	Nj
22,771.86	g	CFj
f IRR		1.00
12x		12.00

› HP17B11+

	☐	CLEAR DATA
100,000	+/-	INPUT
3,000		INPUT
12		INPUT
2,771.86		INPUT
23		INPUT
22,771.86		INPUT
1		INPUT
		EXIT
		CALC
IRR%		1.00
x12	=	<u>12.00</u>

Winning With Leasing!

SUMMARY

1. Pricing a lease entails arriving at a linear or straight line rental (where one rental equals another) given a pretargeted IRR. On the other hand, structuring a lease entails meeting lessee cash flow needs or, occasionally, lessee tax needs.

2. There are an infinite number of structures basically falling into one of the following categories: step-up or low-high; step-down or high-low; skip; and grace period.

3. Structuring is a win-win situation for both the lessee and the lessor. The lessee gets what it desires—a structured lease; the lessor gets the deal done and that, too, possibly at a higher IRR as the focus has been shifted from rate to cash flow.

4. Lessors arrive at the pretargeted IRR in the lease by taking their average cost of debt and adding a spread to this number. The eventual IRR should be competitive in the marketplace; as importantly, it should, after covering all expenses of doing business, provide the shareholders with an adequate return on equity.

5. A refined approach to arriving at IRRs is to compute the firm's cost of capital or WACC. Leases, on an average, should then be priced at WACC plus the expenses of doing business.

6. Leases are generally priced on a pretax basis. Such approach ignores taxation and treats the lease as though it is a loan.

7. Marketing/sales tips

   a. Do not assume that all lessees want linear leases
   b. Ascertain if some have certain cash flow needs
   c. Once cash flow needs are understood, structure the lease accordingly
   d. Take additional collateral if structure imposes additional risk
   e. Increase the IRR in structured leases, where possible. Such may not be possible with step-down or high-low leases where the lessee is paying more cash in the early periods
   f. Structuring is a win-win situation for both the lessee and the lessor. The lessee gets what it desires—a structured lease; the lessor gets the deal done and, that too, possibly at a higher IRR

GLOSSARY

after-tax pricing
Where a lease is priced in a manner that any and all tax aspects of the transaction are a part of the pricing equation. Generally used to price large transactions and/or true (tax) leases.

cost of capital
The cost of debt plus equity or simply put the cost of money to the leasing company. When computed on a weighted average basis, it is known as the weighted average cost of capital—WACC.

delivery and acceptance certificate
An important legal document signed by the lessee certifying that the equipment received is what was ordered and that it is in proper functioning condition. Only after receipt of this certificate does the lessor pay the vendor.

initial direct cost
A cost directly associated with a specific lease such as fees paid by a lessor to a lease broker for originating the transaction.

interim rents
The rental paid by a lessee at the inception of a lease for the stub (short) period from the inception date (the date the lessee signs the delivery and acceptance certificate) to the commencement date (the date regular lease payments begin). Also known as stub or pro rata rents.

pretax pricing
The more common approach (more common than after-tax pricing) used in pricing a lease whereby a lease is priced as though it is a loan. Any and all tax aspects are ignored in such approach.

pricing
Whereby a lessor uses its pretargeted IRR to arrive at a periodic rental amount which is linear (straight line) over the term of the lease.

structuring
Whereby a lessor tailors a lease to meet the cash flow or tax needs of a lessee.

HOMEWORK!

1. Arrive at the rental for the following lease:

Equipment cost	$1,000,000.00
Term in months	48
Rentals	advance
Residual	0
Lessor pretargeted IRR	20%

2. Arrive at the rental for the following lease:

Equipment cost	$1,000,000.00
Term in months	48
Rentals	advance
Residual	$200,000
Lessor pretargeted IRR	20%

3. Arrive at the rental for the following lease:

Equipment cost	$1,000,000.00
Term in months	48
Rentals	2 in advance, 46 remaining
Residual	$200,000
Lessor pretargeted IRR	20%

4. Arrive at the proof for the above.

5. Arrive at the rentals for the following lease:

Equipment cost	$1,000,000.00
Term in months	48
Rentals in advance	1 step with 10% increase at midpoint
Residual	$200,000
Lessor pretargeted IRR	20%

6. Arrive at the proof for the above.

7. Arrive at the rentals for the following lease:

Equipment cost	$1,000,000.00
Term in months	48
Rentals in advance	first 6 at $30,000
Residual	$200,000
Lessor pretargeted IRR	20%

8. Arrive at the proof for the above.

HOMEWORK ANSWERS

Answer 1

> HP12C

	f	REG
	g	BEG
1,000,000	CHS	PV
48		n
20	g	12÷
PMT		<u>29,931.50</u>

> HP17B11+

		CLEAR DATA
		FIN
		TVM
1,000,000	+/-	PV
48		N
20		I%YR
PMT		<u>29,931.50</u>

Pricing and Structuring **401**

Answer 2

› HP12C

		f	REG
		g	BEG
	1,000,000	CHS	PV
	48		n
	200,000		FV
	20	g	12÷
	PMT		27,223.89

› HP17B11+

		☐	CLEAR DATA
			FIN
			TVM
	1,000,000	+/-	PV
	48		N
	200,000		FV
	20		I%YR
	PMT		27,223.89

Answer 3
Present value of residual

> HP12C

		f		REG
	200,000	CHS		FV
	48			n
	20	g		12÷
	PV			90,460.28

> HP17B11+

		☐		CLEAR DATA
	200,000	+/-		FV
	48			N
	20			I%YR
	PV			90,460.28

Net investment in lease:

Equipment cost	1,000,000.00
PV of residual	(90,460.28)
	909,539.72

Assume initial rent is $1. Solve for present value of cash flow from rents.

Pricing and Structuring **403**

> HP12C

	f	REG
2	g	CFo
1	g	CFj
46	g	Nj
20	g	12÷
f NPV		33.949774

> HP17B11+

	□	CLEAR DATA
		FIN
		CFLO
2		INPUT
1		INPUT
46		INPUT
		EXIT
		CALC
20÷12	=	I%
NPV		33.949774

Solve for rent

$$\frac{909{,}539.72}{33.949774} = \$26{,}790.74$$

---

404 Winning With Leasing!

Answer 4

> HP12C

	f	REG
946,418.52	CHSg	CFo
26,790.74	g	CFj
46	g	Nj
0	g	CFj
200,000	g	CFj
f IRR		1.67
12x		<u>20.00</u>

> HP17B11+

		CLEAR DATA
		FIN
		CFLO
946,418.52	+/−	INPUT
26,790.74		INPUT
46		INPUT
0		INPUT
1		INPUT
200,000		INPUT
1		INPUT
		EXIT
		CALC
IRR%		1.67
x12	=	<u>20.00</u>

Answer 5

Present value of all known cash flows from QUESTION 3

$909,539.72

Assume initial rent is $1. Solve for present value of cash flows from rents.

> HP12C

	f		REG
20		g	12÷
1		g	CFo
1		g	CFj
23		g	Nj
1.1		g	CFj
24		g	Nj
f NPV			34.753030

> HP17B11+

	☐	CLEAR DATA
		FIN
		CFLO
1		INPUT
1		INPUT
23		INPUT
1.1		INPUT
24		INPUT
		EXIT
		CALC
20 ÷ 12	=	I%
NPV		34.753030

Initial rent
909,539.72   ÷   34.753030   = $26,171.52

Next set
            x   1.10   = $28,788.67

Pricing and Structuring **407**

Answer 6

> HP12C

	f	REG
973,828.48	CHSg	CFo
26,171.52	g	CFj
23	g	Nj
28,788.67	g	CFj
24	g	Nj
200,000	g	CFj
f irr		1.67
12 x		<u>20.00</u>

> HP17B11+

		CLEAR DATA
		FIN
		CFLO
973,828.48	+/-	INPUT
26,171.52		INPUT
23		INPUT
28,788.67		INPUT
24		INPUT
200,000		INPUT
1		INPUT
		EXIT
		CALC
IRR%		1.67
x12	=	20.00

Answer 7

Present value of all known cash flows (QUESTION 5)	$(909,539.72)
+ Present value of six known rents of $30,000 each	172,782.23
	$(736,757.49)

Assume each subsequent rent is $1. Solve for present value of cash flows from rents.

Pricing and Structuring **409**

> HP12C

	f	REG
20	g	12÷
0	g	CFo
0	g	CFj
5	g	Nj
1	g	CFj
42	g	Nj
f NPV		27.650207

> HP17B11+

		CLEAR DATA
		FIN
		CFLO
0		INPUT
0		INPUT
5		INPUT
1		INPUT
42		INPUT
		EXIT
		CALC
20 ÷ 12	=	I%
NPV		27.650207

Solve for subsequent rent

$$\frac{736{,}757.49}{27.650207} = \$26{,}645.64$$

Answer 8

> HP12C

	f	REG
970,000	CHSg	CFo
30,000	g	CFj
5	g	Nj
26,645.64	g	CFj
42	g	Nj
200,000	g	CFj
f irr		1.67
12 x		<u>20.00</u>

Pricing and Structuring   411

> HP17B11+

	☐	CLEAR DATA
		FIN
		CFLO
970,000	+/-	INPUT
30,000		INPUT
5		INPUT
26,645.64		INPUT
42		INPUT
200,000		INPUT
1		INPUT
		EXIT
		CALC
IRR%		1.67
x12	=	<u>20.00</u>

412 Winning With Leasing!

Operating Leases

Operating Leases

Defining the Product

Unique Advantages to Lessees

Unique Advantages to Lessors

Managing Varied Risks

Residual Risk

Techniques to Mitigate Residual Risk

Operating Leases Without Asset Risk

Summary

Glossary

Homework!

Homework Answers

DEFINING THE PRODUCT

620. What exactly is an operating lease?
To begin with, it depends whether the question is being asked from a marketplace point of view or an accounting point of view.

621. How about from both points of view?
Let's begin with the marketplace. As explained in the Overview Section, the difference between a finance lease and an operating lease solely has to do with the full payout/nonfull payout aspects. Operating leases are nonfull payout where the lessor has reliance on residual; in other words, the lessor has an asset risk. On a finance lease, the lessor only has credit risk; on an operating lease, the lessor has both credit and asset risk.

> *Operating leases are invariably nonfull payout owing to the residual position assumed by the lessor.*

622. Are operating leases mostly full-service?
There is a common misunderstanding that operating leases are mostly full-service where the lessor provides the financing bundled with say maintenance and insurance. In reality, operating leases can either be net or full-service depending on the lessee's intent.

623. Can this be further explained?
Yes. If a lessee desires the transaction to resemble outsourcing, then the operating lease will be full-service. A real world example would be a brewery leasing 20 delivery trucks. The lessee is only interested in using these trucks to distribute beer from the brewery to various distribution outlets and does not care to be bothered with the maintenance of the fleet. The lessor, therefore, will provide a lease which is likely to include maintenance, repairs, insurance and a host of other services. On larger fleets, the lessor can provide replacement trucks whereby if one of the

trucks needs to be in the garage for repairs, the lessor will provide a replacement truck such that there is no down time.

624. But this presupposes that the lessor has an inventory of trucks configured for the narrow use of a certain lessee?

Yes. This type of service (replacement assets) would only be provided by lessors who have such inventory. A lessor who focuses on such equipment type is likely to invest in additional inventory to be able to offer the extra service (of course, for an extra fee!).

625. What about net operating leases?

Many computer leases are net where the lessee maintains and insures the equipment. Of course, the lessor is well advised to have a strict maintenance clause requiring the lessee to maintain the equipment properly; for, if the lessee were to return the equipment at the end of the lease, the lessor would certainly like the equipment to come back in good condition.

626. What are the various end of term events that are possible in an operating lease?

The following diagram best describes what can happen at the end of term in an operating lease:

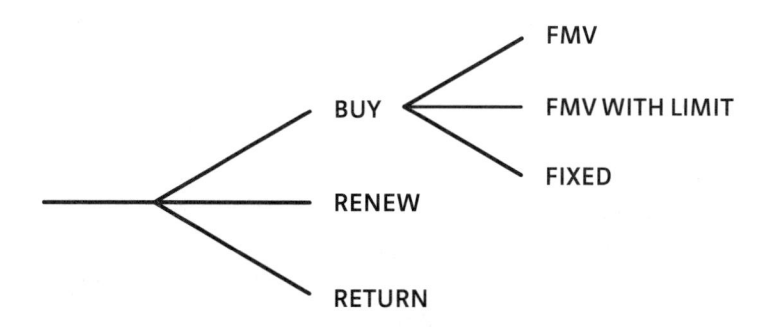

```
                    FMV
         BUY   <    FMV WITH LIMIT
    <          <    FIXED
         RENEW

         RETURN
```

627. Can the above be embellished?

Yes. At the end of term, the lessee has one of three options: it can purchase the equipment, return the equipment or renew the lease.

628. Are these options contained in the lease agreement?

It depends and varies from country to country and lessor to lessor. Many jurisdictions preclude the existence of purchase options. In such cases, the lease will be silent with regard to the various options and simply state that the lessee must return the equipment at the end of lease term. This does not prevent the two parties from negotiating a sale/purchase at the end of the lease.

629. Is the lessee not disadvantaged in a situation as described above?

Possibly, in that the lessor may ask for an unrealistic purchase price particularly if the lessee is keen on purchasing the equipment. A sophisticated lessee will generally, in those cases where leases are silent with respect to varied end of term options, not enter into operating leases on essential or core equipment which the lessee is likely to want to purchase at the end of the lease term. Thus, many such operating leases are for noncore assets such as vehicles.

> *Astute lessees do not like to be subject to FMV uncertainties; they prefer fixed purchase options.*

630. How does it work when a lease agreement contains a purchase option?

Purchase options have three variations. The most common is "fair market value" or FMV. When a lease contains a FMV purchase option, this means that at the end of the lease term the lessee has the option (not the obligation) to purchase the equipment at the then FMV.

631. Who arrives at the FMV at the end of the lease term?

It depends on how sophisticated the lessee is. At two extremes: an unsophisticated lessee is likely to enter into a lease where it is stated that the FMV is arrived at solely by the lessor; on the other hand, a sophisticated lessee will insist that the equipment be valued by an independent appraiser. If it is a very large transaction, it is likely that the FMV will be the average of valuations from three appraisers: one chosen by the lessor, one chosen by the lessee and the last one jointly chosen by the two parties.

632. What is meant by the expression "FMV with Limit"?
Prudent lessees often negotiate an upper limit or a ceiling to FMV. As an example, a lease purchase option may state that the lessee can purchase the equipment at the end of the lease term for its FMV not to exceed 30% of original equipment cost. This gives the lessee the assurance, up-front, that the maximum they will pay for the equipment is 30% of the original equipment cost; but, depending on FMV, it could be less.

633. Why would a lessor agree to such a limit?
To get the deal done! Of course, the lessor would not agree to a ceiling unless the residual position booked by the lessor was equal to or less than the ceiling.

634. Can this be embellished?
On a lease with equipment cost of $100, let's assume the lessor took a 27½% residual position in pricing the lease. The lessor would be willing to enter into a lease agreement with an FMV purchase option not to exceed $30. The lessor is no more at risk than otherwise; yet, has a 2½% upside.

635. What about fixed purchase options?
Again, a prudent lessee would prefer a fixed purchase option. Using the same illustration as before, a lessee who would like such a fixed purchase option is most likely to find a lessor who is willing to offer say a 30% fixed purchase option. The lessee has absolute assurance up-front that if it desires to purchase the equipment at the end of the lease term, it can do so for a known amount; on the other hand, the lessor is satisfied with the possibility of a 2½% upside and is willing to forgo additional upside to get the deal done. Of course, the lessor still has residual risk of 27½% as the lessee has the right to return the equipment.

636. What about renewal options?
Similar to purchase options, renewal options have three variations: fair rental value (FRV), fair rental value with limit or fixed rental value.

637. Can the differences between an operating lease and a finance lease be summarized?

The following diagram does that from a marketplace point of view:

LEASE CHARACTERISTICS

CHARACTERISTIC	FINANCE LEASE	OPERATING LEASE
Credit risk	Yes	Yes
Asset risk	No	Yes
Lessee intent	To buy	To use
Structure	Full payout	Nonfull payout
Bundling	Net	Net or full service

638. What is the correlation between the marketplace and the world of accounting?

In describing the correlation let's assume that the country in question has adopted accounting standards (such as IAS 17, FASB 13 or something similar) whereby there is an accounting distinction between finance and operating leases. An overwhelming majority of the countries in the world have indeed adopted such standards.

The following begins to describe the correlation:

CORRELATION

Party	Marketplace	Accounting
Lessor	Finance Lease	Finance Lease
	Operating Lease	Operating Lease
Lessee	Finance Lease	Finance Lease
	Operating Lease	Operating Lease

639. Can the above be embellished?

Yes. As can clearly be seen, the two parties (lessor and lessee) can either have a finance lease or an operating lease in the marketplace with the distinction solely having to do with full payout/nonfull payout status as described earlier.

What is important to note is that the character of the lease, from a marketplace point of view, will be the same in the hands of both parties. If the lessor has a finance lease owing to its full payout status, then the lessee too has a finance lease; on the other hand, if the lessor has taken on a residual risk causing the lessor to have an operating lease, the lessee too has an operating lease.

The above can be visually embellished in the diagram as follows:

CORRELATION WITHIN MARKETPLACE

Party	Marketplace	Accounting
Lessor	Finance Lease	Finance Lease
	Operating Lease	Operating Lease
Lessee	Finance Lease	Finance Lease
	Operating Lease	Operating Lease

640. What about from an accounting point of view?

The accounting distinction was clearly explained in the Accounting Section. In essence it has to do with "substance over form." As was seen in that section, if one or more of certain criteria is met, the lease will be classified as a finance lease. Remember, a finance lease in the hands of the lessee in the U.S. is known as a capital lease.

641. If a lessor has a finance lease will the lessee, too, have a finance lease?

Not necessarily! It was explained in the Accounting Section that from an accounting point of view it is possible, and even likely, for a lease to have a different character in the hands of the two parties.

642. Can this be embellished?

A lessor can have a part or all of its residual (on a marketplace operating lease) be guaranteed by a third party such as an insurance company or the supplier. This is often done to deliberately meet the 90% present value test thereby causing the lease to be a finance lease from an accounting point of view. As was studied in the Accounting Section, lessors prefer finance leases from an accounting point of view.

> *From an accounting point of view, the same lease can have a different character in the hands of the lessor and the lessee.*

The same lease, however, can be an operating lease to the lessee where none of the finance lease criteria have been met.

Though the above is not uncommon, generally if the lessor has a finance lease, so does the lessee; and if the lessor has an operating lease, so does the lessee. Given the nuance described above (having to do with the character possibly being different in the hands of the two parties), there are four permutation/combinations from an accounting point of view:

CORRELATION WITHIN ACCOUNTING

Party	Marketplace	Accounting
Lessor	Finance Lease	Finance Lease
	Operating Lease	Operating Lease
Lessee	Finance Lease	Finance Lease
	Operating Lease	Operating Lease

643. Now what about the correlation between the marketplace and accounting?

Full payout marketplace finance leases will always be accounting finance leases.

644. Why is this so?

One of the criteria distinguishing a finance lease from an operating lease is the present value test: if the present value of the minimum lease payments (essentially the rentals) is equal to or greater than 90% of the fair value of the equipment (essentially the equipment cost), the lease is classified as a finance lease.

In a marketplace finance lease where the residual is zero the present value of the minimum lease payments will invariably be equal to 100% of the fair value of the equipment. Thus, marketplace finance leases will always be accounting finance leases.

645. What about the marketplace operating leases?

Marketplace operating leases are nonfull payout where the lessor has taken a residual position. Ignoring other accounting criteria (automatic ownership transfer; bargain purchase option; lease term equal to or greater than 75% of the asset's economic life; and in the case of IAS 17, the customized asset test); and focusing on the 90% present value test, it is easy to understand that some marketplace operating leases will be finance leases from an accounting point of view while some other marketplace operating leases will be operating leases from an accounting point of view.

646. Easy to understand? Perhaps an illustration?
Let's take the following illustration:

Equipment cost	$1,000.00
Term in months	36
Residual	$200.00
Rental in arrears	$27.48
Lessor pretargeted IRR	10%
Lessee discount rate	8%

Looking at the lease from the lessee's point of view, the present value of the minimum lease payments (the rentals) is as follows:

> HP12 C

		f		REG
36				n
27.48		CHS		PMT
8		g		12÷
PV				876.94

424 Winning With Leasing!

> HP17B11+

	☐	CLEAR DATA
		FIN
		TVM
27.48	+/-	PMT
36		N
8		I%YR
PV		**876.94**

Given that the present value of the minimum lease payments is less than 90% of the equipment cost, the lease will qualify as an accounting operating lease. As stated earlier, it is being assumed that all other finance lease criteria have not been met.

647. How can some marketplace operating leases be classified as accounting finance leases?

Using the same illustration, let's change the residual to $150. This will cause the rental to increase to $28.68. The present value of the rentals at the lessee's 8% discount rate is as follows:

> HP12 C

	f	REG
36		n
28.68	CHS	PMT
8	g	12÷
PV		**915.23**

Operating Leases 425

› HP17B11+

	☐	CLEAR DATA
		FIN
		TVM
28.68	+/-	PMT
36		N
8		I%YR
	PV	<u>915.23</u>

Given that the present value is greater than 90% of equipment cost, the lease will now be classified as an accounting finance lease.

648. A summary would be helpful?

The diagram below correlates the marketplace to the world of accounting:

CORRELATION BETWEEN MARKETPLACE AND ACCOUNTING

Party	Marketplace	Accounting
Lessor	Finance Lease ⟶	Finance Lease
	Operating Lease ⟵	Operating Lease
Lessee	Finance Lease ⟶	Finance Lease
	Operating Lease ⟵	Operating Lease

UNIQUE ADVANTAGES TO LESSEES

649. What advantages do operating leases offer to lessees that finance leases do not?
Given what was studied in the first subsection, it is important to note that operating leases are divided into two categories: marketplace operating leases whether they qualify as accounting finance or operating leases, and marketplace operating leases which qualify as accounting operating leases leading to off balance sheet financing.

Also, it is important to note that the Section on Lease Marketing fully addressed the advantages of both (finance and operating) types of leases to the lessee; thus, this subsection will only address the unique advantages of operating leases.

650. What then are the unique advantages of operating leases?
Marketplace operating leases (whether they qualify as accounting finance or operating leases) offer the following unique benefits to the lessee, the type of which are not offered by full payout finance leases:

- Hedge against technology
- Technology refresh
- Early termination options
- Lower rentals
- Bundling of services
- Approval from operating budgets
- Tax benefits
- End of term flexibility

Though many of these advantages were detailed in the Lessee Reasons for Leasing subsection of the

Operating leases offer numerous benefits to lessees that finance leases do not; as such, they are increasingly popular.

Lease Marketing Section, they are being discussed here again for cohesiveness—also, repetition never hurts!

651. Why do operating leases offer a hedge against technology?

In a lease, whenever a lessor takes a residual position, the market value asset risk is borne by the lessor and not the lessee. Though this applies more to assets which are high tech in nature (such as IT equipment); it applies in general as well. This is even more true in a highly competitive operating lease market where lessors, often foolishly, take higher residuals than they should.

Regardless, when the lessor assumes the residual risk, the lessee in essence is entering into a usage agreement and the risk from obsolescence is borne by the lessor.

652. Why do lessors often take foolishly high residual positions?

It is done for a simple and obvious reason—the higher the residual, the lower the periodic rental. Just as much as a large part of the finance lease market is interest rate driven, a large part of the operating lease market is cash flow driven. All other things being equal, the lessor with lower rents will win the transaction.

653. What is meant by the expression "technology refresh"?

Technology refresh is a benefit offered generally by captive lessors who have a good understanding of equipment as well as a large customer base. (This is not to say that independents do not offer this benefit; highly focused independent lessors sometimes do).

654. How does the benefit work?

A lessee who has leased high technology equipment such as computers often would like to terminate the lease prior to its expiry and have the lessor "take out" the existing equipment and have it be replaced with newer technology equipment.

The lessor would be willing to do this in particular if they have a very good remarketing group that continually seeks to find alternate users for used equipment.

655. How does the lessee benefit?

The benefit is straight forward—the lessee's objective is to replace the older technology with newer technology and the lessee accomplishes this objective through technology refresh. The lessor will charge the lessee a penalty to accomplish this. The lessee has concluded that it is better to pay the penalty than be stuck with older technology.

656. How does the lessor benefit?

The lessor benefits in many different ways. To begin with, it has accommodated the lessee's need to be "taken out"; this helps in relationship building for future transactions. Secondly, the lessor has monetarily computed that receiving a penalty plus used equipment with a certain value is at least as good as, if not better than, receiving the remaining rentals and the equipment (with a much lower value) at the end of the lease term. Thirdly, the lessor has placed the lessee into a new lease with newer technology; obviously, there is profit in this new lease for the lessor just as much as there is profit in every lease!

657. Any other benefit?

If three benefits are not enough, there indeed is a fourth! The lessor will either lease or sell the used equipment to another lessee or purchaser who is not as technologically conscious as the first lessee. If the lessor in question is a captive lessor, it is possible that the old equipment may go through some refurbishment as well which will cause it to command a higher value in the marketplace.

To summarize from a lessee's point of view, technology refresh benefits the first lessee as well as a second lessee/user who is not as technologically conscious.

658. How do early terminations work?

Early termination options provide comfort to those lessees who, at inception date, are not 100% sure that they will use the equipment till the end of the lease term. The reason for lack of certainty could either be with technology or any other reason such as the lessee, say two years down a three-year lease, contemplating strategic changes in its manufacturing process.

The early termination option works exactly like technology refresh except that the lessee is not replacing older assets with newer ones.

659. How can operating leases offer lower rentals to the lessee?
The mere existence of residual as versus lack thereof causes rentals on an operating lease to be lower than on finance leases, under the premise that all other things such as term and interest rate are equal.

> *Operating leases facilitate "one-stop shopping" but only when the lease is full-service; many operating leases are net.*

As discussed earlier in this subsection this is even more true when lessors take aggressive residual positions.

660. What is meant by "bundling of services"?
Bundling of services has to do with full-service operating leases where the lessee asks for a lease with many services bundled or packaged along with financing.

661. What are some examples of services that can be bundled into leases?
Generally, maintenance and insurance are two of the most common items that are bundled into leases. However, depending on the extent of outsourcing desired by the lessee and the extent of services offered by the lessor, many additional services can be packaged into operating leases.

662. Such as?
Perhaps it would be best to illustrate via a full-service fleet lease say for 100 delivery trucks for a large retail outlet. The lessee's objective is

simply to use the trucks and not be one bit bothered with any aspects of administration or maintenance.

The full-service lessor will purchase the trucks based on detail specifications received from the lessee. This service benefits the lessee as follows: the lessee does not have to spend the time and effort in the procurement activity; more importantly, the lessee could possibly benefit from any volume purchase discounts the lessor may receive.

663. How does this work?

Specialized lessors purchase a large number of similar assets from one supplier for many different lessees thereby enabling the lessor to negotiate and receive a volume purchase discount. More often than not, particularly in large transactions such as the one being discussed here, a part or all of the discount is passed onto the lessee in the form of lower rentals.

664. What are some of the other additional services?

The lessor will license the vehicles, register them and obtain any special permits that may be needed such as in the case of trucks carrying hazardous materials.

Maintenance, which was mentioned earlier, is provided on an exhaustive basis to include items such as preventative maintenance and predictive maintenance. Repairs are undertaken and services such as roadside assistance and washing and cleaning are also provided.

Of course, all types of insurance coverage will be included; items such as casualty, theft, third party liability and the like.

Depending on the country in question, large fleet lessors often have arrangements with gas or petrol stations enabling the lessee to purchase fuel at a discount from retail prices.

Routine inspections of the fleet will be conducted by the lessor such that both lessor and lessee are continually aware of the condition of the fleet.

665. What about replacement vehicles?

On large fleets, lessors will provide lessees with replacement vehicles when a certain truck is being repaired. This enables the lessee not to have any down time with its distribution fleet.

666. Can lessors also provide the lessee with administrative assistance?

This is commonly done. The lessor will often provide the lessee with software to track the fleet on its computer system such that the lessee can monitor the location and efficiency of the fleet; daily, weekly and monthly management reports will be provided enabling the lessee to fully understand the total kilometers/miles driven by each truck and the routes taken; down time for each truck will be detailed providing reasons, etc.

667. Can human beings be bundled into these types of leases as well?

This is not uncommon. A full-service lessor can indeed meet such needs for those lessees who desire to achieve total outsourcing. The lessor will hire and train licensed drivers for the delivery trucks, provide (and launder) their uniforms and if one driver is sick or on vacation for a certain period of time, provide a replacement driver. This indeed is total outsourcing!

668. Moving on to the next unique benefit, what is meant by the expression "approval from operating budgets"?

Large entities, and often governmental agencies as well, have two types of budgets—capital budgets and operating budgets. When the entity desires to purchase equipment, such acquisition has to be authorized from the entity's capital budget. Authorization from the capital budget can be a real tenuous process for many entities. To begin with, depending on the size of the transaction, a fair amount of cost/benefit justification may have to be provided. Subsequent to this someone will analyze the request for acquisition, ask a hundred questions and eventually the proposal will go to the 32nd floor for committee approval. All of this can take a very long time!

On the other hand, preapproved operating budgets will facilitate procurement of the asset through an operating lease as rent expense is often a preapproved line item on such a budget. This enables the entity to skip the bureaucracy and get delivery of the asset faster than otherwise.

669. What possible tax benefits can lessees receive from operating leases?

If an entity were to purchase equipment for cash (or through a full payout finance lease which will, in some countries, be deemed to be a nontax lease and thereby a purchase), the entity can claim tax depreciation as a deduction on its tax return. On the other hand, operating leases (which are almost invariably considered to be true leases from a tax point of view) allow the lessee to claim rent expense on its tax return. This is true in all countries.

670. How does this help?

For those lessees who are tax motivated, which means that they are seeking to minimize taxable income, it is possible that rent expense can be claimed faster if the term of the lease is shorter than the otherwise tax depreciable life of the asset and/or the method of depreciation is not accelerated.

A major tax benefit is derived by lessees when rent expense can be claimed faster than depreciation.

671. Can this be illustrated?

Let's use the following illustration:

Equipment cost	$1,000.00
Depreciable life, in years	5
Method of depreciation	Linear
Lease term, in months	36
Monthly rental in arrears	$27.48
Inception date	January 1

Operating Leases

The above lease is an operating lease where the lessor has priced the lease at 10% with a residual of $200.

Had the entity purchased the asset for cash, the tax benefit in the first year would be $200 of linear or straight line depreciation; on the other hand, if the entity had entered into an operating lease, the first year's rental of $329.76 ($27.48 x 12) would be tax deductible. This illustration assumes the lessee has a fiscal year end of December 31 and ignores tax conventions (such as in the U.S.) which permit an entity to claim half of the first year's depreciation. The higher rent deductibility gives the entity a larger tax deduction causing the taxable income to be lower in the early years.

672. Any other tax benefits?

In the U.S., operating leases can prevent a lessee from triggering the alternative minimum tax (AMT) and the midquarter convention under MACRS. The underlying premise here is that operating leases are generally considered to be true (tax) leases from a tax point of view thereby allowing the lessee to claim rent expense on its return. In the context of the AMT, depreciation is a preference item; rent expense is not. Large amounts of preferences will tip an entity into AMT.

In the context of the midquarter convention, it is purchased property (more than 40% in the fourth fiscal quarter) which triggers this convention which then reduces the total amount of MACRS that can be claimed. True leases (operating leases) help an entity not to tip the 40% threshold, thereby avoiding the midquarter convention.

Both the AMT and the midquarter convention are discussed in greater detail in the Tax Section.

673. What about end of term flexibility?

Typically at the end of an operating lease, as was discussed in QUESTION 626, a lessee can either purchase or return the equipment or renew the lease. The ability to make this decision at the end of the lease term prevents the lessee from being "locked in" at the inception. It allows the lessee to choose the best option based on where the entity is many months after having signed the lease as versus at the onset. As a certain credit card advertisement puts it, this benefit is "priceless"!

674. A summary of lessee benefits from marketplace operating leases would be helpful?

Marketplace operating leases have the following benefits:

- Hedge against technology
- Technology refresh
- Early termination options
- Lower rentals
- Bundling of services
- Approval from operating budgets
- Tax benefits
- End of term flexibility

675. Now that all the benefits of marketplace operating leases have been discussed, is it time to discuss the benefits of marketplace operating leases which qualify as accounting operating leases?

Yes. When marketplace operating leases are classified as operating leases from an accounting point of view this leads to off balance sheet financing for the lessee.

Off balance sheet financing, as seen in an earlier section, offers the lessee the following distinct benefits not offered by finance leases:

- Ratio enhancement
- Possible improvement in earnings
- Possible avoidance of restrictive covenants
- Increased bonuses to management
- Asset tax avoidance
- Book loss avoidance

676. How can ratios be enhanced or improved through off balance sheet financing?

As a review of material previously studied both in the Lease Marketing as well as the Lease Accounting Sections, off balance sheet financing has the following impact on the financial statements of the lessee: on the balance sheet, neither an asset nor a liability is booked; on the income statement, rent expense is shown.

Starting with the balance sheet and picking three important ratios, it is easy to understand how ratios are enhanced.

677. What is the first ratio?

The first ratio is the current ratio which is as follows:

$$\frac{\text{Current assets}}{\text{Current liabilities}}$$

When the liability is not booked, both current (that which is due over the next 12 months) and noncurrent liabilities are lower than otherwise. This causes the denominator in the above formula to be lower than otherwise, thus causing the current ratio to be higher than otherwise. Most entities prefer a higher current ratio.

678. Which is the next ratio?

Return on assets which is:

$$\frac{\text{Net income}}{\text{Total assets}}$$

As a result of the asset not being booked, total assets are lower than otherwise causing ROA to be higher than otherwise. Who would not like a higher ROA?

679. And lastly?

Debt to equity ratio which is simply the ratio of a firm's total debt to total equity, otherwise known as leverage or gearing.

When the liability is not booked, the ratio of debt to equity is lower than otherwise; most, if not all, entities seek to keep this ratio on the low side.

To summarize –three critical ratios: the current ratio, a measure of liquidity; return on assets, a measure of profitability; and the debt to equity ratio, a measure of capital structure are all improved!

680. But is this not window dressing?

Yes it is; yet, through GAAP (generally accepted accounting principles) one is able to show a stronger balance sheet and enhanced ratios.

Of course, the astute reader will be able to pick up detailed disclosures through the footnotes to the financial statements and will be able to adjust the ratios after incorporating the asset and the liability back into the balance sheet. The moral of the story is simple: you cannot fool all the people all the time; you can only fool some of the people some of the time! This is what off balance sheet financing accomplishes.

> *Off balance sheet financing can strengthen the balance sheet and enhance key ratios causing the entity to appear stronger than otherwise.*

681. How can off balance sheet financing possibly improve a company's earnings?

To understand this, one needs to compare the impact of an operating lease to another mode of acquisition (a finance lease or a loan) on the income statement of the lessee.

When a lessee enters into an operating lease, rent expense is shown on the income statement. Rent expense almost invariably appears as a straight line:

Rent expense
_____

However, if the lessee were to enter into a finance lease or a loan, the income statement would show depreciation expense and interest expense as follows:

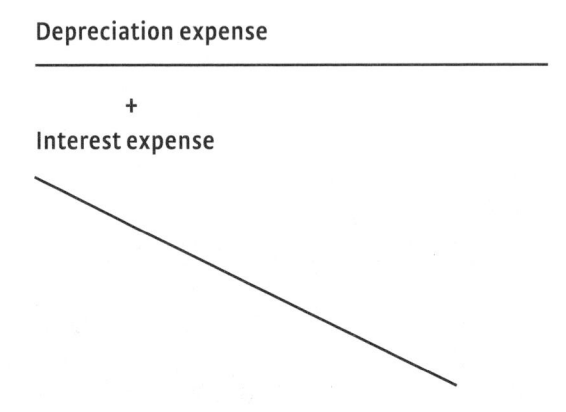

Depreciation expense
_____

\+

Interest expense

\\\\\\\\\\\\\\\\\\\\\\\

Note that depreciation for accounting (and not tax) purposes is almost invariably linear as entities do not desire to take accelerated depreciation which will cause earnings to be lower in the earlier periods. Interest expense, on the other hand, has a downward slope to it as there is more interest in the early periods of a finance lease, or a loan, and less in the latter periods.

682. How does this all help in improving earnings?

In the early periods, a linear line (and that, too, having been lowered due to residual in the lease) when compared to the sum of a linear line and downward sloping line will, more often than not, cause rent expense to be less than depreciation plus interest thereby causing earnings to be higher via off balance sheet financing.

683. Is this not going to reverse in latter periods?

It will only if the lessee stops doing additional operating leases. However, even if it does reverse later most, if not all, lessees strongly prefer to show higher earnings from one quarter to another particularly if they are a company listed on the stock exchange where there is a substantial correlation between earnings and share price. The reversal is of low significance to such lessees.

684. Is all of this window dressing as well?

Not really. Generally accepted accounting principles, such as a choice in depreciation methods between straight line and sum of the years' digits (an accelerated method) or a choice in inventory methods such as LIFO or FIFO, are used by entities often to show the highest earnings possible. Similarly, many entities opt for off balance sheet financing to boost earnings within the realm of generally accepted accounting principles.

685. How can off balance sheet financing aid in avoiding restrictive covenants?

Restrictive financial covenants are commonly imposed by banks on borrowers. These are meant to protect the lender against any undue financial impairment in the borrower's financial position. A typical example is where a bank requires a borrower to agree to a limit to its debt to equity ratio. Often, off balance sheet financing is not considered by the banker to be a part of this ratio thereby enabling an entity to circumvent the covenant through operating leases.

Of course, this is increasingly changing to a point where most, if not all, lenders look at off balance financing with far greater scrutiny than ever before.

686. How can off balance sheet financing increase the amount of bonuses paid to management?

Top management in most companies is provided with incentive compensation; often, this is based on a very common measure of performance — ROA.

Earlier it was clearly shown how off balance sheet financing can improve or enhance ROA. Through operating leases management is able to put a little extra money into its pocket! This is not to suggest that this is a common reason for seeking off balance sheet financing.

687. What is meant by "asset tax avoidance"?
In many countries, local jurisdictions, such as municipalities, impose a nominal tax based on total assets. Also a few countries, trying to plug tax loopholes, have recently arrived at a formula for corporate income tax whereby the taxpayer is to pay the higher of x% of taxable income or y% of total assets.

Whether a jurisdiction has an asset tax or uses a tax on assets as a part of its direct corporate tax approach, off balance sheet financing aids the lessee in reducing its tax liability.

688. But would this not cause the lessor to be in a worse tax position than otherwise?
Overall tax planning generally comes to the rescue.

689. If the lessor does have to bear an incremental tax, is this passed on to the lessee?
Maybe, maybe not. It all depends on how competitive the market is.

690. The last benefit is shown as "book loss avoidance." Can this be explained?
Yes. If an entity were to purchase a high tech asset, it is possible that an accounting loss may occur in those situations where the fair market value of the purchased asset is substantially below its book value. The following illustration embellishes:

Equipment cost	$1,000.00
Accumulated depreciation	(600.00)
Book value	$400.00
Fair market value	$100.00

Assuming the above numbers are material (large enough to make a difference to the entity's stated earnings), the external auditors will require the entity to write down the asset, thereby causing an unanticipated expense or loss of $300.

691. How can operating leases prevent such losses from happening?

No asset is recorded through off balance sheet financing; thus, there is no asset to write down!

692. A summary of lessee benefits from operating leases that lead to off balance sheet financing would be helpful?

Off balance sheet financing offers the following benefits:

- Ratio enhancement
- Possible improvement in earnings
- Possible avoidance of restrictive covenants
- Increased bonuses to management
- Asset tax avoidance
- Book loss avoidance

693. A final summary?

Operating leases offer lessees numerous benefits that finance leases do not. These are categorized as follows:

TECHNOLOGY
- Hedge against technology
- Technology refresh

CASH FLOW
- Lower rentals

CONVENIENCE
- Early termination options
- Bundling of services
- Approval from operating budgets
- End of term flexibility

TAXATION
- Faster write-off
- Mitigation of AMT and midquarter (U.S. only)

FINANCIAL REPORTING
- Ratio enhancement
- Possible improvement in earnings
- Possible avoidance of restrictive covenants
- Increased bonuses to management
- Asset tax avoidance
- Book loss avoidance

UNIQUE ADVANTAGES TO LESSORS

694. What advantages do operating leases offer to lessors which finance leases do not?

Both types, finance and operating, obviously offer one common benefit referred to as spread or margin. Every lease has a pretargeted lessor IRR (interest rate) in it. The spread or margin is the difference between the IRR in a lease and the lessor's pretax cost of debt. If a lessor borrows at 6% and has an IRR of 11% in a lease, the pretax spread or margin is 5%.

Spread is an important reason to be in business. In finance leases, it is the "be all and end all" as it is from this spread that the lessor has to cover all expenses of doing business and have a bottom line (net income after tax) that is satisfactory to the shareholders.

695. What then are the unique advantages of operating leases?

In answering the question there is no need, as was done in the case of lessees, to separate operating leases into marketplace operating leases (whether these are operating leases or finance leases from an accounting point of view) or accounting operating leases.

Operating leases offer the following unique advantages to lessors:

- Niche market
- Additional profit opportunities from bundling
- Residual upside
- Entry into vendor leasing programs
- Tax benefits
- Skills gained benefit all leases

Operating leases can be, and are, far more profitable to the lessor than finance leases—this should explain their popularity.

696. Why are operating leases considered to be a niche product?

In the earlier subsection, it was clearly seen that operating leases offer the lessee over a dozen possible benefits that finance leases do not. A product that delivers substantial incremental benefits is indeed a niche product; the lessor is operating in a niche market.

697. What are the benefits of a niche market?

Niche markets, to begin with, obviously impose certain risks; in this case, the varied residual and other attendant risks that will be discussed in subsequent subsections.

The advantages of a niche market are two-fold: such markets allow for higher returns and also help create a barrier to entry.

698. Can lessors have higher returns on their operating lease portfolios compared to their finance lease portfolios?

They can and they must. Higher risk (from the asset risk) must be accompanied with higher returns. Otherwise, why take such risk?

699. How can returns be higher?

Three ways—front end, duration and back end.

700. Can this be embellished?

Front end means when the lease is priced. The lessor, particularly when operating leases have been recently introduced into a country, will price its operating leases at higher IRRs than its finance leases. This is because the operating lease is a new and premier product compared to the "vanilla" finance lease. Premium products command a higher price; thus, the lessor has a higher spread or margin.

As operating lease markets get competitive, IRRs are not necessarily higher than on finance leases; additional/higher returns are generated at the back end as the lessor has developed its skills in asset management.

701. What about returns during the lease?

This is what is meant by the second benefit listed earlier, "additional profit opportunities from bundling."

When operating leases are full-service, the lessor bundles additional services such as maintenance and insurance into the lease. This "one stop shopping" convenience to the lessee comes at a price.

The lessor is most likely to profit from these services in that the extra monthly rent charged to the lessee is not just what it costs the lessor to provide the extra services but includes a markup.

Also, as noted earlier, when a lessor "takes out" a lessee through technology refresh or an early termination during the lease, there are many pieces of profit for the lessor in these activities.

702. What about the back end?

The back end has to do with residual. If the lessor is an astute asset manager, there is always the possibility for residual upside. This was the third bullet in QUESTION 695.

703. Can this be embellished?

Yes. Lessors who have developed very good skills in residual evaluation (arriving at the future value of an asset) and remarketing (selling or re-leasing equipment when it is returned by the lessee at the end of the lease) are able to profit from the difference between the residual position taken at the onset and the eventual amount the asset is sold for at the end of the lease.

704. How do operating leases facilitate entry into vendor leasing programs?

A vendor leasing program is essentially an alliance or joint venture between a vendor and a lessor whereby the lessor gets the right of first refusal to finance the vendor's equipment that is leased to its customers. Vendor leasing programs are coveted by the lessors as these programs offer a steady source of volume at a low cost.

A vendor would obviously prefer such an alliance with a lessor who offers operating leases as versus a lessor who does not as the vendor is aware that a lessor who offers operating leases and finance leases has more to offer to the vendor's customers.

705. What tax benefits are unique to operating leases?

In some countries, such as the U.S. and China (at least as of the date of this publication), finance leases are generally considered to be loans from a tax point of view. Thus, the lessor cannot claim tax depreciation on finance leases in these countries. On the other hand, throughout the world, lessors can claim tax depreciation on operating leases.

706. How does tax depreciation benefit the lessor?

Though this has been embellished in the Taxation Section, it is quite simple to review. Using the U.S. as an example, when a lessor enters into what is called a true lease (generally an operating lease), the lessor gets accelerated depreciation. Using a five-year asset as an example, and assuming the lessor's fiscal year ends December 31, if a lease is incepted say December 31, 200X, over the 366 days between December 31, 200X and December 31, 200Y, the lessor is able to depreciate 52% of the asset.

Using the following illustration, it is easy to quickly understand the tax benefit:

Equipment cost	$1,000.00
Term in months	48
Residual	$200.00
Pretargeted IRR	10%
Monthly rental in advance	$21.78

Over the 366 days, the lessor will receive 13 rentals or a total of $283.14 in taxable income; yet, the tax depreciation will be $520 (52% of $1,000).

This creates a tax loss of $236.86 over the first two fiscal periods. Using a tax rate of 34%, this generates tax savings equal to $80.53 or approximately 8% of equipment cost, not an insignificant number.

707. Does this not reverse later?

Yes it does but this is where the concept of the time value of money helps. Most lessors, just like most entities in general, would prefer to pay less in taxes in early periods even if this means a greater tax liability later.

708. What about the last unique benefit?

To enter, remain and succeed in the operating lease business, lessors have to gain excellent asset management skills primarily having to do with fully understanding the equipment that is being leased. This skill undoubtedly helps the lessor in general for even on full payout finance leases, understanding the equipment helps the lessor to liase better with the lessee and in the event of a default, the lessor can perhaps gain more value from the sale of the equipment that has been repossessed.

A summary of lessor benefits from operating leases would be helpful?

Operating leases offer the following unique benefits to the lessor:

- Niche market
- Additional profit opportunities from bundling
- Residual upside
- Entry into vendor leasing programs
- Tax benefits
- Skills gained benefit all leases

MANAGING VARIED RISKS

709. What are the risks inherent in operating leases for the lessor?
The common risk having to do with both finance and operating leases is, of course, credit risk or the risk of default.

710. What then are the unique risks in operating leases?
Other than the most significant risk, the asset risk or residual risk, which will be discussed in detail in the next subsection, operating leases impose the following unique risks for lessors:

- Financial reporting risk
- Managerial reporting risk
- Funding risk
- Pricing risk

711. How can leases have a risk associated with financial reporting or financial statements?
As was seen in the Accounting Section, operating leases cause the lessor to have lower earnings in the earlier periods of the lease as compared to finance leases. Lower earnings can indeed be a hazardous to the financial health of a lessor!

712. Why do operating leases create lower earnings in the earlier periods?
Operating leases impact the income statement of the lessor as follows: rental income is taken almost invariably on a linear basis and the leased equipment (which appears as an asset on the lessor's balance sheet) is depreciated also on a linear basis. The margin, which is the difference between rental income and depreciation expense, is shown on a linear basis as well.

Given that depreciation is synonymous to principal, the margin on an operating lease, as described above, conceptually is the same as interest. Thus, "interest" on an operating lease is linear.

Lessors beware—operating leases are potentially harmful to the bottom line!

713. What is meant by depreciation being synonymous to principal?
In the Taxation Section it was discussed that both depreciation and principal represent the recovery of cost and therefore conceptually they are akin to each other.

714. What is the consequence of linear margin?
One has to compare it to the margin (interest) on finance leases.

715. How is margin taken into income on a finance lease?
As seen in the Accounting Section, interest income on a finance lease is a downward sloping line. Thus, linear income from operating leases compared to the downward sloping impact from finance leases causes operating leases to have lower earnings in the early periods.

716. But will this not reverse in later periods?
On a single lease it will; however, if the lessor adds more and more operating leases to its portfolio, the reversal may never come! Even if there is a reversal lessors, like any other entities in the world, prefer to show higher accounting earnings in the earlier periods.

717. What is the solution to this risk?
Lessors who are earnings conscious often will convert a large operating lease to a finance lease for accounting purposes without affecting the operating lease status at the lessee end. (As was studied in QUESTION 642, the same lease can have a different character in the hands of the lessor and lessee).

Lessors will generally do such conversion on large leases as the larger the lease, the greater the adverse impact it will have in lowering earnings in the early periods.

718. How can an operating lease be converted to a finance lease by the lessor and, that too, without affecting the status at the lessee end?

This is best illustrated as follows:

Equipment cost	$100,000
Rentals in advance	$2,321
Term, in months	48
Residual	$28,280
Lessee discount rate	12%
Maintenance per month	$500

The first thing to do is to ascertain whether the lessee has a finance or an operating lease. The 90% test is the only test that will be applied here under the assumption that the other accounting criteria are not an issue.

The minimum lease payments (MLPs) have to be discounted at 12%.

719. What constitutes MLPs for the lessee?

Only the 48 rentals of $2,321 each. The residual is not an MLP as it is not guaranteed by the lessee and, as explained in the Accounting Section, maintenance is not an MLP either.

720. What is the present value of the MLPs to the lessee?

It follows:

› HP12 C

		f	REG
	1		i
	2,321	CHS	PMT
	48		n
		PV	89,019

› HP17B11+

			CLEAR DATA
			FIN
			TVM
	12		I%YR
	2,321	+/-	PMT
	48		N
		PV	89,019

With a present value less than 90% of equipment cost, the lessee has an operating lease. Again, the other accounting criteria are being ignored as it is being assumed that they have all not been met.

721. What about the lessor?

The first step is to compute the lessor's implicit rate in the lease as this is the rate which is to be used as the discount rate for the 90% test.

722. What is the implicit rate in the lease?

The calculation follows:

> HP12 C

	f	REG
100,000	CHS	PV
2,321		PMT
48		n
28,280		FV
	i	1.25
	12x	<u>15.01%</u>

> HP17B11+

	☐	CLEAR DATA
		FIN
		TVM
100,000	+/-	PV
2,321		PMT
48		N
28,280		FV
	I% YR	<u>15.01%</u>

Note that the residual, though unguaranteed, is a part of the lessor's implicit rate.

723. What is the present value of the MLPs to the lessor?

The calculation follows:

> HP12 C

	f	REG
15.01	g	12÷
2,321	CHS	PMT
48		n
	PV	84,425

> HP17B11+

	☐	CLEAR DATA
		FIN
		TVM
15.01		I% YR
2,321	+/-	PMT
48		N
	PV	84,425

Note that whereas the unguaranteed residual is a part of the computation of the implicit rate, it is not an MLP. Also, as stated earlier, maintenance is not an MLP.

With a present value less than 90% of equipment cost, the lessor has an operating lease. Again, the other accounting criteria are being ignored.

724. How can the lessor convert the lease to a finance lease?

To achieve a present value greater than $84,425 either the discount rate must be lower (lower the discount rate, higher the present value) or the MLPs must be larger. The discount rate cannot be altered without altering the economics of the transaction to the lessee as the discount rate here is the IRR in the lease.

Thus, the MLPs must be increased. MLPs to the lessor comprise rents and guaranteed residual. The rents cannot be altered as this once again affects the economics of the transaction to the lessee.

Thus, the only way to increase MLPs is to work with the residual. The lessor can seek to have a part of the residual guaranteed either by the supplier or an insurance company. This does not affect the lessee's MLPs if these parties are unrelated to the lessee. It is important to note, therefore, that the lessee's operating lease status remaining unchanged.

725. Will all of the residual need to be guaranteed?

For purposes of converting the operating lease to a finance lease this is not necessary as will be seen below. Only a part of the residual needs to be guaranteed.

For the lease to be classified as a finance lease the present value of the MLPs needs to be at least $90,000. Currently it is $84,425; thus there is a shortfall of $5,575. The $5,575 is a present value number; while residual being sought to be partially guaranteed is a future value number. Thus, $5,575 needs to be future valued at the implicit rate. This results in a future value of $10,125.

The calculation is shown below:

> HP12 C

	f	REG
15.01	g	12÷
5,575	CHS	PV
48		n
FV		10,125

> HP17B11+

		CLEAR DATA
15.01		I% YR
5,575	+/-	PV
48		N
FV		10,125

Operating Leases

726. If $10,125 of the residual is guaranteed by a third party, what is the consequence?

The present value of the MLPs are now as follows:

> HP12 C

	f	REG
15.01	g	12÷
2,321	CHS	PMT
48		n
10,125	CHS	FV
PV		90,000

> HP17B11+

		CLEAR DATA
		FIN
		TVM
15.01		I% YR
2,321	+/-	PMT
48		N
10,125	+/-	FV
PV		90,000

With a present value of $90,000, the lease now will qualify as a finance lease for the lessor; yet, the lessee continues to have an operating lease!

456 Winning With Leasing!

727. The second risk is the managerial reporting risk. What does this mean vis-a-vis operating leases?

This is best illustrated using the following example:

Equipment cost	$200,000
Term, in months	36
Residual	$60,000
Rental	$5,600
Inception date	1/1/0X
Economic life of asset, in years	5

Based on the above, the lessor's income statement for the three years of the lease will appear as follows:

	200X	200Y	200Z
Rental Income	$67,200	$67,200	$67,200
Depreciation	(40,000)	(40,000)	(40,000)
Margin	$27,200	$27,200	$27,200

The annual rental is $5,600 x 12 = $67,200, while the annual accounting depreciation is $200,000 ÷ 5 = $40,000. The lease generates an annual margin of $27,200.

The balance sheet at the beginning of each of the above three years will show the following amounts for the book value of the equipment:

	200X	200Y	200Z
Net asset at beginning	$200,000	$160,000	$120,000

A key measure of performance for managerial analysis is ROA which for purposes of this illustration is being computed on a gross basis (without taking into account expenses of doing business). ROA for each year follows:

	200X	200Y	200Z
ROA	13.60%	17.00%	22.67%

728. But the above ROAs do not make sense. How can ROA increase when the lease, so as to say, is performing equally each year?

Exactly! ROA is increasing each year as the numerator is constant ($27,200) and the denominator is decreasing ($200,000, $160,000 and $120,000).

Increasing ROAs on a lease that is performing equally creates managerial distortion. Imagine a portfolio of operating leases showing management increasing ROAs. This will create false exuberance within the firm!

729. What is the solution?

The distortion is caused because of the relationship between the numerator and the denominator in the formula for ROA. The numerator is margin; the denominator is the asset. The numerator is rent minus depreciation. Rent is a given; depreciation is arbitrary, left to management's discretion. The arbitrary depreciation affects both the margin as well as the book value of the asset and needs to be adjusted using a different method of depreciation.

730. What method of depreciation should be used?

Keeping in mind that depreciation is synonymous to principal, the amount of depreciation each year should equal the principal portion of the rental such that the margin exactly equals the interest portion. This is shown below:

	200X	200Y	200Z
Rental	$67,200	$67,200	$67,200
Depreciation	(41,067)	(46,432)	(52,501)
Margin	$26,133	$20,768	$14,699

Note that depreciation is increasing each year as it has been computed based on the amortization of a $200,000 loan (equipment cost) over three years (the period of the lease) at the interest rate inherent in the lease. Also, the equipment has been depreciated down to its residual value of $60,000; in other words, the total depreciation over three years is $140,000, which is exactly what principal would have been had the lease indeed been a loan.

731. Why has the asset been depreciated down to residual?

Residual is synonymous to a bullet or balloon payment on a loan. Such bullet or balloon payment is all principal, thus the lease is being depreciated (amortized) as though it is a loan down to its principal.

732. Based on the above what is the annual ROA?

First let's look at the balance sheet. It would show as follows at the beginning of each year:

200X	200Y	200Z
$200,000	$158,933	$112,501

and ROA would be as follows:

200X	200Y	200Z
13.07%	13.07%	13.07%

Operating Leases

Lessors are advised not to blend finance and operating leases into one portfolio; this causes analytical chaos.

733. A summary would be helpful?

A lease which performs equally over its term should not show increasing ROAs each year. The distortion is resolved by treating the operating lease as though it is a loan for internal analysis purposes.

Lessors are advised not only to use this approach; they are also advised to maintain two distinct portfolios, one for finance leases and the other for operating leases. Combining two portfolios into one is a recipe for analytical disaster!

734. What is meant by the third risk, the funding risk?

The risk inherent in funding a portfolio of operating leases can be best understood through a simple illustration dealing with just one lease as versus an entire portfolio. The funding risk is also best understood when compared to finance leases.

Let's begin with a finance lease:

Equipment cost	$100.00
Term, in months	36
Residual	0
Pretargeted IRR	17.50%
Rental in advance	$ 3.54

Even though in the real world funding is accomplished on a pooled basis—whereby a variety of debt is used to fund a variety of leases – for purposes of this illustration, let's assume (both for simplicity and given the fact that the illustration is indeed a single lease) that the lease is funded via discounting the rental stream at 12%.

Though the above is a single lease, one needs to look at it as though it is a portfolio of leases. This will help in better understanding the funding risk.

735. What exactly is meant by discounting?

Discounting the rentals means borrowing against the cash flow on the lease; the ownership of the asset remains with the lessor.

736. What will the proceeds be from discounting?

The computation follows:

> HP12 C

		f	REG
3.54		CHS	PMT
36			n
12		g	12÷
PV			107.65

> HP17B11+

			CLEAR DATA
			FIN
			TVM
3.54		+/-	PMT
36			N
12			I% YR
PV			107.65

The present value of the rentals (the cash flow in the lease) discounted at 12% is $107.65. This funding mechanism will enable the lessor to pay $100 to the supplier for equipment cost and the $7.65 represents the present value of the future profit in the lease. The lessor will not be the beneficiary of the rental stream as this has been sold to a lender.

Another way of looking at this is as follows: assuming there are no expenses of doing business, the lessor does not have to put any equity into the lease as it is fully funded with debt.

737. What about operating leases?

Using the same illustration, let's convert the finance lease to an operating lease by changing the residual from zero to $25. Keeping everything else the same, the monthly rental will drop from $3.54 to $3.01.

738. What are the proceeds from discounting?

Discounting the rentals at 12%:

> HP12 C

	f	REG
3.01	CHS	PMT
36		n
12	g	12÷
PV		91.53

> HP17B11+

		CLEAR DATA
		FIN
		TVM
3.01	+/-	PMT
36		N
12		I% YR
PV		91.53

462 Winning With Leasing!

In the case of the operating lease, the present value of the rentals or the amount of debt is $91.53. As to why this is far less than the $107.65 for the finance lease is obvious – lenders do not loan against the lessor's residual; if they did, in essence they would take the residual risk. Lenders are not in the business of assuming the lessor's residual risk.

739. How is the shortfall made up?
As the supplier needs to be paid $100, the shortfall is $100 - $91.53 = $8.47. Again, using the same assumption as made earlier for the finance lease that there are no expenses of doing business, the lessor has to come up with equity of $8.47.

740. What does this all mean?
What it means is as follows: operating leases require more equity than finance leases. (The reason for this is as explained above: lenders do not fund residual.)

> *Funding a portfolio of operating leases is costlier than funding a portfolio of finance leases.*

741. And what is the consequence of this?
Equity is invariably more expensive than debt. All other things being equal, this means that the cost of capital (cost of debt + equity) in the operating lease business is higher than that in the finance lease business.

742. What is the solution?
A higher cost of capital requires a higher return. In the operating lease business, this can be achieved one of three ways as described earlier: front end, duration or back end.

743. The last unique risk in operating leases was mentioned as the pricing risk. What does this mean?
Just as much as residual is the nuance that brings forth the funding risk, so also does residual cause a pricing risk.

744. How so?

Again, this is best illustrated as follows:

Equipment cost	$1,000
Pretargeted IRR	12%
Residual	
at the end of first lease (3 years)	$400
at the end of next lease (2 years)	$100

For simplicity, the rentals will be computed on an annual basis in arrears. Note that the estimated term of the second lease and the estimated value of residual at the end of this lease is depictive of reality. Astute remarketing requires the lessor to estimate (based on experience, history and judgment) what is likely to happen at the end of the first lease.

In the above illustration, the lessor is of the opinion that if the equipment is returned by the lessee at the end of three years, another lessee is likely to lease it for two years, at the end of which period the residual is anticipated to be $100.

There are two approaches to pricing the first lease.

745. What are the two approaches?

The first approach is the normal or prudent approach, the time line for which is shown below:

0	297.81	3
(1,000)	12%	400

The lease is priced as follows:

> HP12 C

		f	REG
1,000		CHS	PV
400			FV
3			n
12			i
PMT			297.81

> HP17B11+

		☐	CLEAR DATA
			FIN
			TVM
1,000		+/-	PV
400			FV
3			N
12			I%YR
PMT			297.81

The annual rental in arrears is $297.81

Operating Leases **465**

746. How is the second lease priced?

Let's assume that when the asset is returned at the end of three years, it is worth that which it was estimated to be worth, $400. Based on this, the time line for the second lease is as follows:

0	189.51	2
(400)	12%	100

And the pricing computation follows:

> HP12 C

	f	REG
400	CHS	PV
100		FV
12		i
2		n
PMT		189.51

> HP17B11+

	☐	CLEAR DATA
400	+/-	PV
100		FV
12		I% YR
2		N
PMT		189.51

466 Winning With Leasing!

Thus, the two leases together look as follows:

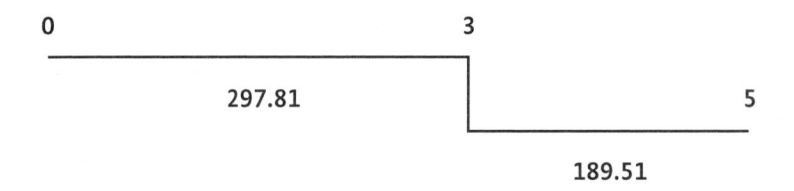

```
0                              3
|——————————————————————————————|
            297.81             |                    5
                               |————————————————————|
                                      189.51
```

which is how most operating leases look over the periods that cover more than one lease, as used equipment typically commands a lower rental than new equipment.

747. What is the second approach to pricing?

The second approach is the "foolish" approach where an aggressive competitor takes a five-year amortization to pricing a three-year lease where the time line looks as follows:

```
0                              3                    5
|——————————————————————————————|— — — — — — — — — —|
(1,000)                     261.67                 100
```

748. What is meant by the expression "a five-year amortization to pricing a three-year lease"?

The lessor is glaringly aware that it needs to price a three-year lease; yet, it acts as though it is pricing a five-year lease by combining the information from the illustration that indicates the anticipated residual value to be $100 at the end of five years.

The pricing computation follows:

> HP12 C

	f	REG
1,000	CHS	PV
100		FV
12		i
5		n
PMT		**261.67**

> HP17B11+

		CLEAR DATA
1,000	+/-	PV
100		FV
12		I%YR
5		N
PMT		**261.67**

749. Now what?

Remembering that the first lessor quoted a rental of $297.81 and that the foolish competitor is quoting $261.67, it is obvious as to who wins the deal—the foolish competitor!

However, when the asset is returned, its fair rental value is $189.51. For the foolish competitor to achieve its 12% overall return, it must price the re-rental at $261.67 which will be close to impossible in a highly competitive market.

Thus, though the first lessor lost the deal to the second lessor, the second lessor in turn merely deferred its pain!

750. What is the moral of the story?
Lessors should price prudently and not succumb to foolish price cutting!

751. A summary of the four risks would be helpful?
The summary follows:

Risk	Impact	Solution
1. Financial reporting	Lower earnings in earlier periods	Convert large operating leases to finance leases
2. Managerial reporting	ROA distortion	Adjust depreciation for internal purposes
3. Funding	Higher cost of capital	Need higher returns
4. Pricing	Losing business to foolish competitors	Exercise pricing discipline

RESIDUAL RISK

752. What are the factors that can affect the future value of an asset?

Residual estimates are arrived at when the lease is priced at the inception of the lease; the $ amount of residual is the most critical component of pricing an operating lease. Obviously, the lessor needs to estimate what the future value of the asset will be at the end of the lease term. Such future value is indeed influenced by many factors, most of which are beyond the lessor's control.

753. What are these factors?

The factors fit into the following broad categories;

- Supplier related
- Economic and regulatory
- Lessee related
- Asset related
- Lessor related

Let's discuss each of the above in detail.

754. How can a supplier affect the future value of an asset?

Ongoing supplier support is critical in the context of asset values. Supplier support comes through items such as arriving at and updating maintenance requirements, stocking and making available parts needed to keep the equipment functioning properly, refurbishing (and where appropriate, issuing a certificate for such refurbished equipment) the equipment when it comes off lease, etc.

If a supplier is unwilling or unable to support its used equipment, the value of such will be adversely affected. Some suppliers deliberately do not support their used equipment as they strategically choose to focus on their new equipment sales. Also if a supplier is in financial difficulties and is say headed toward legal reorganization; or worse yet bankruptcy, then the marketplace loses confidence in the asset and used asset values can plunge. This has unfortunately happened once too often—recent situations in the automobile and computer industries come to mind.

755. What about economic and regulatory factors?

The general economic climate itself can affect the future value of assets. Residual values are actually countercyclical in nature. When the economy dips, business investment slows down and entities spend less on new equipment acquisitions. This in turn causes used equipment to be in greater demand; also, lessees are more apt to renew leases or purchase the equipment at the end of the lease term as versus returning the used equipment. This helps preserve residual values.

Another broad market-based factor that can substantially impact the future value of an asset has to do with the depth or lack thereof of the secondary market. (Of course, this is also a significant factor in arriving at the value of residual at the inception of the lease; but, given that leases typically are three- or four-year agreements, changes can take place with regard to the depth of the secondary market during the lease term.)

Automobiles typically have a very deep secondary market throughout the world; on the other hand, medical equipment may or may not—it depends on the country in question. In the U.S., there are equipment brokers who specialize in narrow equipment types—even within the broad category of medical equipment there are those who focus solely on CT scanners and that, too, say in the western U.S. This is a good example of depth.

Government regulations can affect the future value of assets. Not too long ago, the European Commission passed a new ordinance requiring aircraft flying below so many meters/feet to reduce noise levels. This required aircraft owners, most of whom are lessors, to invest the needed funds so as to be in conformity with the new ordinance. Making unanticipated investments in an asset midstream on a lease is the same thing as taking a residual hit!

756. How can lessees influence the future value of an asset?

As much as in the world of credit there is a gem that states "lessees must have the ability and the willingness to pay"; similarly, in the world of asset management there needs to be a gem that should state "lessees must have the ability and the willingness to maintain the asset"! Many lessees are simply unwilling to take appropriate care of leased assets and this can affect residual value. It certainly behooves a lessor to gauge up-front the type of the lessee it is dealing with and if the lessor has concluded that a certain lessee is unwilling to maintain its equipment, then the lessor should not enter into an operating lease with such lessee.

Another lessee related factor that can affect residual has to do with whether the lessee is likely to renew the lease or purchase the equipment at the end of the lease term—this is referred to as "in place remarketing." If a lessee has a history of renewing its leases or buying the equipment, the lessor is reasonably assured of residual values being maintained at least in those cases where the lease has a fixed purchase option.

757. What asset related nuances can affect residual?

Technology is a big unknown. Even experts in asset management cannot totally predict when and what type of new technology will come forth and how this will affect the value of used equipment.

758. Lastly, what is meant by lessor related items?

This is the only category truly within the control of the lessor—its own asset management skills in areas such as arriving at reasonably accurate residual values, understanding maintenance requirements, having a good grasp on the secondary market, enforcing a strict inspection policy, working with suppliers, gauging which lessees should not be targets for operating leases, and having a sharp and strong remarketing department.

Unless a lessor hedges its asset risk, thereby transferring it to third parties, it should not be in the operating lease business without excellent asset management skills.

> *Arriving at the future value of an asset is a combination of an art and a science.*

759. How exactly does a lessor arrive at the future value of an asset?

If the author knew the answer as to how one precisely predicts future values, he would not be writing another book; he would be a billionaire and retired on a beautiful island!

Arriving at an estimate of what an asset will be worth at the end of the lease term, or in other words to know what residual position to take at the beginning of the lease term, is a combination between an art and a science.

760. How is this done?

To begin with, lessors have history as a guide. If they have been doing operating leases for a while, they certainly have tracked actuals to estimates; if they do not have a history of operating leases and have only begun to do such leases, they can still rely on history from their finance leasing portfolio.

Through lessee defaults and repossessions, at least they have some historical perspective of asset values.

761. History alone is obviously insufficient. What tools/data exist to guide the lessor in estimating residual values?

Many countries have guidebooks that are of substantial benefit. This is mostly true in the automobile industry where guidebooks track, in great detail, used car values. In mature markets, such guidebooks also exist in the IT and aircraft industry. Unfortunately, guidebooks are generally not yet available in emerging lease economies.

762. So what do lessors do in such markets?

They can get counsel from the supplier who generally knows the equipment better than the lessor does. Also, many markets have appraisers or consultants who are experienced in estimating future values of certain asset categories. The Internet, too, is a good source. Many websites exist which provide a great amount of detail on used equipment prices.

763. Is this it?

By and large, yes. Of course, eventually all of the intelligence gathering is to be reduced to just one number—the residual estimate, and this is done by augmenting the data with the lessor's judgment.

764. Can judgment be quantified?

On large transactions, lessors use a technique commonly used in other fields called "expected value analysis."

765. How about an illustration?

Let's assume that based on data gathered and augmented by judgment, a lessor concludes as follows:

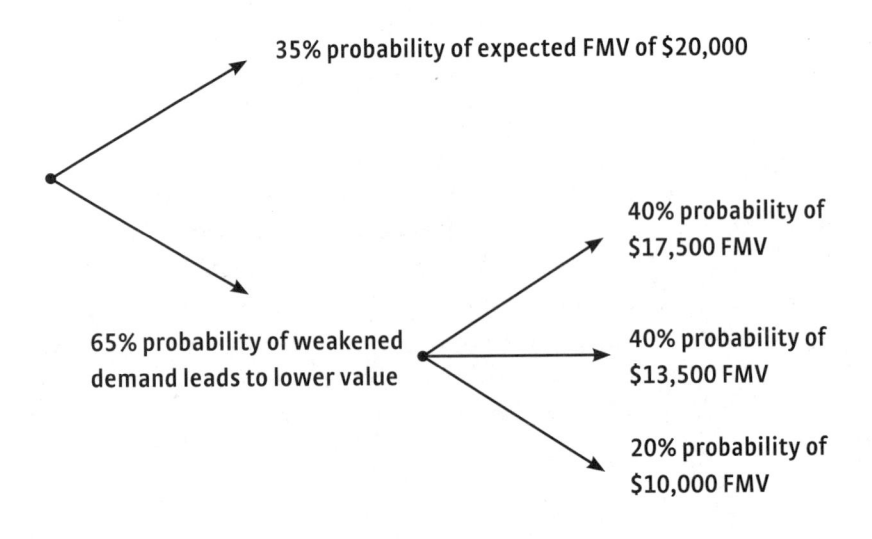

35% probability of expected FMV of $20,000

65% probability of weakened demand leads to lower value

- 40% probability of $17,500 FMV
- 40% probability of $13,500 FMV
- 20% probability of $10,000 FMV

Based on the above, the lessor arrives at the following estimate of residual value:

Probability of 1st Event	x	Probability of 2nd Event	=	Joint Probability	x	Expected Outcome	=	Value
.35				.35	x	$20,000	=	$7,000
.65	x	.40	=	.26	x	$17,500	=	$4,550
.65	x	.40	=	.26	x	$13,500	=	$3,510
.65	x	.20	=	.13	x	$10,000	=	$1,300
								$16,360

The lessor, using expected value analysis or joint probability analysis, arrives at a residual estimate of $16,360.

Good luck in arriving at estimated residual values!

TECHNIQUES TO MITIGATE RESIDUAL RISK

766. How can residual risk be mitigated or eliminated?
Let's discuss the elimination part first. To completely eliminate residual risk a lessor has to pass the entire risk to another.

767. Who would be willing to assume such risk?
There are three parties who may be willing to do so:

- The lessee
- The supplier
- An insurance company

768. Why would a lessee ever be willing to assume residual risk in a lease?
Lessees are not fools—well at least not all of them! Often a lessee has the same amount of knowledge, sometimes even more, as a lessor has about the future value of an asset. As an example, a large electric utility which uses hundreds of trucks as its repair fleet understands trucks well enough to reasonably predict their future value.

769. But why would they guarantee the lessor's residual?
For one and one reason only—to negotiate a lower rental! A lessor would indeed be willing to reduce the rental amount if the lessee were willing to guarantee a part or all of its residual. An astute lessee will get two rental quotes from the lessor, one without any residual guaranty and one with. The lessee will then quantify the economics by taking the difference between the present value of the rent difference and the present value of the possible exposure on the residual. Depending on how these numbers turn out, the lessee will decide whether to guarantee the residual or not.

770. Residual guaranties by suppliers are common, are they not?

Yes, they are. A supplier is generally willing to guarantee a lessor's residual, on a transaction by transaction basis, within the realm of a vendor leasing program. After all, in such a program the lessor and the supplier are partners and a "quid pro quo" approach is beneficial to both parties.

771. Can such residual guaranty be found outside of a vendor leasing program?

Yes, typically on large transactions. If a lessor asks a supplier to help out with say a partial residual guaranty, the supplier is likely to do so if the amount being guaranteed is reasonable. The supplier will be willing to do so to prevent the transaction from falling through.

772. Why would a transaction fall through?

Let's assume that the supplier's customer wants off balance sheet financing and that for the present value of the MLPs to be less than 90% of equipment cost, the residual needs to be 14%. Let's further assume that the lessor's asset management group is comfortable taking a maximum residual position of 10%. Unless the supplier steps in and guarantees the top 4% of the 14%, the deal could fall through as the lessee is unwilling to do a finance lease and the lessor is unwilling to take a residual risk greater than 10%.

773. What about insurance companies?

Residual insurance exists in mature leasing markets such as the U.S., U.K. and Australia where insurance companies have made it a business to offer such a service.

774. How does it work?

In the same complicated manner that life insurance works! The insurance company through careful and exhaustive study ascertains its exposure on a transaction-by-transaction basis and arrives at the insurance premium (fee) accordingly.

Excellent asset management skills are needed to enter, remain and succeed in operating leases.

775. How can residual risk be mitigated?

A lessor can mitigate its residual risk through sound asset management. Also, lessors should choose to focus on an asset type rather than diversify at the onset. This enables their asset management group to initially focus on one asset category, say automobiles.

They then begin to understand how residual values are arrived at and how best to remarket used cars when they are returned. The lessor is then likely to diversify within a broader category of transportation equipment by adding say trucks and busses to its portfolio.

OPERATING LEASES WITHOUT ASSET RISK

776. How can a lessor do operating leases without any asset risk?
As seen in the previous subsection, a lessor can have its residual be guaranteed by either the lessee, the supplier or a third party such as an insurance company. Thus, one way to avoid asset risk is to simply transfer it in its entirety to another.

777. Is there a cost to such a transfer of risk?
Of course, there is. Lessees will demand a lower rental; insurance companies will need to be paid an insurance premium; and suppliers (who rarely take on the entire residual risk), too, will often ask for a fee similar to an insurance premium.

778. Is there any other way to engage in operating leases without asset risk?
A common practice in many countries is to do an operating lease with a "side letter."

779. What exactly is a "side letter"?
This is how it works. The master lease agreement will either contain no purchase option or an FMV purchase option and the rentals will be low enough to not meet the 90% test.

Thus, on the surface the lease qualifies as off balance sheet financing to the lessee. However, the two parties will also enter into a separate agreement (the side letter) that requires the lessee to purchase the equipment at the end of the lease term.

780. Come again?

The two agreements in combination economically cause the lease to be a full payout finance lease to both parties. However, the side letter is not disclosed to third parties—such as independent auditors and tax authorities. Therefore the lease, as far as the master lease agreement is concerned, is an operating lease.

781. Is such a practice proper?

No comment.

SUMMARY

1. There is only one difference between a marketplace finance lease and a marketplace operating lease: full payout versus nonfull payout. This is caused by residual on operating leases. Thus, operating leases entail two types of risks: credit risk and asset risk.

2. Operating leases can either be net or full-service. This depends on what the lessee desires.

3. At the end of term on an operating lease, the lessee can either return the equipment, purchase it or renew the lease. If the equipment is to be purchased via a purchase option, it is purchased either at the end of term FMV, the FMV with a ceiling or at a mutually preagreed amount stated in the lease contract. If no purchase option exists, the two parties will arrive at a negotiated purchase price at the end of the lease.

4. Marketplace operating leases can either be finance or operating leases from an accounting point of view. Its accounting classification primarily has to do with the 90% present value test. If the residual is high enough for the rentals to be low enough not to meet the test, the lease will generally be classified as an accounting operating lease.

5. Marketplace operating leases offer the following unique benefits to the lessee:

   - Hedge against technology
   - Technology refresh
   - Early termination options
   - Lower rentals
   - Bundling of services
   - Approval from operating budgets
   - Tax benefits
   - End of term flexibility

6. Off balance sheet financing (marketplace operating leases that are classified as operating leases from an accounting point of view) offers the following unique benefits to the lessee:

- Ratio enhancement
- Possible improvement in earnings
- Possible avoidance of restrictive covenants
- Increased bonuses to management
- Asset tax avoidance
- Book loss avoidance

7. Ratio enhancement, through window dressing, makes the financial statements appear stronger than otherwise.

8. Earnings can be improved via off balance sheet financing as rent minus depreciation on an operating lease is a straight line compared to the downward sloping interest expense line on a finance lease.

9. Operating leases offer the following unique benefits to the lessor:

- Niche market
- Additional profit opportunities from bundling
- Residual upside
- Entry into vendor leasing programs
- Tax benefits
- Skills gained benefit all leases

10. There are four unique risks inherent in operating leases. These are:

- Financial reporting risk
- Managerial reporting risk
- Funding risk
- Pricing risk

11. The risks and their impact and the solutions are presented below:

Risk	Impact	Solution
1. Financial reporting	Lower earnings in earlier periods	Convert large operating leases to finance leases
2. Managerial reporting	ROA distortion	Adjust depreciation for internal purposes
3. Funding	Higher cost of capital	Need higher returns
4. Pricing	Losing business to foolish competitors	Exercise pricing discipline

12. Residual risk emanates from the following five categories:

    - Supplier related
    - Economic and regulatory
    - Lessee related
    - Asset related
    - Lessor related

GLOSSARY

fair market value purchase option
A purchase option in the lease contract allowing (not obliging) the lessee to purchase the leased asset at the fair market value at the end of the lease term.

finance lease
A lease from a marketplace point of view, which is full payout with no reliance on residual; and a lease from an accounting point of view, which meets one or more of five (four for FASB) IAS 17 criteria.

financial covenants
Restrictions placed on borrowers by lenders with a view to protect the lender's interest.

fixed purchase option
A purchase option in the lease contract allowing (not obliging) the lessee to purchase the leased asset at a fixed price at the end of the lease term.

full payout
A lease where the lessor assumes a residual position of zero in pricing the lease; thus, the sum of the rentals equal the equipment cost (principal) plus the pretargeted interest in the transaction.

full-service
A lease in which services such as maintenance and insurance are included. Also known as a "wet" lease.

marketplace
The commercial framework as contrasted with the accounting, tax or legal frameworks.

net
A lease in which no services are included thereby requiring the lessee to be responsible for items such as maintenance and insurance. The lessor is only providing one thing, the financing. Also known as a "dry" lease.

nonfull payout
A lease where the lessor assumes a certain residual position thereby causing the sum of the rentals to be less than equipment cost (principal) plus the pretargeted interest in the transaction.

operating lease
A lease from a marketplace point of view, which is nonfull payout owing to the residual position assumed by the lessor; and a lease from an accounting point of view, which is not a finance lease.

purchase option
An option in the lease contract allowing (not obliging) the lessee to purchase the leased asset at the end of the lease term.

remarketing
The process whereby the lessor sells or leases the equipment to a third party when the lessee returns the equipment either during the lease term or at the end of the lease term.

renewal option
An option in the lease contract allowing (not obliging) the lessee to extend the lease term either at a stated rental or the then fair value rental.

residual
The estimated fair market value of the leased asset at the end of the lease term. The lessor arrives at such estimate at the inception of the lease.

residual guaranty
A guaranty obtained by the lessor either from the lessee or a third party such as the vendor or an insurance company, whereby a part or all of the lessor's residual risk is hedged.

residual insurance
Insurance available in developed lease economies whereby an insurance company guarantees part or all of the lessor's residual.

technology refresh
Where a lessee negotiates with a lessor to have existing leased assets be taken out prior to the expiration of the lease term and where the existing assets are replaced with newer assets which are technologically more conducive for the lessee.

vendor leasing program
An arrangement between a seller of goods and a lessor whereby the lessor typically obtains an exclusive agreement to finance the vendor's sales.

HOMEWORK

1. Are operating leases always full-service leases?

2. What are the varied end of term events in an operating lease?

3. Under what circumstances will marketplace operating leases qualify for off balance sheet financing?

4. What eight unique advantages do marketplace operating leases offer the lessee?

5. What six unique advantages does off balance sheet financing offer the lessee?

6. What unique advantages do operating leases offer to the lessor?

7. What are the four unique risks in operating leases?

8. Why do operating leases lead to financial reporting risk?

9. How can such risk be mitigated?

10. Why do operating leases lead to managerial reporting risk?

11. Why do operating leases impose a unique funding risk?

12. What is the solution to the above risk?

13. Why do operating leases cause a pricing risk?

14. What is the solution to the above?

HOMEWORK ANSWERS

Answer 1
There is a general misunderstanding that operating leases are always full-service; in fact, many lessors erroneously believe that for a lease to be an operating lease it must be full-service. Operating leases can either be net or full-service. Net operating leases are extremely common.

Answer 2
At the end of the lease term, a lessee can either return the equipment, purchase it or renew the lease.

Answer 3
Marketplace operating leases will generally qualify for off balance sheet financing to the lessee when they do not meet any of the five (four for FASB 13) IAS 17 criteria. The essence has to do with the 90% present value test; residual needs to be high enough for the rentals to be low enough such that the present value of the rentals is less than 90% of the equipment cost.

Answer 4
- Hedge against technology
- Technology refresh
- Early termination options
- Lower rentals
- Bundling of services
- Approval from operating budgets
- Tax benefits
- End of term flexibility

Answer 5
- Ratio enhancement
- Possible improvement in earnings
- Possible avoidance of restrictive covenants
- Increased bonuses to management
- Asset tax avoidance
- Book loss avoidance

Answer 6
- Niche market
- Additional profit opportunities from bundling
- Residual upside
- Entry into vendor leasing programs
- Tax benefits
- Skills gained benefit all leases

Answer 7
- Financial reporting risk
- Managerial reporting risk
- Funding risk
- Pricing risk

Answer 8
The margin on operating leases, rent minus depreciation is linear; the margin on finance leases, interest income, is a downward sloping line. Thus, operating leases cause income to be lower in the earlier periods.

Answer 9
Lessors will often seek a guaranty for a part of the residual either from the supplier or an insurance company. Guaranteed residual is an MLP and as such can help in increasing the present value of the MLPs causing present value to be equal to or greater than 90% of equipment cost.

Answer 10
Linear margin is the numerator and a decreasing asset base the denominator in ROA. This causes ROA distortion.

Answer 11
Lenders will not typically loan against residual. All other things being equal, a portfolio of operating leases therefore will have less debt and more equity. Equity is more expensive than debt resulting in a higher cost of capital.

Answer 12
The solution is to have higher returns either from spread, bundled services or astute asset management resulting in residual upside.

Answer 13
Pricing risk exists due to aggressive competition resulting in foolish residuals.

Answer 14
The solution is obvious: one needs to walk away from deals when competition gets ugly; in other words, lessors must exercise residual discipline.

Advertisements

ACC Capital Corporation

International Customers / Local Financing Solutions

$ 5,000,000 Trucking 60 months TRAC Lease	**$ 1,000,000** Golf Course Equipment 60 months True Lease
$ 1,500,000 FF&E 60 months Operating Lease	**$ 400,000** Computer Hardware 24 months Capital Lease $ 1.00 Out
$ 500,000 Resort Maintenance Equipment 48 months Operating Lease	**$ 1,217,300** Scrap Metal Shear 84 months Capital Lease

ACC Capital Corporation is a diversified middle-market financial services company that specializes in structuring, origination, servicing a broad array of lease products. We offer equipment financing for all types of industries and equipment with transactions ranging from $ 50,000 to in-excess of $ 10 million.
$ 100,000 Application Only Program for your well-established clients who need a quick response.!

Contact
ACC Capital Corporation

Email : info@acccapital.com www.acccapital.com

Amembal & Associates
in conjunction with
Odessa Technologies, Inc.
proudly announces the launch of

Lease vs. Purchase

LEASEWAVE LEASE/PURCHASE WILL:

- Use present value after-tax as the approach
- Show simple conclusions through spread sheets and bar diagrams
- Solve for break even discount rate and salvage value
- Have clear instructions for your sales team to use it immediately
- Allow you to recover its total cost by winning your next transaction

---

- Are you losing transactions to cash & varied financing alternatives?
- Are your margins under pressure?
- Are your lease vs. purchase software options costly and complex?
- Are you lacking a simple tool to convince customers that cash is generally more expensive than leasing?

Did you answer "yes"?

Most emerging market lessors are likely to answer with a resounding "Yes!" to all of the above questions. Having taught leasing in over 60 countries, Mr. Sudhir Amembal recognized the need for a simple yet inexpensive software package that can be used to clearly show potential customers that cash is indeed more expensive than leasing!

Odessa Technologies   **AMEMBAL & ASSOCIATES**

DO NOT WAIT! ACT NOW! E-MAIL
sudhir@amembalandassociates.com
FOR MORE INFORMATION

Annual Asian Leasing School

EACH NOVEMBER ~ BANGKOK, THAILAND
INSTRUCTED BY SUDHIR P. AMEMBAL

Winning With Leasing
3 DAYS

Winning With Leasing is our flagship workshop. For those not in sales/marketing, it will broaden your horizons enabling you to interact better with customers and insiders. For those in sales/marketing, it will provide you with tools which will lead to incremental transactions and profits. The novice will learn; the experienced will fine tune their skills.

Operating Leases: Benefits & Risks
1 DAY

Operating Leases: Benefits & Risks is a must for those contemplating entry into this niche market as well as those already offering it. You will learn the varied unique benefits the product offers; as importantly, five unique risks will be addressed including techniques to mitigate and eliminate them.

Management Strategies for Success
1 DAY

Management Strategies for Success is a must for those desiring to learn from mature markets. You will learn a variety of strategies and techniques in areas such as customer development, operational efficiencies and product innovation.

FOR MORE INFORMATION, CONTACT ANNA@AMEMBALANDASSOCIATES.COM

AMEMBAL & ASSOCIATES PROUDLY ANNOUNCES THE FIRST-EVER

2006 ASIAN LEASING YEARBOOK

COUNTRIES PRESENTED:

Australia	Korea	Philippines
Bangladesh	Malaysia	Singapore
China	Maldives	Sri Lanka
Indonesia	New Zealand	Taiwan
Japan	Oman	Thailand
	Pakistan	Turkey

- Detailed, focused information from 17 countries in the region (the data is presented in a consistent format for each reporting country)
- The accounting, tax, legal and regulatory approaches used
- Key financial data such as ROA, ROE and spreads
- A listing of members of domestic leasing associations
- Articles on topics such as international best practices, internet technology, and other strategic managerial issues
- Over 250 pages of relevant data

Gain a better understanding of one of the fastest growing regions in the world. This first-ever regionally focused compilation gives a full flavor for how leasing is done in each country, including constraints and opportunities.

To order, go to www.amembalandassociates.com

AMEMBAL & ASSOCIATES

Clean up your image...

Contact creates effective design that highlights and enhances your message. You won't find design for design's sake here. No sir.

We are a small design group with four guys who love to make you look better. Contact doesn't have account reps or salesmen. You deal with the designers from concept to finished project. Nothing is lost in the translation and there's no static in the transmission of your message.

Let Contact help you with your next print or web project and save money while raising your company's profile. We'll help clean up your image without cleaning you out.

We've helped several leasing companies take their image to a new level. We even designed this book. Now, let us help you.

...make contact.

⬛CONTΔCT
BUSINESS COMMUNICATIONS

350 South 400 East, Suite 320
Salt Lake City, UT 84111
801.363.0101 / fax 801.363.6095
www.gomakecontact.com

Merger and Acquisition Advisory Services For the Equipment Leasing Industry

Kropschot Financial Services has arranged the sale of over 140 equipment leasing and specialty finance businesses in the past 19 years.
The following are some of the services we can provide to your organization:

- Representing owners in the sale of businesses and portfolios
- Performing acquisition searches for buyers
- Developing joint ventures and strategic alliances
- Securing lease funding and lines of credit
- Arranging subordinated debt and equity financing
- Valuation of businesses and portfolios

Visit our website at www.kropschot.com

Kropschot
Financial Services

Bruce Kropschot
70 Beachside Drive, #101
Vero Beach, FL 32963
Phone: 772-228-9808
Fax: 772-228-9899
bkropschot@kropschot.com

Jim Billings
309 Windfern Court
Millersville, MD 21108
Phone: 410-729-1800
Fax: 410-729-8550
jbillings@kropschot.com

IMAP
INTERNATIONAL NETWORK OF M&A PARTNERS

LeaseInspection.com
tomorrow's technology today

LEASE INSPECTIONS: Find out the facts BEFORE you fund!

It only makes sense to protect your investment when financing leased equipment. Unfortunately, fraud is a fact of life, but it doesn't have to be your fact of life. If it's your money on the line, **let us be your eyes and ears in the field.**

- ✓ IT equipment
- ✓ Medical equipment
- ✓ Industrial equipment
- ✓ Telecommunications equipment
- ✓ Automobiles and other vehicles
- ✓ Farm equipment
- ✓ Printing equipment
- ✓ Tanning equipment
- ✓ Airplanes
- ✓ Office furniture and equipment

We offer nationwide inspections, photos on every job, weekend service, intuitive web-interface, instant job-status notification, check pick-up, site inspections, and more. Find out the facts before you fund.

Lance Black
LeaseInspection.com
801.523.8449
lance@leaseinspection.com

P.S. Or you can visit us on the web at www.leaseinspection.com

ELA ONLINE
Equipping lease professionals for success

UAEL
United Association of Equipment Leasing

AMEMBAL & ASSOCIATES Publications

📖 The Handbook of Equipment Leasing

Is it possible to learn everything you ever wanted to know about equipment leasing from one book? Of course not. That is why The Handbook of Equipment Leasing is actually two books — two volumes to be exact! Within its 1300 pages, you will find the most comprehensive, detailed and accurate body of leasing knowledge ever compiled about the subject of equipment leasing. Written by the world leader in lease education and consulting services, these volumes are already an indispensable part of thousands of leasing and asset financing professionals' libraries. Topics include tax, financial reporting, structuring, yield analysis, lease vs. buy, international, credit, documentation, legal, asset management, leveraged leasing, captive and vendor programs, securitization, and many more.

📖 International Leasing: The Complete Guide

Leasing, like every other financial product, exists within the framework of a global economy. This book is for those who wish to understand the leasing marketplace in its entirety, thereby expanding their horizons. Whether one desires to enter such markers or not, each lessor, regardless of location, is impacted by the global leasing arena. International leasing markets are at varied stages of development—from nascent to mature. Lessors in nascent and emerging markets need to keep current on the issues in mature markets, as well as learn from each other's experiences. Lessors from mature markets, on the other hand, realizing the potential of newer markets, need to understand the unique leasing infrastructure—legal, regulatory, and tax aspects—that exists in each market. Reading and understanding the subjects contained in this 880-page book will benefit lessors and lessees, regardless of size or country of origin, and the professionals who serve them.

📖 Operating Leases: The Complete Guide

The operating lease is the product of the future. It is one of the most complicated products in an already complex industry. Mature markets add value to this product as it evolves in new shapes and forms. Emerging markets are probing the operating lease; some have introduced it, others will do so shortly. The operating lease has numerous nuances that need to be fully understood. Whereas, the benefits of operating leases are obvious (increased volume and profit to the lessor, and off balance sheet financing and a hedge against technology to the lessee) the risks are substantial. Understanding the risks is critical to success in this highly competitive market. This 850-page book provides the reader with a complete understanding of asset risk and varied techniques to mitigate or eliminate such risks. This book is for those who need to gain a complete understanding of operating leases. Asset management, equipment nuances, and a complete discussion of off balance sheet financing — its benefits, potential, and future — are discussed in detail. This book is a must for lessors, lessees, and the varied professionals serving the leasing industry.

order: WWW.AMEMBALANDASSOCIATES.COM OR EMAIL TO ANNA@AMEMBALANDASSOCIATES.COM

Amembal & Associates Lease Training

Current offerings include:

> Winning With Leasing

Our flagship workshop, providing you with tools which will lead to incremental transactions and profits, and allow those not in sales to broaden their horizons. The novices will learn; the experienced will fine-tune their skills.

> Operating Leases

Risks and Benefits—a must for those contemplating entry into this niche market, as well as those already offering it. Learn the varied unique benefits this product offers; as importantly, unique risks will be addressed including techniques to mitigate and eliminate them.

> Management Strategies for Success

A must for those desiring to learn from mature markets. Learn a variety of strategies and techniques in areas such as customer development, operational efficiencies and product innovation.

Available in-house or in-country. Customizable from two to five days duration.

For more information, contact Sudhir Amembal
SUDHIR@AMEMBALANDASSOCIATES.COM

Register Today for **monitor**_daily_.com
FREE Daily
E-News Update

The Equipment Leasing Industry's Best Daily News Broadcast

- *Industry News*
- *Personnel Announcements*
- *Employment Opportunities*
- *E-News Advertising Opportunities*

Register today...
It's **FREE**!

www.monitordaily.com/app_enews/members_registration.asp

Odessa Technologies®

FLEET & LEASE MANAGEMENT SOFTWARE
Internet-based
customizable
end-to-end

FUNCTIONALITY Integrated Fleet & Lease Contracts • Maintenance & Fuel • Cards • Vehicle & Vendor Mgmt.
TECHNOLOGY Microsoft.NET® • SQL Server® • Oracle® • Crystal Reports®
ONLINE ACCESS Customers • Sales Reps • Dealerships • Maintenance Facilities • Other Third Parties

Are you riding the LeaseWave?™
The world's premier leasing software suite

www.odessatech.com　　　+1-215-231-9800　　　leasewave@odessatech.com

Odessa Technologies®

LEASE MANAGEMENT SOFTWARE
Internet-based
customizable
end-to-end

FUNCTIONALITY Origination • Funding • Lease / Asset Management • Fleet Management • Remarketing
TECHNOLOGY Microsoft.NET® • SQL Server® • Oracle® • Crystal Reports®
ONLINE ACCESS Customers • Funding Sources • Vendors • Brokers • Other Third Parties

Are you riding the LeaseWave?™
The world's premier leasing software suite

www.odessatech.com +1-215-231-9800 leasewave@odessatech.com

SUCCESS requires VISION.

VISION COMMERCE DELIVERS
Internet Based Front-End Systems for

Automated Application Processing
Credit Profiling, Scoring & Analysis
Electronic Documentation & Proposal Delivery
Automated Tasking & Workflow
Application Tracking with Automated Notification
Integration with Accounting, CRM, Pricing & Other Resources
Private Branding for Vendors, Brokers & Lessees
Extensive Tools for Pre-Tax & After-Tax Pricing
Custom Designed Solution for Every Client

*"OUR TECHNOLOGY DOES NOT GET
IN THE WAY OF YOUR BUSINESS."*

www.visioncommerce.com

866-707-9929

VISION COMMERCE

Winning With Leasing!
PUBLIC SEMINARS   NOW OFFERED IN THE U.S.

Mr. Sudhir Amembal,

Chairman and CEO of Amembal & Associates (the world leader in lease education, consultance and publications) will begin teaching public leasing seminars in the United States.

The first workshop to be introduced will be Amembal & Associates' most popular one: Winning With Leasing. This three day flagship workshop includes the following topics:

- **Leasing Overview**
- **Lease Finance**
- **Lessee Benefits**
- **Lessor Benefits**
- **The Equipment Acquisition Process**
- **Lease Versus Purchase Analysis**
- **Lease Versus Lease Analysis**
- **Lease Accounting**
- **Lease Taxation**
- **Pricing and Structuring**
- **Operating Leases**

FOR FURTHER DETAILS INCLUDING LOCATION, DATES AND FEES, PLEASE CONTACT anna@amembalandassociates.com OR VIEW OUR WEBSITE: www.amembalassociates.com